WEEKEND
JOURNEYS

D1590720

WEEKEND
JOURNEYS

SIXTY-TWO GETAWAYS

WITHIN A DAY'S DRIVE

OF PHILADELPHIA

FROM THE

PHILADELPHIA INQUIRER

ANDREWS AND McMEEL
A Universal Press Syndicate Company
Kansas City

Weekend Journeys: 62 Getaways within a Day's Drive of Philadelphia
©1995 by The Philadelphia Inquirer.
All rights reserved. Printed in the United States of America.
No part of this book may be used or reproduced in any manner
whatsoever without the written permission of Andrews and McMeel
except in the case of reprints in the context of reviews.
For information, write Andrews and McMeel,
a Universal Press Syndicate company,
4900 Main Street, Kansas City, Missouri 64112.

Additional copies of this book may be ordered by calling
(800) 642-6480.

Library of Congress Cataloging-in-Publication Data

Weekend journeys : 62 getaways within a day's drive of Philadelphia /
from the Philadelphia Inquirer.
p.   cm.
ISBN 0-8362-7037-1
1. Middle Atlantic States—Guidebooks. 2. New England—Guidebooks.
3. Philadelphia Region (Pa.)—Guidebooks.
4. Automobile travel—Middle Atlantic States—Guidebooks.
5. Automobile travel—New England—Guidebooks.
6. Automobile travel—Pennsylvania—
Philadelphia Region—Guidebooks.
I. Philadelphia Inquirer.
F106.W42 1995
917.404'43—dc20   95-1613
CIP

First Printing, April 1995
Second Printing, January 1996

Photo credits: pages 2–3, April Saul, Philadelphia Inquirer;
pages 130–31, Maine Development Commission;
pages 212–13, Washington Convention and Visitors Bureau.

Design and composition by Hillside Studio, Inc.

Contents

Introduction

1
PENNSYLVANIA, DELAWARE AND NEW JERSEY

2
NEW YORK CITY AND NEW YORK STATE

3
NEW ENGLAND

4

WASHINGTON, MARYLAND, AND VIRGINIA

Introduction

IN A WORLD OF HOT TRENDS AND FADS, anything that lasts for 20 years has got to be either good, lucky, or both. "Weekend Journey" has been a standing feature in *The Philadelphia Inquirer*'s Sunday Travel section for about that long.

There's got to be only one reason—people find it useful. This book is a collection of a few dozen "Weekend Journey" installments from the early 1990s—and we think they will be just as useful through the permanence of a book as in the newspaper they came from.

If you live in the Philadelphia region—and Philadelphia is the starting point for all the "Weekend Journey" destinations—you may already be familiar with the feature from reading your Sunday *Inquirer*. But if you're not, you'll want to know a bit about it and how it works.

It's not a substitute for a comprehensive tour guide, and for a simple reason. As the name of the feature suggests, these are quick hits—meant for helping with an impulsive getaway. They'll give you a weekend's worth of entertainment when you have a hankering to go somewhere but not the time, money, or inclination to do much more. Our hope is that these stories will mesh with some of your interests and show you a good way to spend a few days somewhere relatively close.

Each installment is just that—a story. You won't find anything here about the Statue of Liberty or the Washington Monument. That's for the big tour guides. Rather, these features are one person's, couple's, or family's highly subjective impressions of a destination focused on activities a bit more unusual. They were chosen for this book because we think they have broad enough appeal that many readers would want to give them a try, too.

The ground rules are simple. To qualify as a Weekend Journey, these destinations have to be different enough to make you feel that you've gotten away but close enough so you can get there by car in a relatively short time. Generally, six hours of driving is the maximum. But that's loose. Some of these destinations stretch that limit a bit, but our expectation is that you'll also be stretching your definition of a weekend, too, and be planning a three- or four-day excursion.

A few things should be kept in mind when you read any travel book, including this one.

Restaurants, inns, other places of accommodation, and shops come and go constantly. That's one reason why you won't see mention of too many of them in these pages. Unlike the newspaper where these reports originated, such establishments are too perishable to be included in a book, so the articles that follow concentrate instead on streets, sights, sounds, and local flavor. The few that are included are generally historical places that can be expected to be around for decades to come. Most prices, too, have been removed from these reports because most can be outdated before you read them. Any that we've left in should be considered guidelines, likely to change soon—or to have already changed.

Instead of giving you lists of restaurants and hotels, we've tried when possible to provide a reference to local tourism bureaus or chambers of commerce. Remember, though, those addresses and phone numbers are also subject to change. When traveling, even for a short trip, it's always best to do a bit of advance planning and phone work.

•

The stories were edited by Mike Shoup, travel editor of *The Philadelphia Inquirer,* and Jack Severson, executive travel editor. Roger Hasler of The *Inquirer's* editorial art department provided the maps.

WEEKEND
JOURNEYS

1

Pennsylvania, Delaware and New Jersey

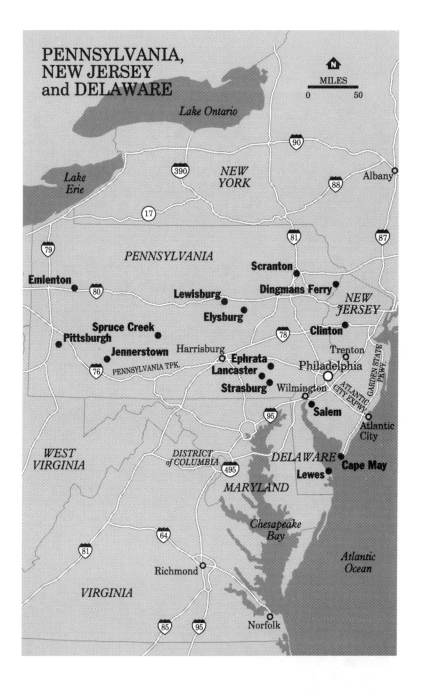

Knoebels Grove

ELYSBURG, PA.

GRAB THE CAR KEYS. Pack the kids. Here's fun you can afford. It's Knoebels Grove, an amusement park that draws nearly a million folks each season. Yet, you may never have heard of it.

That's not really so surprising, since the place is just about smackdab in the middle of nowhere (actually, the middle of Pennsylvania is more like it, about 160 miles northwest of Philadelphia).

It's an unlikely location for an amusement park—one with a roller coaster that enthusiasts have ranked fifth-best in the nation—sandwiched as it is between the east branch of the Susquehanna River on the north and the fringe of the anthracite coal region on the south.

Still, this rural setting is a large part of Knoebels Grove's appeal to its clientele—largely middle-class families, with more than a few farm boys and locals thrown in for good measure.

And they don't call this place a grove for nothing. Unlike most modern amusement parks that were built on cleared land, Knoebels (pronounced kuh-NO-bulz) gives the impression that nary an old oak was downed to make room for the rides.

But part of the park's appeal is what it doesn't have: There are no fees for parking, no admission fee, generally no long waits for the most popular rides, no piped-in Muzak, no billboard with a long list of don'ts to spoil your good time, and few, if any, unruly teenagers.

Like many others, I had never heard of Knoebels Grove—until, first, my dentist, then a couple of colleagues told me about the place. After their rave reviews, I grabbed the car keys on a late-spring weekend, packed my daughter and her friend, and headed for some affordable fun.

Now I've strolled Walt Disney World's Main Street U.S.A., so I know the feeling of fake—surrounded by enough restored cuteness to make you puke without the aid of a looping roller coaster. But this place is for real.

There's a stream (not a manmade waterway) that cuts through the park, sweetening the air and necessitating a series of covered wooden bridges. There are ancient oaks and elms and gravel paths and good food and reasonable rides—you can even bring your dog.

On opening day, July 4, 1926, Knoebels was just a swimming pool, a carousel, and a restaurant. Today, there's a giant crystal pool with filtered mountain stream water as well as four water slides, and I'll bet you could safely tell your kids to wander off and meet up with you later.

I am predisposed to enjoy all this because I was reared on the carousel at Ninth and Hunting Park and on the Alps at Willow Grove Park. But on this day I am with Sally and Julia, 13-year-olds accustomed to $30 haircuts.

Sally, my daughter, has been to Disney World five times, Dorney Park three, Busch Gardens once, Canada, the Grand Canyon, and Las Vegas. Julia is not a roller-coaster enthusiast. She has, however, been to "almost all the islands in the Caribbean." Every spring, she and her mother take a week-long vacation alone so they can bond.

If the weather had been a touch warmer, we might have camped here overnight amid the tall pines. There are tent sites with platforms to cushion your behind from the rocks, RV sites with all the right hookups, hot showers, tile baths, and a camp store, and, with the right planning, you can rent a log cabin or—get this, Wild West fans—a teepee that sleeps six.

We chose the pedestrian route, checking into one of the many inexpensive motels off Interstate 80, a scant 13 miles from Knoebels. Then we embarked with near-seriousness to answer the question: Are we too jaded, too sophisticated, and, for me at 40-plus, too old to have fun here?

On the advice of my advisers among the Knoebels cognoscenti, we started our visit with a ride on one of the park's three mini-railroads. We select the Pioneer Railway, a train pulled by an 1865 diesel engine. It's really a train ride to nowhere because instead of riding through the park, the tracks meander at a walloping 8 mph through the nearby woods. The mile-and-a-half path loops around a small clearing, where ears of hog corn have been stuck on strips of wood to attract deer, and passes a black ash bearing a sign proclaiming it the Black Ash Champion for 1990. "Still is the tallest and the widest, far as we know," the conductor says.

After the ride, we are tempted to eat. The Oasis is serving meat loaf, barbecued chicken, or roast pork with potato or stuffing, two vegetables, plus roll and butter for $5.25. But our stomachs face other challenges first: the 16-car Ferris wheel, the Hi-Speed Thrill Coaster, the Whirlwind (the park's only upside-down event and "the only one of its kind in the U.S.A.; subjects rider to forces three times as great as the Earth's gravitational pull"). And the park's prize: the Phoenix, a giant vintage wooden roller coaster.

Inside Track, a magazine for amusement-park enthusiasts, rates the Phoenix the fifth-best roller coaster in the country. It was called the Rocket at its first home in San Antonio. But in 1985, the endangered ride was rescued, moved, and restored at Knoebels. The first incline is staggering.

But there's more—much more. Knoebel's Bumper Cars are the "Best Bumper Cars in America," according to Tim O'Brien, author of the *Amusement Park Guide*; my two testers concur.

We pass the Wharf: crab cutlets, chicken Parmesan sandwiches, steaks, hamburgers, hot dogs, pizza (in a poll, readers of *Inside Track* magazine named it "the best park pizza in America" six years in a row), nachos with extra cheese, onion rings, pink lemonade, and some terrific white birch beer. ("It's birch beer that's white," the girl at the counter explains simply.)

Peg Knoebel, who died in 1990, was a carousel nut. So the park boasts a Kiddie and a Grand Carousel, plus a carousel museum starring Peg's collection of ancient prancing horses, zebras, and camels. The Grand Carousel, hand-carved in 1912 and bought by Knoebels in 1941, is one of the largest surviving merry-go-rounds in the country. We rode twice—once on the up-and-down horses with the real horsehair tails and, later, hanging astride the stationary horses so we could reach for the brass ring. Sally won on her third try.

From the carousel, you can see the birthday-party picnic pavilion, where parents who plan ahead can arrange parties under a roof shaped like a giant pink cake adorned with roses and topped with candles. There are scads of other picnic pavilions that can be reserved elsewhere in the park. (Leave the liquor at home.)

Can we eat yet? There are french fries with vinegar, shrimp rolls, burritos, grilled chicken, tuna hoagies, pita pockets, and taco salad. Then there are candy apples, caramel apples, and apple juice served from a booth shaped like a giant Winesap with windows. Did I overlook the Belgian waffles with ice cream, the snow cones, and six flavors of cotton candy?

Nice touches abound throughout Knoebels Grove: park benches aplenty, a changing table in each ladies' room, plus a pink-and-blue baby booth with an electric bottle warmer and some chairs for nursing. There's the usual free entertainment: country music, magic shows, song-and-dance routines by the not-so-talented locals. And the unusual: a free anthracite coal-mining museum (eat your heart out, Dorney). See the 10-ton lump of coal; see the Lost Logger turn tree trunks to dust with his mighty chainsaw.

Of course, there is a Log Flume and a 13-minute mechanical-bear show. Yes, there is a MAC machine. Sure, you can rent movie cameras and baby strollers.

And did I mention the food?

The Old Mill (thick chocolate milkshakes; peach ice cream; sundaes with hot fudge, wet walnuts, whipped cream, and a cherry) sits next to an authentic old mill. At the next booth they pitch waffle fries, Rib-B-Q sandwiches, baked potatoes with chives, and cheese-filled pierogis.

Ready for more rides?

Our vote for the blue-ribbon best goes to the Haunted Mansion. Who knew a laid-back family park a stone's throw from Nowheresville would have such first-class frights? "Better than Disney World," the girls proclaimed.

A metal car padded with red leather traverses a maze of dark, darker, pitch-black rooms, separated by slamming wooden doors, pierced by truly scary sounds. Julia made me promise not to reveal the "big surprise" at the end of the ride. It's probably enough to say that at the close of the day, we rode this one more time.

Knoebels Grove isn't the only attraction in this part of Pennsylvania. The area is full of pastoral beauty and a driving tour of the region reveals it as a treasure trove of covered bridges—one of the richest concentrations of such structures in the country. You can get a map showing the location of the bridges from the Columbia-Montour Counties Tourist Promotion Agency in Bloomsburg.

Each autumn, near the height of foliage season, there's a covered-bridge festival, headquartered at Knoebels Grove, with arts and crafts, music and entertainment, food, games, and hay rides.

In nearby Ashland, you can tour a coal mine and ride a steam train at the Pioneer Coal Mine Tunnel. For more in-depth knowledge on the rich history of coal mining in the region, stop in at the state-run Museum of Anthracite Mining, just up the road from the tunnel.

These and other area attractions can round out a weekend visit to Knoebels Grove, the greatest little amusement park you may never have heard of—until now.

—Dianna Marder

Directions from Philadelphia: Take the Northeast Extension of the Pennsylvania Turnpike north to Interstate 80 West. Continue on I-80 west to Exit 35 and go 13 miles south on Route 487. Knoebels Grove (717-672-2572) is open daily from late April (call for the exact date) through Labor Day from 11 a.m. to 10 p.m. It is also open the two weekends after Labor Day.

For a covered-bridge map and information about the area, contact the Columbia-Montour Counties Tourist Promotion Agency, 121 Paper Mill Rd., Bloomsburg, Pa. 17815.

The Poconos' other face

DINGMANS FERRY, PA.

COME THE ECO-REVOLUTION, all tacky resorts will go the way of the Pocono Environmental Education Center:

No more heart-shaped bathtubs, poolside cocktail lounges, or servile waitpersons cadging tips. Bedding will be bunk, decor will be minimal, and the only in-room convenience will be a broom and pail so you can clean up before you leave. Off the wall go the romantic paintings, replaced by posters for recycling and government land-use planning.

Meal service? Line up in the mess hall (don't be late), help yourself, and don't forget to wipe down the table after you've bused it. Entertainment? The endangered mud toad expedition leaves at dawn, and tonight there's a lecture on snake habitat.

That isn't entirely fair, of course. In fact, we had a ball on our family camp weekend here at the Pocono Environmental Education Center. We hiked, we canoed, we stared at the moon and sang campfire songs. Our 4- and 2-year-olds studied pinecones and waterbugs, touched snakes, and roasted their first marshmallows. And if the setting was sub-plush, the price was quite reasonable for a midsummer mini-vacation 2 1/2 hours from Philadelphia.

It's just that the ironies of the place, a converted "couples" resort once called the Honeymoon Haven, continued to peep out at us throughout our three-day midsummer stay.

Bits of heart-shaped mirror remain on the walls of the cabins, which have been otherwise gutted of honeymoonesque furnishings in favor of two-by-four bunks and plastic-covered mattresses. The path to the main lodge-cum-education center winds by a stone loveseat, inscribed with doggerel mythologizing sweethearts of old. And evidence of old shuffleboard courts and swimming pools sits around like the ruins of a lost civilization.

What happened here was not a coup by radical environmentalists. But it does represent a triumph of sorts for people who like their recreation with a public-sector, or at least public-spirited, flavor.

The federal government took over Honeymoon Haven's property in the early 1970s as part of a dam project, which was to flood the nearby upper Delaware River. The National Park Service invited Keystone Junior College, near Scranton, to use the 38-acre site as an environmental lab and classroom. Keystone did so until 1986, when the Pocono Environmental Education Center, or PEEC, incorporated as an independent, nonprofit organization.

PEEC's main mission was to make good environmental scouts out of urban schoolchildren. It still is, but the center has been gradually adding programs aimed at bird-watchers, cross-country skiers, and (this is where we came in) families with small children.

"We were doing workshops for the teachers that would help them learn how to use nature for instruction," PEEC president Jack Padalino said. "And a lot of the teachers were saying, 'Hey, this would be a nice place to bring my family.' Now it seems that's one of our major growth areas—and to this day, a lot of the families are related to educators."

We hadn't heard of PEEC until early in 1993, but it sounded right up our alley. Not only were we a family with small children, but my wife was a former elementary-school science teacher whose fondest memories involved showing pupils the wonders of pond slime.

Me, I can take pond slime or leave it. But I was delighted to find an inexpensive country place where we could catch at least a few moments of off-duty time from parenting. Not having deep roots or close relatives in the area, we've found it next to impossible to get away from the daily routines of feeding, changing, and amusing our preschool-age kids. As we'd learned from two or three earlier unrelaxing trips by ourselves, having other families with kids around is a major plus, affording both little and big people the chance to occasionally get away from each other. Some solve the problem at full-service family resorts, complete with camp counselors and organized activities. Others opt for tents and campgrounds. But we consider the former too expensive and the latter too much hassle; while we're still juggling naps and diapers, beds and bathrooms are de rigueur.

PEEC had what we wanted. The three-day Fourth of July weekend we spent offered more than enough activity to keep our kids amused and us interested but was loose enough to let us follow our own schedule for naps and meals. And there were indeed plenty of families just like us, so that after we finished busing our tables at the mess hall, we could sit and schmooze with grown-ups—ah, the simple pleasures— while the kids played with their peers nearby on the lawn.

When we weren't eating, we took advantage of the PEEC staff's informal yet organized activities. On a "sensory hike" through the woods, the guide had our daughter, Sophie, put on a blindfold to better get the feel and smell of pine cones, bark, and other common items. Later, Sophie and I donned life vests and went for a paddle around the pond, mostly failing to find the beaver dams and snake hangouts identified for us by the canoe instructor.

Mom and son Eli listened to bullfrogs and looked at woolly worms near what once was Honeymoon Haven's main lake, which PEEC has let silt up to create a more environmentally instructive wetland. The area now features muck, algae, wildflowers, and dozens of noisy critters you won't find in the cast of "Sesame Street."

Some other families we met, whose kids were older, opted for more rigorous hikes around the nearby Delaware Water Gap, or early-morning hikes to watch the birds and beavers around the pond. The center's staff tries to build in as many options as possible and varies the programs for each camp according to the ages of the families who sign up.

In the afternoon, we all went for a swim in PEEC's indoor pool, a useful holdover from the Honeymoon Haven days. And after dinner, we returned to the main lodge for lectures and stories, the highlight of which was a lengthy show-and-tell on Poconos reptiles by a local naturalist. The kids were agape when he planted a tree frog on the wall, and appropriately fascinated when he let them pet the giant bullfrog.

But the biggest hit was the campfire, which the PEEC staff organized on our last evening. It had everything: ghost stories, goofy skits, corny camp songs—and s'mores, those classic sandwiches of toasted marshmallow and melted chocolate between graham crackers. Those were two happy, sticky kids we dragged back to the cabin.

About that cabin—well, you can't have everything. And if you're 4, sleeping on a narrow plastic mattress with eau de Pine Sol in your nostrils isn't really much of a sacrifice, especially when you get s'mores in the bargain. But I hadn't bedded down that way since my own summer-camp days, and with good reason. Three nights in a row like that was more than plenty, thanks.

On the other hand, the weather was warm and the moon full after we put the kids down, so we plunked down the lawn chairs we'd brought with us outside the cabin door for an hour or so and just stared. And that was enough to justify the whole weekend.

—Andrew Cassel

Directions from Philadelphia: Follow Route 611 north for about 80 miles, Route 8 west for about five miles, and 209 north for about 25 miles.

PEEC Family Camps take place throughout the year. The 1995 rates were $89 per person for two-day weekends, $119 for three-day holiday weekends, and $159 for five-day camps. Children 1 to 4 go half-price, those under 1 for free. For more information, contact Pocono Environmental Education Center, R.D. 2, Box 1010, Dingmans Ferry, Pa. 18328, 717-828-2319.

The old oil town

EMLENTON, PA.

WE AWOKE IN OUR second-floor bedroom to the melodic twitterings of our feathered neighbors nesting under the eaves of the roof.

The sight that greeted us from our window was the Allegheny River sliding past, strong and silent, black eddies in the water gleaming like oil in the morning sun.

Downstairs, mild bedlam had commenced, as the hunger of seven children aged 10 and under expressed itself in grumpy chorus. The adult heads of our two families were too content to react.

The need for contentment was part of what had brought us to this quiet town on the north shore of the Allegheny, some 65 miles north of Pittsburgh. We were occupying a bed-and-breakfast in Emlenton, just five minutes off Interstate 80. Indeed, we lay in the shadow of one of the engineering marvels of the road, the 1,668-foot-long Allegheny River Bridge that looms 270 feet above the water. All to the good. But why Emlenton?

There was no doubting the attraction of a once-booming oil town gone to bed—a picturesque river village in a hilly part of Pennsylvania rife with history.

The more practical reason, however, was the need for a convenient rendezvous with friends who live in the Detroit suburbs. Emlenton, we discovered, was almost precisely smack dab in the middle between their home and ours in a Philadelphia suburb.

Most people have a less geocentric reason for coming to this area of western Pennsylvania. The attraction is oil—bubblin' crude.

They don't come to drill for it, but to see where the Pennsylvania oil industry began. To see, in fact, the first oil well in the world.

Many visitors use Emlenton as a base to explore north into the region that a top-hatted former railroad conductor named Edwin Laurentine Drake made famous around the globe. That includes Oil City—headquarters for the Quaker State Corp. (the company dropped the words "oil refining" a while back when it began to diversify)—and Titusville, where Drake drilled his first well.

Today, Emlenton is a peaceful town of about 850 residents who manage just fine without a traffic light. Who would guess that this place was once one of the wealthiest small towns in America, boasting more millionaires per capita (37!) than any comparably sized place in the United States?

Emlenton's history began in 1790, when settlers started arriving by boat and overland trail. In 1820, it was laid out as a town on farm lands owned by Andrew McCaslin and Joseph M. Fox, and was named for the latter's wife, Hannah Emlen.

Around the new town were 20 crude stone furnaces in which Pennsylvania ore was reduced to iron. Along with timber and building stone, the iron was floated by barge down the Allegheny to Pittsburgh.

Richer sources of ore were found elsewhere, however, and the furnaces had closed down by 1845.

Then came the oil boom. Sparked in 1859 by Drake's discovery of oil near Titusville, about 45 miles to the north, and the opening of a new rail line, Emlenton was ideally placed. Several hotels, livery stables, and bars sprung up practically overnight.

Oil wells were drilled in the immediate vicinity. The Emlenton Refining Co. grew into the well-known Quaker State Oil and Refining Corp. Natural gas was also discovered and by the 1880s was being piped into homes.

Made wealthy by the boom, area residents had to have the proper shelter. And the place where they chose to build some magnificent homes was Emlenton. On Second Street, we admired the beautiful Eleanor Daubenspeck Home, built by one of the founders of the First National Bank. Later, oil and gas magnate T.B Gregory lived here.

On Hill Street, one of the terraces that ascend the mountain up from the river, a number of homes can fairly be described as houses that oil built.

At the corner of Hill and Seventh streets stands the magnificent Queen Anne–style residence built for Harry Jennings Crawford around the turn of the century. Like the Daubenspeck Home and others, it's still a private dwelling.

Crawford, a native son of Scots ancestry, parlayed an initial investment of $800 in three oil wells near Emlenton into a fortune of many millions in gas and oil ventures. He was one of the founders of Quaker State, a canny businessman who also invested in a radical new product—the hookless fastener, or zipper.

A number of buildings in and around Emlenton were constructed with Crawford's financial assistance, including the school—the Elizabeth Crawford Memorial School. It was state-of-the-art when it was built in 1928. Now it's used as an elementary school.

Crawford died in Oil City in 1953. Although his house is quite striking, it is nowhere near Rockefelleresque standards. Local historian Joanne Long says this was intentional.

"The wealthy people in this area have never paraded that wealth before the general public, and so the homes were never representative of the dollar value of the individual. There has always been an effort not to flaunt wealth before others here in town."

There is more to see than just the houses. On Main Street is the Old Emlenton Mill Co., billed as America's first steam-powered grist mill.

Built in 1875, the mill still displays some original machinery and artifacts on five floors, and the kids had a great time poking around this stuff.

Still, the main purpose of this converted, modern-day mill is commerce—antique/boutique style.

We tried lunch at an unpretentious little luncheonette that was perfectly serviceable for two famished families, but Emlenton is a bit short on places to eat, so one should be prepared to leave town to get a real meal.

Foxburg is one such destination, and it's a good one for reasons besides food. The Foxburg Country Club was founded in 1887 and is the oldest golf course in the United States in continuous use. The course is also the site of the American Golf Hall of Fame, whose museum houses a pictorial history of the game dating back four centuries. Complete sets of antique golf clubs dating from 1770 are also displayed.

Next to the Silver Fox Inne, a popular tavern-type restaurant, Foxburg Livery and Outfitters offers canoe "fun floats" on the Allegheny and Clarion rivers. The livery is located on Main Street at the bridge in Foxburg and is open daily in the summer; weekends in spring and fall.

The Drake Well Museum is part of a larger park that runs along picturesque Oil Creek, a favorite of trout fishermen. The reconstructed sites in the outdoor portion of the museum exhibit are an ideal place for curious eyes and young legs.

After an early museum closed in 1923, local oilmen banded together to get a permanent one built on the site of Drake's original well. In the 1930s, the American Petroleum Institute acquired the land, built a small museum, and turned it over to the Commonwealth. In 1963, the present museum building replaced the original.

The well replica on the original site, the extensive museum, and the working oil machinery depict the once booming industry.

Another attraction in Venango County is the Oil Creek and Titusville Railroad, a 13-mile line "through the valley that changed the world."

You may begin your ride at Perry Street station, a restored 1893 freight house in Titusville, or at Drake Well Park. At the southern end of the line, you may board at Rynd Farm, four miles north of Oil City.

There is a flag stop at Petroleum Centre, once one of the oil boom towns and now a recreational park that provides hiking, hunting, fishing, bicycling, and camping opportunities. The railroad operates weekends from mid-June through October.

The Barnard House has a few beat-up bicycles for local cruising, but serious recreationists should consider bringing their own mountain bikes or hybrids.

Emlenton will eventually be linked up with three regional bicycle trails: the 5.8-mile Samuel Justus Recreational Trail, the 9.7-mile Oil Creek State Park Bicycle Trail, and the 14-mile Allegheny River Trail. The latter is in various stages of development.

Ultimately, the trail will stretch from Drake's Well Museum south to another river town, Kennerdell, and then to Emlenton.

—Steve Goldstein

Directions from Philadelphia: Emlenton is about a six-hour drive from the Philadelphia area. Take the Pennsylvania Turnpike's Northeast Extension to Interstate 80, and take I-80 west to Exit 6. Emlenton is five minutes off the exit.

Places to stay: There are several bed-and-breakfast places in Emlenton, and lodging is available in surrounding communities such as Oil City, Titusville, and Franklin, the historic Venango County seat. For more information, contact the Franklin Area Chamber of Commerce (814-432-5823) or the Titusville Area Chamber of Commerce (814-827-2941).

New Jersey's Hunterdon County

CLINTON, N.J.

DESERTED ROADS WIND through green pastures and rolling farmland, where horses, sheep, cows, even an occasional llama or emu can be glimpsed from the car window.

Abandoned farm buildings are followed by bright, newly painted red barns and restored farmhouses, followed in the next mile by squat, newly landscaped mansions, or an occasional older estate receding behind the proper stretch of lawn, or just a clutch of ranches and Cape Cods.

An antiques shop doubles as a tea shop, serving up scones along with the afternoon's herbal selections. It's autumn, and geese honk, as do the ubiquitous four-wheel-drive vehicles when they get stuck behind slow, rusty tractors.

Until relatively recently, New Jersey's Hunterdon County was nothing more than a cluster of sleepy farming towns and riverside hamlets. But in the 1980s, land values soared in Hunterdon, and the interstate-highway system began to turn it into a weekend-getaway destination, as well as a bedroom and second-home community for wealthy New Yorkers.

For shoppers, the area is rife with outlets, galleries, gourmet stores, and antiques shops selling everything from Mr. Peanut salt shakers to Victorian library chairs, reupholstered by the man who does some of the leather at Buckingham Palace. And for those overburdened by civilization, there are still miles of infrequently traveled and well-paved country roads and expanses of forested parkland.

Within Hunterdon is the quaint county seat of Flemington, which has become an outlet center known all over the East—in itself a weekend destination for many shopper-travelers. And there is also the scenic portion of the county that borders the Delaware River and includes the river towns of Lambertville, Stockton, and Frenchtown.

But we're talking today about a weekend in the other Hunterdon County to the north, and about towns close to Interstate 78. The town of Clinton—a Victorian jewel at the juncture of the Raritan and Spruce Run rivers, just off the interstate—is a good base for exploration.

Clinton has been around long enough to have been a recruiting outpost for the Revolutionary War. For many years, the village was a stagecoach stop for travelers en route from Manhattan to Easton, while also building an industrial base of mills and quarries.

Contemporary Clinton might at first seem like an idealized version of small-town America, the sort of place Ma and Pa Kettle would go to pick up some dry goods and get a shoe repaired. But a second glance reveals that those quaint Main Street shops cater more to tourists and well-to-do locals than to farmers. In fact, the small-town charm results from the fact that many of its buildings and homes are on the National Register of Historic Places.

And if Clinton seems oddly familiar to some visitors, it's because film companies and television crews have been filming and photographing it for years, whenever they need a quaint Victorian town for the movies or for advertising shots.

Downtown Clinton begins on the far side of an ornate, yellow wrought-iron bridge spanning a waterfall over the Raritan River. On the far side of the one-lane bridge is one of the town's older attractions, a living museum featuring exhibits on the area's agricultural and industrial heritage. The Clinton Historical Museum Village closes its blacksmith shop, schoolhouse, and working mill from October until mid-April, but the grounds and gift shop are open every day except Sundays.

Many artists live in or around Clinton, and they meet and show their work at the Hunterdon Art Center, a community artists' facility and gallery housed in the converted mill across the river from the museum. This stone gristmill, built in the mid-1800s, was in use until the 1950s. When it was purchased by the Art Center and restored, stucco applied in the 19th century was removed to reveal the original gray fieldstone.

On a visit there, I strolled alone through the center's three floors of whitewashed gallery rooms, creaking an occasional board under my feet. The exhibit of illustrations from children's books was charming but not exactly compelling. I spent about as much time sitting in the narrow mill window bays, contemplating the mallards spiraling in the water below, as I did contemplating the artwork.

Outside, once you've explored the perimeters of the Raritan waterfall, it's time to decide how you'd like to spend your afternoon—shopping or schlepping. The more sedentary might choose to browse in downtown Clinton, which offers a lot of shopping in a relatively compact space. The buildings are sometimes at least as charming as the merchandise; many were originally homes and sport big bay windows, gingerbread detail, gables, and porches. Almost all of the town's 20 or so antiques stores are crammed into just one such old Victorian, Pyewacket's Porch, on central Main Street.

Pyewacket's has the atmosphere of a house sale thrown by one's periodically psychotic, but moneyed, Aunt Chloe. There is merchandise everywhere—army-green crocheted afghans, faded oils of forgotten ancestors, kitsch items from the 1970s, nice old pine and mahogany pieces, and a scattering of reproductions.

Nearby, The Attic seemed to have the best prices for antiques. And if you tire of the old, there's always the new: gourmet shops, Orvis fishing gear, even a shop that sells sheepskin and wool products.

For those ready to get away from downtown, Spruce Run Recreation Area is only a few miles north on Route 31. The park has an enormous reservoir (15 miles of shoreline) and, in winter, offers iceboating, ice-skating, and ice-fishing, weather permitting.

During my visit, the weather didn't permit, but the ground was covered with newly fallen snow and the park was deserted, to my eyes, except for a pair of persistent fishermen casting off a small pier. I sat and watched the wind ripple the unfrozen lake against the frozen shore, and saw a few misplaced seagulls glide overhead.

About eight miles east of Clinton is a larger state park, Round Valley Recreation Area. There's another reservoir here, not quite as large, surrounded by denser woods. In the winter, visitors to Round Valley can ice-skate, iceboat, ice-fish, and also cross-country ski—though skiers should be warned that the park's trails are steep and can be rocky. And if you see what looks like an emu or llama grazing the green somewhere, don't be surprised. Some of the more eccentric New York types are raising them as pets. They've even showed up at the annual Hunterdon County Fair, which has, for well over a century, been accustomed to the equine or bovine.

Leaving Clinton, I drove east to spend the afternoon in a few smaller, less-developed towns where signs of development—sometimes of modernity—have been more strictly monitored.

Tewksbury Township, an affluent cluster of towns that have also become progressively less rural, has controlled development through very strict zoning. In other words, it's not that towns such as Oldwick and Mountainville haven't been discovered yet; it's just that they're zealously protected.

Antiquing is really a serious pastime—and business—here. Many shops are frequented by dealers and collectors from New York or Philadelphia. There's even an "antiques trail" with about 50 businesses listed.

The Central New Jersey Antiques Trail Map is the brainchild of Ellie and Bob Haines of Pluckemin Country Antiques. For a copy, send a request, along with a stamped and self-addressed return envelope, to Country Antiques, Route 202-206, Pluckemin, N.J. 07978.

Using a brochure, I followed a small, clockwise loop on the antiques trail, starting in Oldwick, about 15 miles east of Clinton, and going through Mountainville, Lamington, and Pottersville.

Oldwick, the largest town of my loop, was founded in the early 1700s by German immigrants from Philadelphia.

The town was originally named New Germantown, but the name was changed during World War I because of local anti-German sentiment. Zion Lutheran Church, built in 1751 by these settlers, is said to be the state's oldest. Faded and skewed tombstones in the graveyard bear names such as Moses, Elijah, Baltus, and Experience.

The Oldwick General Store, a functioning general store and deli, is a great place to grab a bite with the locals, and eavesdrop on tables full of carpenters—or retired CEOs.

When you've had your fill of the store, walk up tree-lined Main Street from the short-steepled Lutheran church to the Oldwick Methodist Church, dating from the mid-1860s. Just as in Clinton, you'll notice that many of the businesses on the street are housed in former residences.

There also seems to be a zoning law in Oldwick that requires shops to carry antiques, no matter what else they may sell.

Up Route 512 about four miles, a tiny sign marks the Sawmill Road turnoff for Mountainville, perhaps the only town in this vicinity that has actually shrunk over the past century.

Downtown Mountainville consists today of only a few shops. Still, it's worth a visit, partly because of the winding wooded drive along Sawmill Road, which is punctuated by dignified old stone farmhouses and the occasional fleeing deer.

—Lisa Lynch

Directions from Philadelphia: Take I-95 north to 31 north. Take 31 and 202 north to 78, and follow 78 west to Clinton.

For information about shopping or accommodations in Hunterdon County, N.J., contact the Chamber of Commerce at 908-735-5955.

Quaint, but more

LANCASTER, PA.

IF SOMEONE DID A SURVEY, and asked what the word Lancaster called to mind, the top answer would probably be Burt—followed by Amish, buggies, hex signs, and Harrison Ford in the movie *Witness*.

But only Burt would come close to being right.

Lancaster, a city of about 50,000 residents at the heart of the county of the same name, no longer fits any of those other images—if it ever did. Yes, the homey Central Market is still here. So are the quilt displays, the pretzels, the Pennsylvania Dutch festivals, and the hex signs.

But Lancaster in the 1990s is more like a new yuppie, enjoying his or her first trendy car and trendy clothes, and on the prowl for fun times. When my family and I come here for a weekend, it's actually to escape the rural and the quaint, qualities that are ankle-deep in our ex-urban neighborhood.

To us, Lancaster spells e-x-c-i-t-e-m-e-n-t.

Well, OK, maybe just a really nice time.

We come here for the city's good restaurants, pleasant bars, entertaining music clubs, and interesting art galleries. And also to dance, and I don't mean square.

One Saturday night found us at an urban dance club called City Lights, trying to pass for young in a mostly under-30 crowd in painted-on jeans, flailing wildly to such rap hits as "Doo Doo Brown" and "Jump." (This is Lancaster, I had to keep reminding myself.)

"It's not just shoofly pie and potato buns," says Patricia Lawson, a staffer at the city's lovely Franklin and Marshall College.

She tells the story of a Manhattan resident who was astounded when one of the college's students managed to take public transportation the entire way from Lancaster to a nanny's job interview in New York. "We have public transportation here," Lawson sniffs. "We don't just jump on a horse and buggy."

Lancaster was established as a borough in 1742, by which time it was already a large, lively town with nearly 300 houses and an eclectic mix of residents. For those seeking history, some of the oldest surviving homes, from the late 1700s, can be found on the second and third block of East King Street off Penn Square. And some of the oldest churches are also in this vicinity.

The attraction that started us coming to Lancaster was the city's twice-annual "art walk," a tour of special art exhibits at the more than a dozen galleries and print shops stretching three blocks in every direction from Penn Square in the center of downtown. The walk is held the first Sunday in October and the first Sunday in May.

While there for the art walk, we did what practically every new Lancaster tourist does: visited the 257-year-old Central Market on Penn Square, touted as the oldest continually operating farmers market in the nation. (It's open Tuesdays, Fridays, and Saturdays from 6 a.m. to about 2 p.m.)

Don't misunderstand me. I love farmers markets. But as I sat on a Central Market bench, eating a pink caviar cheese roll and a piece of French bread, I had to wonder if civilization hadn't wrought a little too much. The small, 80-stand market is a dizzying mix of tradition and glitz. "We Will Order Lamb, Goats, Hogs," says one stall's sign, across from another reading "Distinctive Affairs . . . Our Own Distinctive Annie's Chocolate Raspberry Dessert Sauce."

The market also has a heap of calico gifts. Across the street from it, there are some high-class shops that would satisfy the most discriminating yuppie's taste, selling everything from coffee beans to beaded dresses in the $500 range.

Also next to the market, and well worth a visit, is the free Heritage Center Museum, open daily from 10 a.m. to 4 p.m. from May through mid-November. It has a collection of breathtaking old quilts and early Lancaster furniture, silver, pewter, toys, and folk art.

As for nightlife, Lancaster's *Intelligencer Journal* headlined a story "Yuppie nightspots becoming toast of the town" back in the early 1990s, and that's still the case. There are many drinking and dining establishments to seek out, but don't exhaust yourself with Saturday night revelry, because there is plenty to do the next day. Try a downtown walking tour, which will take you past America's oldest surviving tobacco shop (the Demuth Tobacco Shop, at 114 E. King St., established in 1770) and into the home and garden of famed 1920s Lancaster artist Charles Demuth. You can also visit Wheatland, the mansion residence of President James Buchanan, at 1120 Marietta St.

There is the reassuringly old-fashioned natural-science museum, the North Museum, on the Franklin and Marshall campus. My son was thrilled with the glass cases filled with examples of local freshwater fish (reproduced in plastic, hanging from metal wires) and mummy heads.

It also includes a planetarium; we enjoyed its story of "The Little Star That Could," featuring a smiley-faced star that hopped around from place to place "in order to become special."

—Fawn Vrazo

Directions from Philadelphia: Lancaster is about 63 miles from Philadelphia. Take the Pennsylvania Turnpike west to Exit 21, follow Route 222 south from there to Route 30, then take Route 30 west. Several exits head south into the city, but Fruitville Pike is the most direct route to downtown.

For a 32-page map and visitors' guide to Lancaster and Lancaster County, call the Pennsylvania Dutch Convention and Visitors Bureau at 800-735-2629, ext. 2322. The bureau is at the Greenfield Road exit of Route 30.

Marietta and Columbia, two charming Susquehanna River towns, are about 12 miles west of Lancaster city. Marietta is noted for its well-preserved 18th- and 19th-century architecture, its restaurants, and bed-and-breakfast establishments. Columbia, a few miles south of Marietta, has antique stores and museums. Wright's Ferry Mansion is the preserved house of a rich ferry owner of the early 1700s (phone: 717-684-4325). Also nearby is the Watch & Clock Museum, the official museum of the National Clock Association (phone: 717-684-8261).

The cloistered community

EPHRATA, PA.

WE ARE HERE TO CONTEMPLATE the contemplative life. To imagine living in a cloistered community. To weigh the pros and cons of seeking utopia in this world.

Actually we're here to spend a weekend away from fractious Philadelphia. We wanted a change of scene that didn't involve long hours in the car.

Ephrata was a perfect choice. It's an easy 65-mile drive from Center City, and wandering around the Ephrata Cloister is as restful as a long soak in a hot tub. Moreover, the town itself is a sleeping beauty, as its neighbor, Lancaster, was before it became commercial and touristy.

Ephrata Cloister is but one of 16 museums that dot Lancaster County like pepper on a fried egg. A ticket stub from any museum in the county is good for reduced admission at any of the others.

In addition, Lancaster County is loaded with other attractions.

If you enjoy visiting the homes of the famous, check out the house in which Robert Fulton, inventor of the steamboat, was born in Quarryville. Wheatland, the Federal mansion of James Buchanan, America's 15th president, is just west of Lancaster.

Railroad buffs can take a nine-mile ride to Paradise on the 150-year-old Strasburg Railroad and visit the Railroad Museum of Pennsylvania and the Toy Train Museum, both also in Strasburg.

And there are myriad opportunities to learn about "the Plain People," such as visiting the Amish Farm and House on Route 30 near Lancaster. Amish in buggies are a common sight in the countryside.

We chose to stick close to Ephrata and the cloister, except for a little Sunday antiquing at nearby Adamstown.

The cloister is a loving restoration of a celibate German religious community that flourished here in the 18th century. While waiting in the reception center for our tour to begin, we watched a short film on the cloister's history. It's quite a story.

In 1732 Conrad Beissel, a German mystic and Seventh-Day Baptist, established the religious society, one of the thousands of communal groups that once flourished in America. Few, though, left a legacy as rich as this one.

The society was based on the medieval concept of service to God through self-denial, meditation, and a life of extreme simplicity. It was made up of a brotherhood and sisterhood and a group of householders—married craftsmen who lived nearby, worshipped at the cloister, and contributed to the community's economy.

Among the few enterprises allowed at the cloister were the making of paper and the printing of books. From 1745 to the 1790s, the brethren printed books in both English and German, and the sisters embellished them with the elaborate Gothic calligraphy called fraktur. These books are considered among the rarest and most precious of early American documents.

The most ambitious work was the translation and publication in 1748 of the 1,200-page *Martyr's Mirror*, a history of persecuted Christians. It was the largest book produced in Colonial America, and it took 15 printers three years to complete 1,300 copies. A copy of *Martyr's Mirror* and a display of the sisters' calligraphy are in the small museum in the reception center.

Beissel managed the funds and kept the members in holy poverty, but he also tried to ease poverty outside the cloister. He fed the needy and gave them clothing and started a free school for neighborhood children.

After the Battle of the Brandywine in 1777, five hundred sick and wounded Continental soldiers were brought here to be cared for. A typhus epidemic broke out, however, swept through the cloister, and killed many brothers and sisters.

The community went into further decline. Old members were dying and there were no new ones to replace them. The celibate orders became extinct about 1800, although householders continued to use the cloister buildings until the 1930s.

Our tour guide was a young woman dressed in a white habit like those once worn by the sisters.

The first stop was the sisters' house, a three-story structure built in 1743, and the attached meetinghouse. Between 1735 and 1749, we were told, the society built log and stone buildings similar to those the members remembered from their German homeland.

We were struck by the quality of the buildings' construction. The stonework was simple but beautiful, and even on outbuildings the woodwork was superb. Apparently there is no German word for slapdash.

These buildings are among the best remaining examples of medieval German architecture in the United States. But saying that makes the buildings sound formal and pretentious, and they're not. Hansel and Gretel would have felt right at home at the Ephrata Cloister.

It takes a little maneuvering to explore these buildings. The halls are narrow, symbolizing the straight and narrow path; the doorways are low to teach humility.

Life at the cloister was highly organized. The brothers and sisters spent their waking hours in labor, meditation, and worship. They slept on wooden planks 18 inches wide, with wooden blocks for pillows. Their diet consisted of bread, roots, greens, milk, butter, and cheese; usually there was only one meal a day. Some members fasted seven days at a time and slept only three or four hours out of 24.

Church services were held on the first floor of the meetinghouse; singing and writing classes were held upstairs. Beissel composed many hymns and taught choral singing with a falsetto intonation that created an otherworldly effect.

The tour includes the 1748 Beissel cabin and a typical householder cabin, which has been restored. We peeked in at the bakehouse, almonry (the almshouse where the homeless could find shelter), the weaver's shop, and the print shop, where we watched a vintage press in action.

Then we dropped off the tour and wandered through the small graveyard where Beissel and many of his followers are buried.

Later, we decided to do Ephrata in style and comfort, which is simple: Just remember the name Doneckers.

The Guesthouse at Doneckers and the 1777 House are the best accommodations in the area, and the restaurant at Doneckers was described by *Gourmet* magazine as "world-class."

In addition, the "Doneckers Community," as it's called, includes attractive shops; a four-story marketplace of working artists and galleries, and a farmers market.

We stayed at the 1777 House, which was built by Jacob Gorgas, a master clockmaker and a cloister householder. The quarters, all different and distinctive, are named for members of the cloister.

We chose Brother Gideon's Loft in the carriage house, a multilevel first-floor suite with a private entrance, fireplace, and Jacuzzi. The whitewashed walls were highlighted with pastels of lavender and peach.

Somewhere between luxuriating in the Jacuzzi, sipping champagne chilled in the suite's little refrigerator, and lights out, we debated the pros and cons of a weekend in Ephrata.

It wasn't much of a debate. Neither of us could think of any cons.

—Chuck Lawliss

Directions from Philadelphia: Take the Pennsylvania Turnpike west to Exit 21 (Denver), go south on Route 222 to Route 322, and take Route 322 west six miles to Ephrata.

For more information on places to stay, or other attractions in Lancaster County, contact the Pennsylvania Dutch Convention and Visitors Bureau at 800-735-2629 or 717-299-8901.

The Ephrata Cloister is at 632 W. Main St., phone 717-733-6600. The cloister is open daily, April through November, and daily except Monday the rest of the year.

The Strasburg Rail Road, on Route 741 east in Strasburg, offers a scenic steam-train ride through Pennsylvania Dutch countryside. Phone 717-687-7522. Across the street is the Pennsylvania Railroad Museum, which you don't want to miss. Phone 717-687-8628.

The Adamstown Antiques Mall is along Route 272 in Adamstown, a few miles north of the turnpike. It is open from Thursday through Monday all year, although Sunday is by far the busiest day. There are numerous motels and restaurants in the area. Phone 717-484-0464.

The other Delaware

LEWES, DEL.

AS DUSK GENTLY SUFFUSED a brilliant fall day, I stood at the crest of a low rise from which a narrow sandspit fell away to the north.

East of the spit, the silvery-gray Atlantic swept off to meet an equally silvery-gray sky at some invisible horizon. To the west, a small bay curved into the land and then out again, the town on its far shore only an indistinct smudge in the failing light.

Suddenly, above the bay, a poppy-colored sun emerged from tall banks of cloud. We watched, hushed, as it charted a careful course precisely between the masts of two anchored sailboats before sinking majestically out of sight.

It was a glorious, quintessentially Caribbean moment.

Except that this wasn't the Caribbean.

It was Delaware—not the familiar du Pont-monied northern part of the state, with its grand mansions and prominent museums, but the flatter, wilder south.

The spit of land was Cape Henlopen, where Delaware Bay meets the Atlantic. The town hidden in shadow was Lewes (pronounced LEW-is), a charming nest of one-of-a-kind shops and carefully preserved 18th- and 19th-century houses.

And Philadelphia was a mere three hours or so away—assuming you were foolish enough to make the trip nonstop, rather than nosing around the salt marshes, wildlife refuges, historic towns and villages, and beaches of the coastal plain that begins just south of Wilmington.

That plain, which for millennia was ocean bottom, covers 94 percent of the state's not-quite-2,000 square miles. Today, corn and soybeans cover much of this former sea floor. But for some 100 miles, where the plain meets the Delaware River and Bay, water and land remain locked in a symbiotic embrace that shapes both landscape and human activity.

Wending its way south through this watery domain is sinuous, two-lane Route 9. Only a few miles south of Wilmington, it offers a stop in New Castle, where cobblestone streets and pre-Revolutionary buildings announce the town's historic past. Here William Penn first stepped onto New World soil in 1682, and here Delaware was governed through much of the 18th century from the still-standing New Castle Court House.

The road next crosses the Chesapeake & Delaware Canal, the heavily used shipping route between Baltimore to the west and Philadelphia and the Atlantic Ocean to the east. South through Port Penn, it runs right next to a narrow, rocky beach, where fishermen can look directly across the Delaware River at the cooling tower of the Hope Creek nuclear plant in New Jersey.

Farther still, the road weaves through thickets of marsh grass high as a man's head, above which a brilliant sky rises clear, no tree or hill breaking its grand sweep. From here, a short detour westward leads to Odessa, another early Delaware town whose historic district is listed on the National Register. Three of the historic houses are owned and operated by Winterthur Museum and Gardens, and many private homes are open during the annual house tour held the first weekend in December.

Beyond Odessa, a turn off Route 9 leads into Bombay Hook National Wildlife Refuge, which stretches for eight miles along the bay near Smyrna, one of a series of refuges along the Atlantic and Delaware Bay coasts that provide vital resting grounds for migrating birds on the North Atlantic flyway. As at the Edwin B. Forsythe Refuge in Brigantine, N.J., and the Prime Hook Refuge farther south in Delaware, hundreds of thousands of birds stop here to feed and rest on their long trips north in the spring and south in the fall.

From Bombay Hook, the road skirts to the east of Delaware's capital, Dover, and ends at Route 113. Not far from the junction, just to the east on Kitts Hummock Road, is the plantation of John Dickinson, the prominent Colonial farmer and lawyer who earned the nickname "Penman of the Revolution" for his essays on Colonial rights and liberty. His *Letters From a Pennsylvania Farmer* (Dickinson owned land in Pennsylvania as well as Delaware) set forth the case for opposition to English taxes, and he set his political views to music in the popular "Liberty Song."

Guides in the house explain pre-Revolutionary farm life and a video in the visitor center gives an introduction to Dickinson and his philosophy. (He eventually freed his slaves.)

From here, there are two routes to Lewes, a good stopping point for a weekend visit to the area. The direct route picks up State Route 1 to the east when it forks off Route 113; the indirect route follows 113 south to Georgetown, the seat of Sussex County and the site of a small but fascinating exhibit of sunken treasure and the adventurers who reclaimed it.

"Treasures of the Sea," at the Delaware Technical and Community College in Georgetown, displays $4 million worth of gold and silver bars, swords and cannon, coins, jewelry, and emeralds retrieved from the sunken Spanish galleon *Nuestra Senora de Atocha* off the Florida Keys, as well as photographs and videos of the expedition that discovered the hoard.

The galleon was carrying treasure from the mints and smelters of Central and South America back to Spain when it sank in a Caribbean hurricane in 1622. Its wreckage was discovered in 1985 by treasure hunter Mel Fisher, whose financial backers included Georgetown contractor Melvin L. Joseph and Delmarva peninsula chicken magnate Frank Perdue.

The exhibit is enchanting despite its small size and gives a vivid portrayal of the mining, smelting, and coining of silver in the 17th-century Americas. Maps of the far-flung mints, established from Mexico to Bolivia and Peru, show the astonishing reach of the Europeans and the great distances the treasure had to travel before it arrived at the ships that would carry it across the Atlantic.

The exhibition also includes a video showing some of the salvage work.

While a trip down Route 9 is one way to imbibe the maritime atmosphere of Delaware, there is also the possibility of approaching Lewes by sea, as Henry Hudson and his Dutch crew did in 1609 when they became the first Europeans to set foot in Delaware. Ferries leave frequently from Cape May for the 70-minute, 17-mile run across the mouth of Delaware Bay.

Lewes is just north of Cape Henlopen, which, like Cape May, was charted and named by a later Dutch captain, Cornelius May. He named the cape on the Delaware side Hindlopen, after his home town.

May was just one of many explorers and traders who made the Dutch a familiar presence on the Delaware River throughout the 17th century in their voracious pursuit of furs for sale in Europe. Emboldened by the success of that trade, the Dutch in 1631 sent 32 settlers to establish a whaling station near Cape Hindlopen, on the site of present-day Lewes. The little town, called Zwaanendael, met the fate of so many other early American settlements: Its inhabitants were all massacred.

But the Europeans persevered, and by the end of the 17th century, Lewes was well-established. Fortunately for visitors, Lewes has made a determined effort to preserve many old buildings, both from the town and from its surrounding countryside. Many, in fact, have been moved into the same neighborhood to create a historic district that displays a wealth of architectural styles spanning two centuries and well repays a few hours' stroll.

Here are one of the earliest cabins, part of a small house dating to 1665, a 1720 fisherman's cottage, the house built for Gov. Daniel Rodney in 1800, and a building that still bears the scar of a cannonball from the British bombardment of 1812. All told, the town boasts about 30 old houses and commercial establishments, including about 20 that date from before 1850.

Unlike Williamsburg, Va., with its stage-set air, most of Lewes' houses are the seats of living history. Aside from a half-dozen or so buildings owned by the Lewes Historical Society, all are privately owned and occupied. The 1720 fisherman's cottage, for example, is a physician's office. Although many owners have meticulously restored interiors, all except those owned by the Historical Society are closed to public view except for rare occasions. One of those occasions is the annual house tour in December.

Also open for the tour are a few of the Lewes Historical Society buildings, including the Thompson general store and the Burton-Ingram House, which dates from 1789 and houses a museum of early Lewes furniture and portraits.

The tour includes the Cannonball House, now a maritime museum, a number of churches, and the Zwaanendael Museum, with exhibitions devoted to the history of Lewes and Delaware. The Zwaanendael, which is not a historic building, should not be missed and, in fact, is almost impossible to miss. Its baroque red brick exterior, which looks like nothing else for miles around, is modeled after the town hall of Hoorn, the Netherlands.

Another interesting stop is Preservation Forge, a working blacksmith shop and museum where ancient tools festoon the walls and such items as pothooks and fireplace tools are for sale.

A walking tour of the town's historic sites also weaves through Lewes' small but tony commercial district. While tacky souvenirs are available here, the offerings run more to one-of-a-kind art glass, casually elegant clothing, and antique jewelry. The stores are a reflection of Lewes' tourist trade, which sees mainly middle-aged affluent visitors, according to the local Chamber of Commerce.

But as a waterfront town, Lewes does have its earthier side. Just across the Lewes-Rehoboth Canal from the historic district is Fisherman's Wharf, from which boats leave for deep-sea fishing, whale-watching tours, and sunset cruises. When the fish are running, its parking lot fills up by 6:30 a.m. with the four-wheel-drive vehicles of sportsmen heading for a day on the ocean.

Of course, the ocean is always nearby as a counterpoint to Lewes' busyness. At Cape Henlopen State Park, there are miles of seashore, and a trail that leads across the famous walking dunes, shifting hills of sand where half-buried trees bear witness to the dunes' restlessness. The park offers 3,300 acres of dunes, pinelands, and marsh, and trails on which to explore them—and, for the lucky, a spectacular sunset to bring the day to a close.

—Andrea Knox

Directions from Philadelphia: Take 95 south. Near Wilmington, pick up 13 south to 113 south, to 1 south, then northeast on 9 to Lewes.

Lewes offers both motel and bed-and-breakfast accommodations. A complete list is available from the Lewes Chamber of Commerce; phone 302-645-8073.

The historic houses of Lewes and other buildings are closed in the winter, and only those owned by the Lewes Historical Society are open during the summer tourist season. (Most shops and craft stores and many restaurants are open Saturdays through the winter.)

A Victorian time capsule

LEWISBURG, PA.

WE WERE AWARE THAT SOME very well-known Americans had made their way to this central Pennsylvania town over the years—such familiar names as Al Capone, Alger Hiss, and Jimmy Hoffa, to mention only a few.

But there would be some significant differences between their visit and ours.

My wife and I would spend the weekend in bed-and-breakfast style, enjoying the pleasant ambience of what is certainly one of America's best-preserved 19th-century towns. Then we would hop in the car and drive home to Philadelphia.

They, on the other hand, spent a lot of their time in cells at Lewisburg Penitentiary—bed and breakfast of a sort, perhaps. But no weekend passes to stroll the historic streets, and certainly no driving home after Sunday brunch.

Too bad for them; like their fellow inmates, they missed a lot. Lewisburg is a time capsule of showcase Federal and Victorian architecture, much of it in exquisite condition. The historic district has more than 600 original structures—not bad for a borough of about 5,000 residents.

But a weekend visit to Lewisburg can be much more than historic architecture.

If the weather's cold and the snow is sufficient, there's cross-country skiing on ungroomed trails at nearby Raymond B. Winter Park, as well as ice skating. And there's antiquing, looking in on several small but excellent museums, exploring other nearby river towns, catching a sporting event or cultural performance at Bucknell University, and furniture shopping at the factory store of Pennsylvania House, a Lewisburg-based manufacturer.

And the scenery is also good anytime. Route 45 runs through Lewisburg and slices southwest into the Buffalo Valley, an agricultural region whose rich, fertile land still supports well-kept old farmhouses, huge bank barns, and herds of dairy cattle. (The valley, like other surrounding places, is named for the animal, although there is no direct historical evidence that buffalo ever roamed here.) On Route 45, or on Route 192 just a few miles north, travelers will encounter, especially on Sundays, the buggies of Old Order Amish who have fled the disintegration of their homeland in Lancaster County in the last few decades.

We arrived in Lewisburg late on a Friday morning, so smitten by the feel of the town that we just parked the car downtown and started walking. Many towns make idle boasts that visitors can "step back in time" on their streets, but this is one of the rare ones where the cliche has a ring of truth about it.

"We haven't had any major revitalizations; it's just been cherished over the years," says Nada Gray, the borough manager.

After a five-minute stroll off Market Street, we came upon the red brick, Greek-revival county courthouse, whose facade is dominated by four huge white pillars. The bell in the tower, a walking brochure informed us, was presented by Simon Cameron, a native Pennsylvanian and Lincoln's first secretary of war. It was built in the late 1850s with private donations; an addition was put on in 1973, but only a trained eye would notice it, so skillful was the work.

Just a few steps away, we paused to admire the detail on a yellow stucco Italianate mansion at 60 Second St. We found this style, also called Tuscan villa, repeated elsewhere, including the Slifer House, once the home of 19th-century entrepreneur Eli Slifer, and now a small museum. The Second Street residence was built in 1870 and had long, narrow windows on the first floor and, unlike Federal-style homes, inside shutters. Several oval windows ran across the top of the facade, below the roof line.

From here, we strolled down Second Street toward Market, noticing all the while the Victorian embellishments that had been added in later years to the plain, Federal facades, which date to the 1830s and 1840s: porches, etched and stained glass, terra cotta, cast iron, or gingerbread wood trim. Assessing the relative merits of all these touches—and dating them—can become something of a game.

It was a game we were playing when, at Second and Market streets, we came upon the granddaddy of Lewisburg buildings—at least as far as we were concerned.

Dominating one corner of Second and Market was a huge brick building whose original Federal lines had been considerably enhanced by porches and gables, mansard roofs, a tower, some finely molded terra cotta decorations on the facade, and beautiful, intricate Tiffany windows. Although it is a private building that includes apartments and a beauty parlor, we were able to step into the vestibule and admire the tile work there, and, through the glass doors, the chestnut paneling on the ceilings and walls within.

What a place! Built in the 1830s, the building was expanded and reworked in 1852 and became the Lewisburg National Bank, then was gradually remodeled in the 1880s and 1890s to become a private home. The current owner seems to have spared no expense in its care—exactly the case with so many other old homes in Lewisburg.

There is a drugstore across the street, and has been since 1845. The Victorian ornamentation and additions on this building, which also contains a bookstore, hide the original 1806 log house. Just across Second Street on the other corner is the Lewisburg Hotel, which dates to the 1830s (the out-of-character portico was added 100 years later).

Before checking in at the hotel, we walked down this last block of Market to the Susquehanna River, on the way encountering Owen Mahon, an affable (strangers will nod or say hello in this town) retired Bucknell professor who owns a small art gallery a few blocks away. Mahon pointed out his home in this block, joking that it was built in 1913 and was, thus, "practically new."

Indeed, most of the homes and buildings on the block date to the 1830s and 1840s, or earlier, except for the First Presbyterian Church (Greek revival, of course), which was built in 1856. The house next door to the church, we noted, was the boyhood home of Norman Thomas, the Socialist who frequently ran for U.S. president earlier in this century. (Speaking of the famous, legendary New York Giants pitcher Christy Mathewson, who attended Bucknell, lived at 129 Market St.)

We saved the Packwood House, at the end of the block, for the next day. After getting our luggage, we checked in at the hotel where the room, although comfortable and furnished with period reproductions, pretty much matched the very cheap price. (We ended up at the Pineapple Inn Bed and Breakfast down the street the next night.) Dinner in the hotel's Governors' Room that night, however, was a successful meld of historic ambience in the original, chestnut-paneled dining room, and quality food from the kitchen.

Early Friday afternoon, we set out on a circuit that took us west through the farm country on Route 45 to Mifflinburg, a Victorian town more than 200 years old. Mifflinburg calls itself "the buggy town" because of its history as a buggy manufacturing center prior to the automobile's arrival. (A buggy museum is open here from spring into fall.)

From Mifflinburg, we hooked southeast to New Berlin, where the accent falls on the "ber" instead of the "lin." New Berlin, founded by Germans despite the local pronunciation, was the first county seat and the region's most prosperous town until the Pennsylvania Canal reached Lewisburg in 1830.

New Berlin is still surrounded by the same fertile farmland that attracted settlers two centuries ago. The sweet, pungent smell of manure lay heavy upon the town on our fall visit, although certainly not unpleasantly so. In the center of the village, the sturdy brick courthouse —built in 1815 when this was the county seat—today functions as the local post office, with a small museum of local artifacts on the second floor.

A stroll around New Berlin turned up those familiar, unadorned brick fronts again. In one backyard was an intriguing, octagonal brick smokehouse, which at first glance could easily be mistaken for an upscale outhouse. There were several old churches, among them the Methodist, which was built in 1873 as an Evangelical Church to replace another of the same denomination that dated to 1816. And that church, according to a nearby historical marker and memorial stone, was the first built in America by Albright's People, the followers of 19th-century preacher Jacob Albright, today merged into the Evangelical United Brethren Church.

Back to Lewisburg we headed, stopping first just outside town to check out the antiques at the Victorian Lady on Route 45. After that, we crossed the highway to Brookpark Farm, a semi-rural shopping center that has, among other things, an indoor antiques co-op, a rug outlet, a bed and breakfast, the aforementioned Pennsylvania House furniture showroom—even a few roosters strutting about the property.

In our earlier ramblings about town, we'd stopped in the antiques-laden Pineapple Inn on Market Street and met the owners, Deborah and Charles North. Now, as we returned to the hotel, we resolved to spend our second night with the Norths, even though our bathroom would be in the hall, because the rooms with bath were already taken. It would turn out to be a wise choice; the Norths were a pleasant couple, and their 1857 home—Federal style, of course—was furnished with an eclectic assortment of antiques that didn't have the usual you-can't-sit-down feel to them.

That night, while strolling Market Street down from the inn, we couldn't help admiring—even chuckling at—Lewisburg's only art deco building, the Campus Theater. We knocked on the door of a small adjoining office and chatted with Jacquie Stiefel, the owner and widow of a man who, with his brothers, ran a chain of Pennsylvania movie houses that bore their name.

When we told her we'd been admiring the touches on the theater—the big blue and orange panels on the facade, with a bas-relief buffalo in the center (Bucknell's colors and the university's sports symbol); the stainless steel marquee, etc.—she took us on a brief tour between movies, pointing out the wall murals and art deco light fixtures, and the striped doors with silhouettes of bison and college sports figures.

On Saturday, we just strolled the town, stopping in to admire the work of several Pennsylvania artists at Owen Mahon's gallery, the Open Door; pausing to read the newspaper and have coffee and doughnuts at the bakery across the street; and generally letting the town just take us where it would.

That included a five-minute walk to the nearby campus of Bucknell, a liberal arts institution whose manicured lawns and fine brick buildings (Greek revival, of course) fairly reeked of affluent academe in a small-town setting. It looked and felt like the kind of place where you wish you'd attended college, or where you hope your children might.

We also managed to look in on the Packwood House for something of a zany tour of the antiques and art collections of its onetime owners, the late John and Edith Fetherston. The guide, Bob Sterner, related the Packwood House tale with wit and the wisdom of somebody who actually knew Edith Fetherston.

Fetherston died in 1972, but not before becoming a legend in her native (and somewhat conservative) town. Her paintings, which range from amateurish strokes populated by stick people to not-so-bad floral designs, hang throughout the place. One, "Lewisburg Scandal," depicts several women cavorting naked in a Garden-of-Eden-type setting. Others bear titles such as "The Top Goat Is the Economist Jumping Into the Unknown," or "In the Moonlight, Drunk With Delight."

That night, after checking in at the Pineapple Inn, we headed for the nearby Temperance House for dinner. Owen Mahon swore he'd had "at least 142 steaks" there and never once been disappointed. It was a crackerjack recommendation; our steak and prime rib were a notch above excellent, on a par with what you'd expect at the finest of steakhouses.

But it was a meal that wanted walking off, and with the late fall temperatures still in the high 50s, we set out up Market Street. Lewisburg is equally pleasant by evening, in no small measure because of the soft, incandescent light thrown from the three frosted globes atop each of its many Victorian light standards.

The light posts are original, 75-year-old Westinghouse stock designs that have long since been discontinued by that company, and scrapped by most cities and towns. But not Lewisburg, and here was yet another insight into why the town is what it is today: Lewisburg kept the molds after Westinghouse gave up making the line, and the town is still casting the standards at a local foundry, and erecting them as the borough coffers permit.

Thus, as you walk down Market Street, you see that most of the intersecting streets in the historic district have the same warm lighting.

Remove the cars from the streets, and some of the more modern signs, and, why, you could almost step back in time!

Lord willing and the river don't rise, we'll take that stroll again soon.

—Mike Shoup

Directions from Philadelphia: Take the Blue Route to 9 north. After about 80 miles, pick up 80 west for about 65 miles to 15. Take 15 south about 8 miles to Lewisburg.

For more information on accommodations, or on the general area, call the Susquehanna Valley Visitors Bureau: 717-524-7234.

No visitor to Lewisburg should miss the campus of Bucknell University, if only just for a walk-through. Those who might want to link their stay to some campus cultural or sporting event should call for a quarterly calendar: 717-524-3260.

The old Lincoln Highway

JENNERSTOWN, PA.

JUST WEST OF THIS VILLAGE about 15 miles southwest of Johnstown, on the north side of the road, are the two stone gateposts for Jenner Pines, a campground where early motoring adventurers pitched tents or slept on the ground beside their cars.

That was before tourist cabins were built along U.S. Route 30—the Lincoln Highway—to accommodate travelers along the nation's first coast-to-coast motor route.

The Lincoln Highway was a concept long before it was concrete: the dream of linking together older byways into a road stretching from New York's Times Square to San Francisco.

Moseying along its original route today, over a stretch through this part of Pennsylvania, can fill a weekend with the sights from ages past—a time when auto travel was slower-paced, gentler than it is today. The weekend wanderer has time to appreciate the natural beauty through which the road passes, to stop and stare and maybe chuckle a bit at the vestiges of roadside attractions long gone to seed.

West of Schellsburg, for example, a giant, sculptured-concrete Little Boy Blue silently blows his horn beside the gate to what once was Storyland, a theme park that enthralled traveling children before there were real, live Mickey Mice, talking Lincolns, buildings that make their own earthquakes, and vast swimming pools that generate their own tidal waves. Today, a visitor can peek through the wire fence and see weeds overgrowing the domicile of the Little Old Woman Who Lived in a Shoe, and an elf who has lost an ear forlornly watching over a Humpty Dumpty forever about to fall.

Tourist cabins were ubiquitous when the Lincoln Highway was the ultimate in American motor travel. A few remain along the route. Some have clearly seen better days—the former Shorty's Place in Fulton County now rents cabins seasonally to hunters and has a nude dancing club next door.

But one cluster of cabins has been refurbished to a 1990s comfort level while retaining the aura of the 1940s Lincoln Highway. Debbie Altizer says she's a country girl who persuaded her husband, Bob, to flee the city in the early 1980s and look for a small business somewhere in the countryside. What they found was the Lincoln Motor Court, five miles west of Bedford, where their sweat, imagination, and entrepreneurship have transformed a near ruin into a most pleasant—and reasonably priced—place to stay.

With a menagerie of pets of their own, the Altizers welcomed the cocker spaniel that was traveling with this moseyer and his companion on a tour of the Lincoln Highway—and even deputized their retriever to guide our spaniel around the adjoining meadow.

The couple is working hard to preserve the tradition of hospitality once so prevalent along this historic route.

The Altizers are not alone in their interest in the highway's history. A movement is now afoot in southwestern Pennsylvania to preserve the relics of bygone eras, and the state of mind that impelled the coast-to-coast roadway they mark, by creating something called the Lincoln Highway State Heritage Park—a 10-mile-wide, 140-mile-long corridor of history, tourism, and hoped-for economic development.

The proposed corridor begins at Caledonia State Park just west of Gettysburg and follows U.S. 30 through Franklin, Fulton, Bedford, Somerset, and Westmoreland counties to Irwin, just east of Pittsburgh.

When the state officially designates the corridor a heritage park—the movement's backers expect that to happen in the spring of 1995—it will perhaps refocus the attention of travelers on a section of roadway that once was famous to the motoring public. Indeed, it was instrumental in kindling the still-smoldering love affair between Americans and their automobiles.

Already, a heritage park task force has produced an excellent driving guide to the area, which is available from visitor information offices, many merchants, or by calling 800-765-3331.

A common misconception is that today's U.S. 30 and the Lincoln Highway are one and the same. It's true that about two-thirds of the Lincoln Highway's original 3,389 miles more or less correspond with today's Route 30, becoming conjoined at Philadelphia and separating again around Granger, Wyo. The original route began at Times Square and ended at Lincoln Park overlooking the Pacific in San Francisco. Motorists drove west on 42nd Street to the Hudson, crossed the river by ferry, and journeyed through New Jersey to Philadelphia along the old King's Highway, which was an Indian footpath long before the first European ever set foot in the New World.

Westward from Philadelphia, the Lincoln Highway followed an existing system of turnpikes to Pittsburgh, collectively known as the Pennsylvania Road, which in turn owed their existence to paths traced long before by migrating animals, by Native Americans, and by early military road builders. Where Route 30 has veered elsewhere on modern bypasses and roadway improvements, the original Lincoln Highway route often can be identified by names such as Forbes Road, Pitt Road, or Penn Road.

The man who dreamed the concept that became the Lincoln Highway was Carl Graham Fisher, owner of the Indianapolis Motor Speedway, who inspired "good roads" groups across the breadth of the country to lobby for his dream.

But the man who provided the concrete was Henry Joy, president of the Packard Motor Car Co., who contributed the first $150,000 in 1912 to the campaign for a paved, coast-to-coast motor route. Joy had originally planned a road from Gettysburg to Washington to honor the martyred president. But when Congress rejected the idea, Joy lent his allegiance, money, and fondness for Lincoln to Fisher's east-west roadway movement. Soon the original dreamer was in the background and Joy led the project to fruition.

As early as 1913, adventuresome souls could get from coast to coast along Joy's Lincoln Highway Route, but the road was never "opened" in today's sense that a strip of concrete is laid from here to there and then formally opened to traffic. State, district, and local groups simply made improvements when they had sufficient support and money; the road evolved and its progress was largely in the hands of dreamers.

Today's dreamer is Joanne Zeigler, a senior planner for the Bedford County Planning Commission and key figure in the Lincoln Highway State Heritage Park movement. Like Fisher's, her dreams are big and will require someone else's entrepreneurship, as well as government encouragement, to become reality.

Among them:

• A transportation museum in downtown Bedford—telling the story of road development in the United States and demonstrating how road transportation shaped the places we live.

• A redeveloped scenic overlook at the "ship hotel" at Grand View Point, the 2,464-foot summit of Allegheny Ridge; the hotel is perhaps the most famous relic of the Lincoln Highway's golden age.

• A scattering of privately owned bed-and-breakfasts along the entire route, which in turn would stimulate the growth of travel-related small businesses and support services.

• A two-week-long annual festival, celebrating the 250-year transportation history of the corridor.

• Designation of large stretches of the Lincoln Highway as a Federal Scenic Highway, which would make available federal funds and private grant money for further enhancements.

Today, the moseying traveler along the highway realizes that the speeding hordes on the freeways will never know the joy of such discoveries as Fulton House and Marty McCullen, historian. Fulton House, built in 1793 as a wayfarer's inn, now serves as an annex to the McConnellsburg Borough Hall and as the home of the Fulton County Historical Society.

Once open only by appointment and during the Fall Folk Festival, the building was open seven days a week as an experiment during the summer of 1994. McCullen, proudly noting that an average of eight visitors per day had toured it, showed off its architecture and period pieces—antique furnishings, a Civil War sword, a late-19th-century disc-driven music box that still works flawlessly—with an avuncular pride.

"Be sure to come back for the Fall Folk Festival," he bade his departing visitors. "Fulton County really comes alive then."

Fulton House is but one of the heritage corridor's many surviving links to the early days of the republic. At the western terminus of the corridor is the Irwin House (1836), a former stagecoach stop. Heading east, at Laughlintown, the Compass Inn (1799) is now a museum. At Jennerstown, the Dennison Tavern (1836) is now an antiques shop. In Buckstown, the John Statler house (1834), originally a tavern, is now a private residence.

In the Schellsburg cemetery west of town, there is the log Reformed and Lutheran Church (1806), where services are still held on special occasions. Three miles west of Bedford, the Jean Bonnet Tavern (1762) still serves its original purpose as a place to dine and lodge. At Bedford, an entire re-created hamlet of 18th-century buildings—Old Bedford Village—has costumed guides who demonstrate the crafts of the era.

Seven miles east of Everett, at a particularly scenic juncture, the Juniata Crossings Tavern (circa 1800) is now a lodge and antiques shop. East of Breezewood on Ray's Hill, long abandoned and deteriorating rapidly, the Mountain House (circa 1800) was once a four-star stop for affluent stagecoach passengers. And in Fayetteville, the Paul-Corbutt House, an early 19th-century manor, holds open house and garden tours in spring and fall and at Christmas time.

Military history is preserved throughout the corridor, as well. There were Civil War episodes around Chambersburg and Fayetteville. Bushy Run Battlefield, east of Irwin, was the site of a 1763 engagement between British troops and hostile Indians. Fort Ligonier, the reconstructed British fort, dating to 1758, is but a short stroll from Ligonier's charming town square. Fort Bedford is a restored 18th-century stronghold on the Juniata River in Bedford's historic district. And just east of the town of Fort Loudon is the reconstruction of the eponymous military post dating to the French and Indian War. Re-enactments and costumed tour guides entertain visitors to many of these sites.

Perhaps the most memorable of all the buildings from the old Lincoln Highway is the "ship hotel." The two-story building shaped like a ship sits on one of the most spectacular lookout points on the entire road. It was built in 1931 by one Herbert Paulson, who, looking out toward Maryland and West Virginia from this scenic spot on a foggy day, was reminded of the view from a ship's deck while at sea.

Imagine chugging up the 7 percent grade of Allegheny Ridge in a '29 Ford, radiator boiling over and engine whining, rounding a last curve to see an ocean liner riding the crest of the hill! Scarcely a motorist could pass without taking on water and permitting the engine to cool while admiring the view from the hotel's second-story deck. The old ship is still a startling sight, although a visitor must maneuver between old truck tires that discourage entrance to the pitted and pockmarked parking area, and a junkyard dog patrols the upper deck snarling reminders that this is privately owned and visitors are no longer welcome. Even on a hazy autumn day, however, the vista is grand enough to justify a stop.

There are eight state parks in the heritage corridor and the Lincoln Highway passes through about 45 miles of state forest lands. Innumerable hiking trails—including the 70-mile Laurel Highlands Trail between Johnstown and Ohiopyle State Park—are accessible from the Lincoln Highway. The corridor's nine summits—from Piney Mountain west of Gettysburg to Chestnut Ridge near Latrobe—offer scenic vistas from 2,000-foot elevations that are denied to drivers of the Pennsylvania Turnpike's tunnels.

Three of the state parks—Keystone, Shawnee, and Cowans Gap—are on lakes. Four of the state parks have rental cabins; five have campgrounds.

Caledonia State Park, the corridor's eastern terminus, also has Totem Pole Playhouse, a summer stock theater that innkeeper Debbie Altizer, a woman who knows where the good times are, recommends highly. To the west, just north of Jennerstown, the Mountain Playhouse offers professional theater from May to October in a converted 1805 grist mill on charming grounds adjoining a rustic pond. And still farther west, at Greensburg, the former Palace movie theater has been transformed into a performing arts center for ballet and stage productions.

With the fast-food chains now clustered around the turnpike, and Lincoln Highway's glamour now tarnished by time, dining facilities on some stretches of the corridor can be, to use planner Joanne Zeigler's term, "sparse." Still, along the western stretch of the highway, there are the justifiably well-known Green Gables Restaurant (adjoining the Mountain Playhouse outside Jennerstown), the Mountain View Inn outside of Greensburg, and several excellent restaurants in and around Ligonier. Elsewhere, let whim and a sense of adventure be your guides.

The Pie Shoppe bakery across Lincoln Highway from the historic Compass Inn Museum in Laughlintown yielded not only choice pastries, but splendid sandwiches on fresh-baked bread for a roadside picnic we stopped for at the next scenic overlook. And this weary, homeward-bound traveler approaching the summit of Scrub Ridge couldn't resist the sign that read "Fish—All you can eat—$5.95" outside the Scrub Ridge Inn.

Aesthetically, the place may have seen better days, but rarely a better repast than the one the co-proprietor, Ruth Seiders, set out on the oil-cloth-covered table beside the ketchup bottle and the A-1 sauce. Seiders and her partner, Wendell Strait, do everything themselves. He's the cook whose sautéed whiting coated with a secret blend of spices comprised the all-you-can-eat special and whose crab cakes pleased my traveling companion.

The principal house specialty is steak—from 12 ounces to 84 ounces—and if you can consume the 84-ounce slab and all the trimmings within an hour, it's free. Pictures of three recent winners are thumbtacked to one rough-pine wall, near the entrance to the dance floor.

"We're like family here," Seiders said. Strait said the inn's upstairs rooms—"more like a dormitory, really," Seiders interjected—are booked solid by hunters during the game seasons in the surrounding forestland. "They keep coming back, year after year," he said.

Sated and vowing to return another day, we finished our moseying journey, optimistic that if Joanne Zeigler can find enough Wendell Straits, Ruth Seiderses, Debbie Altizers, and Marty McCullens, new dreams one day will indeed come to life along the old Lincoln Highway.

—Tom Wark

Directions from Philadelphia: It's about a 2-hour drive from Philadelphia to Chambersburg via the Pennsylvania Turnpike and Interstate 81. The proposed Lincoln Highway State Heritage Park begins eight miles east of Chambersburg at Caledonia State Park.

A heritage park task force has produced an excellent driving guide to the area, which is available from visitor information offices or can be obtained by calling the Bedford County Tourist Information Center at 800-765-3331. Within the Lincoln Highway corridor, there are eight state parks: Caledonia (717-352-2161), Cowans Gap (717-485-3948), Buchanan's Birthplace (717-485-3948), Shawnee (814-733-4218), Laurel Mountain (office closed at this writing), Linn Run (412-238-6623), Laurel Ridge (412-455-3744), and Keystone (412-668-2939).

Places to stay are few and far between along the Lincoln Highway, but the Lincoln Motor Court (814-733-2891), five miles west of Bedford, combines the feel of the route's early days with '90s ambience and amenities.

The Coastal Heritage Trail

SALEM, N.J.

THE MAN ON THE RIDING MOWER glanced up at us as we pedaled past him, then raised his hand in a silent greeting.

In the pasture beyond, a pair of horses also seemed to take an interest, lifting their heads from the grass to stare at us, and swishing their long tails.

Only the cows showed no particular enthusiasm. When they looked our way at all, it was with dull, glazed eyes, as if we were too insignificant to merit acknowledgment from creatures of their social status. Truth be told, they didn't excite us much either.

We followed the road into a shadowy patch of woods, then sped quickly downhill before shooting around a quiet, pine-fringed lake and returning to green, open pastures. In the air, the telltale scent of manure mingled with the damp, salty smell of the ocean, reminding us that we were just a stone's throw from the Delaware Bay and, just beyond, the Atlantic Ocean.

This bucolic panorama on a country road south of Salem was not exactly what I had anticipated when I began contemplating a weekend bicycle journey along the newly opened New Jersey Coastal Heritage Trail. "Coastal" to me meant lighthouses and fishing boats—not cows.

Still, I was pleased with what I found. The mostly flat South Jersey countryside proved perfect for cycling, and the verdant farmland, interspersed with small, pre-Revolutionary War towns, provided a peaceful, scenic atmosphere in which to explore New Jersey's coastal legacy.

Developed by the National Park Service and the State of New Jersey, the 275-mile Coastal Heritage Trail follows the Delaware River southeast from Fort Ott State Park—which lies across the river from New Castle, Del.—to Cape May. It then sweeps northeast along the Atlantic coast to Perth Amboy, near Staten Island.

The trail itself consists of a collection of historic and otherwise significant points of interest linked by a network of roads. Though signs direct cars to these sites from such main highways as Route 49 and the Garden State Parkway, there is no strict route to follow, and back roads can be used—as we happily discovered—to get from one point to the next.

With my friend Andy, a veteran coast-to-coast cyclist who had once worked with me in a New York sound studio, I set out on a cloudy spring morning, hoping to cover about half of the trail over two days.

We dropped a car at Port Norris, a coastal town about 15 miles south of Vineland, where the Maurice River slips into Delaware Bay. Then we drove northwest with our bikes to Fort Mott, just 40-odd miles southwest of Philadelphia. Here the Heritage Trail organizers had set up a welcome center with brochures describing trail sites, photographic exhibits detailing the area's maritime history, and a video highlighting the wildlife and people along the trail.

We perused the exhibits, then explored the nearby ruins of Fort Mott, completed in 1896 in anticipation of the Spanish-American War. The fort's disappearing gun carriages were cleverly designed to drop below the parapet immediately after the guns were fired, allowing them to be reloaded in safety. This sneaky tactic, combined with camouflage on the outer wall, would have left enemy ships baffled about who was firing at them—had any of them been considerate enough to blunder into the trap. As it was, the guns were fired only in practice.

We walked through the damp tunnels inside the fort, then mounted wooden steps to the top of the wall to look across the freshly mown grass at the Delaware River. Below, picnickers dined beneath a pavilion, while kite fliers took advantage of the day's gentle breeze.

Mounting our bikes, we rode a short distance to Finns Point National Cemetery, a peaceful enclave carved out of the surrounding marsh and encircled by a stone wall. Tall reeds, alive with chattering birds, towered above the cemetery on all sides, adding to an overall feeling of seclusion.

The 4.5-acre cemetery is the final resting place of 2,436 Confederate soldiers—all prisoners who died at Fort Delaware during the Civil War—as well as 135 Union soldiers and 13 German World War II prisoners, among others. The Confederate graves are marked by a towering obelisk and several weathered plaques bearing each soldier's name and home state. Though it's sad that these Southern men were buried so far from their homes, it's somehow comforting to note that the cemetery lies in a part of New Jersey that is south of the Mason-Dixon Line.

Shortly after noon, Andy and I finally pedaled away from the park and headed southeast toward Salem, most noted, unfortunately, for its troubled nuclear power plant. We had barely started, though, when we encountered the curious sight of a lighthouse sitting about a mile from the nearest water. We later discovered that the 115-foot-tall Finns Point

Rear Range Light, erected in 1876, had once worked in conjunction with another, now-dismantled lighthouse on the coast; a ship's pilot would sight along the two lights, keeping one positioned atop the other, to ensure that the ship stayed in the channel.

The sun began to break through the clouds as we pedaled past the salt marshes and winding waterways along Route 49. We headed down the main street of Salem, passing the famous 500-year-old Salem Oak and gazing up at the lofty 19th-century steeples of the First Baptist and First Presbyterian churches.

Storefronts quickly gave way to barns, and green fields opened up, speckled with grazing horses and cows. Butterflies flitted through the tall, wind-tossed grass. A weeping willow dropped its stringy tendrils down to brush the tops of the yellow wildflowers sprouting alongside the road. The serenity was only slightly tarnished by the roadside warning signs telling passersby what to do if one of the reactors decided to blow its top.

We paused for lunch by the Hancock House State Historic Site, the next point of interest on the trail. Here, on March 21, 1778, British-led troops massacred dozens of sleeping patriots who had supplied provisions to George Washington's army at Valley Forge. An engraved monument commemorates the fallen heroes.

The two-story, brick Hancock House, bordered by a white picket fence, now serves as a museum, though it was locked and silent during our visit. On the far wall, the initials of William and Sarah Hancock and the year 1734 stand out in gray bricks against a background of brown.

We slowly worked our way southward into Cumberland County, crossing rivers and greeting the fishermen and fisherwomen perched on their bridges. Small general stores cropped up at crossroads, beckoning us inside.

At an intersection labeled Gum Tree Corner on my map, I struck up a conversation with Dale Ferguson, the owner of the sole house on the site. He pointed out the renowned gum tree and thanked the area's voracious insect population for his solitude. "Mosquitoes are your best friends if you don't want neighbors," he said, laughing.

Dale steered us to a pleasant, wooded route that carried us downhill and around a small lake. Soon we entered Greenwich, a village of restored frame homes dating from the 1700s. The town made history in 1774 when a group of men staged their own version of the Boston Tea Party—complete with Indian garb—by stealing and burning a shipment of British tea to protest unfair taxation. A granite marker commemorates the event.

From here, we hastened into Bridgeton, the county seat, crossed the Cohansey River and pedaled toward Fairton, about 10 miles west of Millville. The day was waning, and we had more mileage ahead of us than we cared to ponder.

Eager to hit every Coastal Heritage Trail site, I made a bad judgment call about seven miles later when I decided to make a side trip to the state marina in Fortescue, a small bayside fishing hamlet sitting alone at the end of a four-mile road. The wind blew against us the entire way, and when we got there, winded and weary, we discovered nothing but a deserted marina and blocks of empty summer homes.

Allen Will, proprietor of Al's Bait & Tackle, told us the scene picked up quite a bit when summer filled the marina with fishing boats. "The town is fish-dependent," he explained. This insight did little to cheer us as we retraced our four-mile route, then struggled against a head wind for 10 miles to reach my car in Port Norris.

We had parked near the Delaware Bay Schooner Project, an ambitious effort to restore a 66-year-old oyster schooner, while educating the public about the days when this area was a prosperous oyster-harvesting community.

After riding more than 60 miles, we were too tired to justify a trip to East Point Lighthouse, across the Maurice River. We made the long drive back to Fort Mott to pick up Andy's truck and drove back southeast to North Dennis to spend the night.

The morning dawned cloudy. After a diner breakfast in Clermont, five miles from Avalon, we parked a car in Sea Isle City and headed with our bikes aboard for Cape May.

Our first stop there was the 157-foot-tall Cape May Point Lighthouse. Amazingly, the Coast Guard still uses the 135-year-old structure as an active navigational aid.

Predictably, it was closed for repairs during our visit. We had to settle for "climbing" to the top vicariously through a videotape. The panoramic view out over the town looked marvelous.

After checking out the aquarium exhibits and fossils in the visitors center, Andy and I drove into town. By now, it had started to drizzle, dampening our enthusiasm for touring the quaint shops and Victorian homes that give Cape May its allure.

A minor rift developed at this point between Andy and me. I wanted to ignore the rain and start cycling; he, having more common sense, did not. So we split up, agreeing to meet in Wildwood in a few hours.

As I headed out of town on Pittsburgh Avenue, I chanced upon a somber bayside memorial honoring the many dozens of fishermen lost at sea since 1897. Their names were carved into a wall, while nearby stood statues of a woman and two children, clutching each other and staring sadly out to sea.

Despite my rain poncho, I got quickly drenched as I pedaled along the coast toward Wildwood. Once I arrived, though, a strange thing happened: The sun came out.

I stared out at the ocean for a while, watching the clouds move out to sea, then rode along the empty streets, eerily quiet without the summer's crowds to fill them. When I reached Hereford Inlet in North Wildwood, I almost missed the next Heritage Trail site—the Hereford Inlet Lighthouse—because it looked more like a landscaped Victorian home.

Inside, a small, free museum showcased old photos of the area, antique furniture, and the original whale-oil lighthouse lamp. Then lighthouse keeper Ed Hewitt—whose great-uncle Freeling Hewitt tended the lighthouse from 1878 until 1918—said he had devoted many years to restoring the 50-foot structure to its original look.

I climbed the winding steps to the top of the tower, stopping at each level to admire the photos and nautical displays that Hewitt had carefully set up. The light at the top, automated now, flashes all through the night to warn boats away from the inlet's dangerous shoals and sandbars.

Andy caught up to me here, but decided to head home to Clifton to prepare for a trip to Alaska rather than accompany me farther. We shook hands, then I saddled up for the ride to my car in Sea Isle City.

With the skies now blue and the wind at my back, the rest of my journey unfolded like a dream. I crossed a toll bridge (free to bikes) out of Wildwood and immediately found myself in the middle of a vast salt marsh, teeming with birds. I stopped to chat with birders Roger and Diane Harrison, who let me peer through their binoculars at the blue herons and orange-beaked American oyster-catchers that frequented the wetlands.

The wind propelled me onward, through Stone Harbor and Avalon, and onto the bridge spanning Townsends Inlet. Here I paused to gaze into the water and listen as it lapped the bridge's supports. A low-flying gull skimmed the surface, then headed skyward.

I had seen barely half of the Coastal Heritage Trail, but it had shown me a lot. And with many miles still to explore, I sensed a future bike trip in the cards.

Taking a deep breath of the fresh, salty air, I coasted down the other side of the bridge and headed into Sea Isle City.

—Bob Neubauer

Directions from Philadelphia: Take I-95 south to near Wilmington and pick up I-295 east. After about five miles, take 49 south to Salem.

Get brochures on the New Jersey Coastal Heritage Trail by contacting the National Park Service, Box 118, Mauricetown, N.J., 08329; phone 609-785-0676. A good state map is critical for anyone hoping to venture onto the back roads. You can request one from the New Jersey Division of Travel and Tourism at 800-537-7397.

Though a bicycle will allow you to experience New Jersey's coastal heritage on a more intimate level, numerous blue, green, and tan road signs have been erected to direct automobile drivers to trail sites from Route 49 and from the Garden State Parkway.

Find out about lodging from the New Jersey Hotel-Motel Association, phone 609-586-9000; or Bed & Breakfast Adventures, phone 609-522-4000.

Find out what awaits you at some of the sites by calling or writing for more information: Fort Mott State Park, Box 543, R.D. 3, Salem, N.J., 08079, 609-935-3218; Delaware Bay Schooner Project, Box 57, Dorchester, N.J. 08316, 609-785-2060; Cape May Point Lighthouse, Mid-Atlantic Center for the Arts, Box 340, 1048 Washington St., Cape May, N.J., 08204, 609-884-5404; Hereford Inlet Lighthouse, First and Central Avenues, North Wildwood, N.J. 08260, 609-522-4520.

~

The grime is gone

PITTSBURGH, PA.

PSSST! . . . PITTSBURGH.

Pittsburgh? Pittsburgh? The Pits? Smoky City? That place that Charles Dickens called, "hell with the lid lifted"? That place where men left for the office in white shirts and came home the same evening in gray ones? That place where they turned on the street lights at noon?

Pittsburgh's past has clung to it like a barnacle to a hull, and so the newcomer is not prepared for emerging from the Fort Pitt Tunnel on the Penn Lincoln Parkway to behold a shimmering Oz of glass and metal and marble, set among green hills in the Y of two great rivers.

The Pittsburgh of today is corporate and high-tech, pruned and civic, architectural and artistic. What's more, the air is celery-crisp. Peregrine falcons soar among the downtown's corporate canyons, and those two rivers—the Allegheny and the Monongahela—teem with 102 species of fish. Pittsburgh is a place with more bridges than Venice, and annually vies with Miami for national leadership in the number of registered pleasure boats.

And it's also a great spot for a long weekend.

It's almost worth the trip to Pittsburgh just to look at the city's natural splendor and architectural treasures. But it has a lot more to offer: Extraordinary museums, a world-class symphony orchestra and highly regarded opera and ballet companies, and first-rate restaurants— though one would not expect it in a city where McDonald's chose to introduce the Big Mac in 1961.

The view from Mount Washington, just across the Monongahela, is the urban equivalent of the Grand Canyon: a trowel of land called the Golden Triangle, with the vast, looming geometry of the skyline upon it, and the two rivers stapled by bridges as they flow together to form not just the triangle's apex, but the mighty Ohio. It's even better at night, when the stars are polished to a high glitter.

Downtown Pittsburgh encompasses about 10 blocks that are easily walked and provide some of the finest urban architecture in the world. The Gateway Center, with gardens, trees, and fountains, is home to the Equitable Life Assurance Society. The 40-floor Pittsburgh Plate Glass

Industries building, with five satellite buildings and six Gothic towers (designed by Philip Johnson and John Burgee), is nearby, as is the 64-story USX Tower.

Some of the industrial giants of American history—Andrew Carnegie, Henry Clay Frick, H.J. Heinz, Andrew Mellon—made their fortunes here, and they and their heirs went on to be the city's chief benefactors. Twelve Fortune 500 companies, including USX, Westinghouse, Alcoa, Pittsburgh Plate Glass Industries, and H.J. Heinz, are headquartered here—remarkable for a city of fewer than 400,000 residents.

To counter somewhat the effect of all that steel and glass, look to Trinity Episcopal Cathedral downtown—built between 1870 and 1872 and still soot-blackened from the earlier Pittsburgh years.

And adjacent to all the glitter of the Gateway Center, in the very point of the triangle, is Point State Park, which includes the 1764 Fort Pitt Museum. The museum has exhibits on early Pittsburgh and on Fort Pitt, which the French called Fort Duquesne until the British seized it in 1758 and renamed it after the elder William Pitt, an eminent British statesman of the day. The museum is built on part of the original fort, which afforded the British a clear view of the three rivers, as it still does for the visitor today.

The city's museum complex—collectively known as The Carnegie—is a short drive away in the Oakland section—home also to the University of Pittsburgh.

And the newest kid on the cultural block—also part of The Carnegie—is the $40 million Carnegie Science Center, which opened in October 1991 and features interactive hands-on exhibits designed to educate, inspire, and entertain. You'll find this part of The Carnegie, however, not in the Oakland section but across the Fort Duquesne Bridge from downtown, near Three Rivers Stadium (home to the Pirates and Steelers, but that's another story).

Topographically, the city is a patchwork of valleys and ridges that are sliced up by the serpentine rivers. The resulting maze of tunnels, steep roads, and 451 bridges drove journalist Ernie Pyle to declare in 1937 that "Pittsburgh must have been laid out by a mountain goat." When a book of maps trying to explain it all was published (it's called Pittsburgh Figured Out), many of the first 50,000 copies were bought by longtime Pittsburgh residents.

Mount Washington is best appreciated when reached by the Monongahela Incline or the Duquesne Incline—hill-climbing trolleys, of a sort—that were built in the 19th century to carry immigrant workers to and from their jobs at the riverside factories. The restored inclines still carry workers, as well as tourists.

It was those same immigrants that made Pittsburgh an ethnic hodge-podge. The great waves of immigrant labor flowed to the mills and western Pennsylvania mines between 1800 and 1914, and today more than 80 neighborhoods retain a distinctive ethnic flavor—Bloomfield is Italian, Lawrenceville is German, Squirrel Hill is Jewish, and so on.

However, Pittsburghers are united by a common language: "Stillers" is the local professional football team, "aigs" are what hens produce, a "tahr" is a very tall structure on the Golden Triangle, and "younz" is a second person plural pronoun, as in "Are younz going to the Stillers game?"

If you think you've seen Pittsburgh before, you're probably right. It's a favorite location for Hollywood producers, though Pittsburgh rarely plays itself. Films shot here include *The Dark Half, The Silence of the Lambs, Mrs. Soffel, The Deer Hunter*, and *Flashdance*. In addition, many actors and producers were trained at Carnegie Mellon University, including Ted Danson, Holly Hunter, Jack Klugman, Michael Tucker, and Steven Bochco.

But Pittsburgh's principal export these days is knowledge. The region has some 25,000 scientists, 170 research and development facilities, and 32 colleges and universities. There are 55 hospitals in the area, making Pittsburgh an international medical center.

The new science center has one of those Omnimax theaters with tilted seats, and participants are surrounded by dramatic images and sounds. The Hall of Eating, appropriately sponsored by H.J. Heinz, examines such food issues as nutrition, preservation, and packaging, and you can walk through a huge mechanized model of the human digestive system. The Aquarium has a self-sustaining Pacific coral reef in four interconnected tanks. In a section called Sport, you can race an Olympic sprinter, try to stay on a balance beam, throw a baseball in the strike zone, rock-climb on a 36-foot wall, spin like a Frisbee, and bobsled down a simulated track.

Less than 15 minutes' drive east of downtown is The Carnegie, which primarily comprises two museums.

The Carnegie Museum of Art has an array of the works of the French impressionists, including Claude Monet's "Waterlilies," post-impressionists, and 19th-century American art.

The adjacent Carnegie Museum of Natural History has what is generally considered the world's best preserved collection of dinosaurs, and it prepares you with a brief show of footage from old dinosaur movies—*Godzilla, King Kong, Gorgo, One Million B.C.*—poking fun, but in an instructive way. (The Carnegie complex here also includes the Music Hall and the Library of Pittsburgh.)

Practically across the street is the University of Pittsburgh's 42-story Cathedral of Learning, sometimes called the world's tallest schoolhouse. As a tribute to Pittsburgh's ethnic groups, the Gothic Commons room is surrounded by 22 nationality classrooms, furnished in the style of their land of origin—ranging from African to Yugoslav, from fifth-century B.C. Greece to 18th-century Poland. Nearby is the French Gothic Heinz Memorial Chapel with 73-foot-long stained-glass windows depicting 319 sacred and secular figures, from Moses to Emily Dickinson. If you're there on a Saturday, you'll probably see a wedding; there are six just about every Saturday.

Farther to the northeast is the Pittsburgh Zoo—one of those modern zoos with almost no cages. The animals roam in replicas of their natural habitats—an Asian forest with Siberian tigers and snow leopards; an African savanna with elephants, reticulated giraffes, and a white rhinoceros; an aquarium with sharks, penguins, and octopuses; and a new rain forest with 16 primate species.

You don't have to buy anything to get the definitive Pittsburgh shopping experience—on The Strip, northeast of downtown along Penn Avenue. It's primarily a produce market, but much more—something like Philadelphia's Italian Market, but with more ethnic diversity. At Jimmy and Nino Sunseri's Italian Grocery (1906–1916 Penn Ave.), your sense of smell is greeted with a combination of oregano, fresh anise, and Genoa salami, and it's an aroma that wasn't built in a day. New Sam Bok Oriental Foods (1735 Penn Ave.) offers 50-pound bags of rice, 10-inch hunks of Hawaiian ginger, lotus root, and other fresh ingredients for macrobiotic diets, and takeout kimchi (Korean pickled vegetables). For more than 50 years, Stamoolis Brothers (2020 Penn Ave.) has been selling Greek olives, couscous, falafel, and bulk spices.

Pittsburgh's performing-arts scene continues to grow. The Stanley, an old movie theater in the heart of downtown, underwent an extensive restoration and became the Benedum Center, home of the Pittsburgh Opera, Ballet Theater, Dance Council, and Civic Light Opera. Heinz Hall for the Performing Arts, also downtown, is another renovated movie theater and the home of the Pittsburgh Symphony.

Pittsburgh abounds in fine restaurants. For a meal you'll long remember in a place you'll never forget, try the Grand Concourse at Station Square. This is the old formal waiting room of the Pittsburgh & Lake Erie Railroad Station, built in 1901 and restored to its original Edwardian splendor at a cost of $2.5 million. The airplanes that made this station obsolete now bring in fresh seafood, which is the highlight of the menu.

In short, the city has a feel all its own—an urban sophistication overlaid with friendly, unpretentious people who treat you as though they will see you again soon.

And they probably will.

—William Ecenbarger

Directions from Philadelphia: Pittsburgh is about a six-hour drive west via the Pennsylvania Turnpike, which connects with Interstate 376 into the downtown.

For more information, including information about accommodations, call the Greater Pittsburgh Convention and Visitors Bureau, 800-359-0758.

Coal country

SCRANTON, PA.

IF I EVER THOUGHT about coal mines—and, frankly, I can't say I'd spent much time on them—I pictured warm, perhaps even hot places. Five minutes into my tour of the Lackawanna Coal Mine, I realized I was mistaken. Forty-five minutes later, I was positively chilled—not only by the damp, cold conditions, but also by an experience that vividly brought to life a period in history that should never be forgotten.

A stunningly accurate picture of the not-so-distant past comes alive during the mine tour, one of a number of historic sites in and around Scranton that are well worth visiting. Coupled with visits to the Steamtown National Historic Site and the Pennsylvania Anthracite Heritage Museum, a tour of the Lackawanna County area provides a surprisingly effective hands-on experience of history—the core of an entertaining and informative weekend getaway.

If you like history and trains, chances are you like baseball, too. An added reason to visit the area during the warm-weather months is the presence of the Phillies' Triple-A farm team, the Scranton/Wilkes-Barre Red Barons.

Scranton is an easy two-hour drive from Philadelphia. A leisurely Saturday morning drive will allow you to miss most of the vacationers headed to the Poconos on the Northeastern Extension of the Pennsylvania Turnpike.

I was more than a little skeptical about visiting a coal mine, but the friend who helped plan my itinerary, Dunmore native Dom Keating, insisted it was a must-see.

My wife, citing potential claustrophobia, opted out of the coal-mine tour altogether. While I agreed to it, I imagined it would be a short elevator ride 20 feet or so below the surface, with a bored graduate student reading a script—sort of like a trip on the Broad Street Subway with narration.

Instead, I got Tony Donofrio, Jr., a veteran of 23 years as a miner, who delivered a tough, frequently hilarious walk through more than 100 years of mining.

There were about 15 people in our group, including some children. We squeezed into a flat, rectangular rail car, which was lowered by cable into the ground on a severe incline. It was an eerie sensation when the last specks of natural light disappeared as we descended. We traveled about 1,350 feet and ended up about 250 feet below the earth's surface. Of course, since the tunnel was well fortified with wooden beams, we had nothing to worry about, right?

"Now, if this rock decides to come down, these timbers won't stop it," said Donofrio, explaining that natural arches formed by the rock are what really keeps the tunnel open. The wooden posts serve as warning alarms, cracking if there is a shift.

"When miners say 'the timbers are talking,' that's what they are referring to," said Donofrio. "If you hear the timbers start talking, let me know, because I'll be leaving."

We were in a section of the Lackawanna Coal Basin, a series of seven beds of coal that stretch for seven miles from East Mountain, where we entered the mine, to Montage Mountain. There is still plenty of coal in these mines, but most have been flooded, and the economics of extracting the coal (combined with a scarcity of markets for it) have ended the large mining operations in the area. The mine we were in closed in 1966.

The temperature in the mine is a constant 55 degrees, but it is a damp chill. If you are not prepared for it, you'll quickly begin shivering. Of course, if the weather doesn't get to you, Donofrio's stories will.

At the beginning of this century, the coal companies controlled everything. Miners lived in company-owned houses and bought supplies from the company-owned stores. They worked 10- to 12-hour days and were expected to maintain a high level of production.

The men were in constant danger—accidents were frequent and often fatal. When a miner's body was pulled from a cave-in or explosion, the company hearse would pull in front of his house, drop the body on the front porch, and move along. A few days later, a representative of the company would stop by to order the widow and the rest of the family to leave the house.

Even more troubling was what happened to children. Boys as young as 6 had roles inside the mine, and were considered as expendable as the adults. Besides the "breaker boys" who picked slate, little boys would tend to the mules used for pulling rail cars, and would be charged with the dangerous task of opening and closing ventilation doors.

The lack of light was another reality for the kids. While the Lackawanna mine is well-lit for the tour, Donofrio pointed out that in a working mine our lights would not be available because of the presence of gas. At one point, Donofrio turned out the lights and the tunnel was lit only by the lamp on his hard hat. Covering the light with his fingers until it was quite dim, he approximated the light available to the children while they worked.

It was a sad chapter in our country's history.

Far from being claustrophobic, the mine tour was exhilarating. It wasn't scary in a dangerous sense—but it was frightening as history. It made a past era come alive in a way I hadn't thought possible.

Our visit to the Anthracite Heritage museum served as a companion to the mine tour. While the museum lacks the gritty immediacy of the mine, it is effective in its own way at telling the story of a difficult time.

The permanent exhibits in this state-run museum tell several chronological stories: the history of the area, the introduction of first iron and then coal as the major industries, the growth of the textile milling industry (to take advantage of the labor pool provided by the miners' wives and daughters, a tale often as grim as that of the mines), the formation and repression of labor unions, and the diversity of the various waves of European immigrants.

From 1850 until a bit after World War II, wave after wave of those immigrants settled in the Lackawanna Valley. The ethnic heritage detailed in the museum was evident later as we drove through the Scranton area, from the sign for the American Ukrainian Veterans Association Post, to the Italian restaurants and even the radio polka show that encouraged listeners to call in their requests.

No trip to Scranton would be complete without a short ride down Main Avenue to the little town of Old Forge.

If you look quickly, you might think Old Forge was settled exclusively by restaurateurs and funeral directors. It seems made up of a few houses, churches, and restaurants, with each dining establishment serving "Old Forge–style" pizza. Order some.

After you have had your fill, ask for directions to Moosic Road and Interstate 81 North, which will take you to Lackawanna County Municipal Stadium, about a 15-minute ride.

The approach to this stadium is quite unlike those of any of the many other ballparks I have visited. The stadium first comes into sight from the highway, a modern stadium tucked into the side of Montage Mountain. There is a clearly marked exit and adequate access roads. Most of the parking lots for the stadium are unpaved, and you might be shocked by the low, low prices for parking and admission that's the rule for minor-league baseball.

The stadium seats about 11,000 people in two levels, which in effect makes the worst seat roughly equivalent to the press-box level at Veterans Stadium. Montage Mountain looms over the outfield fences, and is the overwhelming visual signature of the park.

There is little not to like about the park. It's very clean, the fans are friendly and polite, the entire atmosphere relaxed. About the worst thing I can say is that foul balls get to you quickly because you are sitting so close to the field. In other words, you have to pay attention to the game, which is hardly punishment.

The Steamtown National Historic Site has been set up on the site of the former Delaware, Lackawanna & Western rail yard. Our tour of Steamtown began at the visitor center, which is temporarily housed in one of the original buildings. The DL&W operated there from 1851 to 1963, and a series of pictures details a bustling rail yard in its glory days, its decline and eventual abandonment, and the restoration work. There are also several renderings of what Steamtown will look like when it is finished.

Sitting near the visitor center are a number of cars and engines that have been restored as exhibits. You can sit in an engine, operate a handcar, watch several videos about trains, or walk through a small exhibit on the history of steam trains.

We enjoyed walking through the post-office car, complete with the mail bags that were "hooked" as the train passed through small towns without stopping. The mail then would be sorted as the train sped through the night.

My favorite was the caboose, which you could climb into and explore. An elderly man and his wife were sitting in the caboose listening to a tinny transistor radio blaring polkas while he reminisced about when he worked for the railroad. (I tried to convince my wife that they were part of the exhibit, but she wouldn't buy it.)

There is a free train ride through the yard to the roundhouse where the engines are stored and serviced. The roundhouse has been lovingly rebuilt, using the same materials as the original whenever possible.

During our visit, an amiable park ranger, Kenny Ganz, walked us through a history of steam engines, showing us various examples in the roundhouse while explaining their uses and differences.

As we rode back in a beautiful 1920 Jersey Central Day Coach pulled by a 1917 Canadian Railways locomotive, we passed a number of cars and engines that had not yet been restored, most notably the 1941 Union Pacific "Big Boy," one of the largest steam engines ever built.

Steamtown is seen by Scranton as the cornerstone of its redevelopment, along with a downtown shopping mall under construction. The mall will have a food court overlooking the rail yard and a walkway connecting it to Steamtown. By 1995, construction at Steamtown itself is supposed to be complete; that includes the roundhouse work, a new visitor center, museum, and other public areas.

Since being taken over by the National Park Service in 1988, Steamtown has been decried as pork-barrel politics at its worst. It has even been characterized by at least one congressman as a "third-rate collection of engines"—but you couldn't tell that by the faces of the people viewing it on this day.

Among the plans when everything is completed is a 56-mile round-trip steam excursion from Steamtown into the Poconos each weekend from July through October. We plan to return to ride it.

The small engine that normally gives yard tours was being repaired during our visit, which meant the short trip from Steamtown to the Scranton Iron Furnaces was not running. Instead, we drove to the nearby park, which features enough written information for an easy self-guided tour.

Scranton was an iron town before it was a coal town. The Lackawanna Iron & Coal Co. manufactured high-quality "Trails" for many railroads throughout the country. The furnaces worked from 1841 until 1901, when the company abandoned the works and moved to Lackawanna, N.Y., to take advantage of the rich iron ore deposits near the Great Lakes. Overnight, thousands of jobs were lost, one of several economic down-cycles that have befallen the city.

One result of the years of economic scuffling is that much of the architecture of the city has remained frozen in time. Late in the afternoon, some friends treated us to a tour of a part of Scranton quite different from the neighborhoods of "company" houses that still exist in much of the city.

From 1870 to 1900, a time of great prosperity in Scranton, everyone wanted to build in the Hill section of the city. The result is a series of mammoth structures on tiny plots of land. There are examples of Italianate design, variations on Tudor using stone and shingles, and other combinations. It seems that everyone wanted something distinctive and this eclectic architecture was the result.

We traveled up Gibson Street from the center of town, turning on North Webster Street. There, for instance, two large houses sit on the same side of the street, but with their front doors facing each other, supposedly built by a man for his twin daughters. Farther down the street, an imposing set of steps leads to a house with a wide porch with pillars, all made of stone. Distinctive houses abound on Pine, Olive,

North Washington, and Electric streets. Some notable structures include the building on Jefferson Street that now houses the Red Cross and the nearby Woolworth mansion, which is vacant and facing an uncertain future.

The neighborhood is being slowly encroached upon by the University of Scranton and two hospitals, but many of the homes remain as single-family residences, and the neighborhood still retains much of its majesty.

—Bob Cotter

Directions from Philadelphia: Take the Northeast Extension of the Pennsylvania Turnpike north to Exit 37 (Scranton) and follow the signs to Interstate 81 north. I-81 has several exits for downtown Scranton.

For general information, brochures, accommodations and restaurant listings, and information on attractions in and around Scranton and northeastern Pennsylvania, contact the Northeast Territory Visitors Bureau at 800-245-7711.

The Lackawanna Coal Mine Tour, in McDade Park, is open daily from May to November. For information, call 717-963-6463. The Pennsylvania Anthracite Heritage Museum, also in the park, is open Monday through Saturday, 9 a.m. to 5 p.m.; Sunday from noon to 5 p.m. Steamtown National Historic Site is open daily from 9 a.m. to 5 p.m. Information: 717-961-2035.

Fly-fishing country

SPRUCE CREEK, PA.

IN THE BAD OLD DAYS before he won the Medal of Freedom, before he earned revered-elder-statesman status, before he left the White House—in those bad old days—Jimmy Carter occasionally sought refuge from it all in this quiet, leafy, green little corner of the world.

Carter is a fly-fisherman, and this is fly-fishing country, some of the best on the East Coast, but the scenery alone is more than worth the trip to central Pennsylvania.

And, should you crave more than solitude, there's easy access to swimming, boating, antiques shopping, museum-hopping, nature trails, and Indian caves—plenty of activities to more than fill a weekend visit to the area.

It was late spring when my husband and I visited Spruce Creek, and it was difficult to imagine lovelier countryside anywhere, any time of the year. We found it hypnotic just driving around: the profusion of roadside wildflowers, the summery smell of sun-warmed grass, the fleecy white clouds bright with reflected sunlight.

For my husband, it was reminiscent of his Minnesota homeland, and, for both of us, it recalled a trip to Sweden when we drove through the rolling farmland west of Stockholm.

At night, the silence and darkness were absolute. In the morning, we awoke to the snuffling of horses beneath the window of our bed-and-breakfast.

Once you're here, informality is the style, and that includes dining. Spruce Creek is a place to enjoy good food, not fine cuisine. Everyone told us that nearby State College could provide the latter, but we felt like being lazy. Local taverns and diners offered meals both filling and extremely reasonable, which was all we required.

One afternoon, we set out for 7 Points Marina in nearby Hesston, where Raystown Lake and environs attract about a million people a year to the area. We found it after snaking along a meandering road through miles of gorgeous vistas.

The lake—manmade, for flood control, by the Army Corps of Engineers, and shaped like a Chinese dragon—has 118 miles of shoreline; the park surrounding it consists of 8,300 acres.

Fishing, of course, is the main attraction (the lake is famous for its bass), but there are also beaches, boat rides, picnic tables, nature trails, campsites, and restaurants. We wandered along the shore, just enjoying the serenity of the setting—and kicking ourselves for having just missed the double-decker boat that is available for daily cruises at 2 p.m. (more often on Sundays), with a minimum of 10 people.

On the drive back, we tarried a bit in Hesston itself, a tiny village that could have been a set for *Our Town*. Laid out on a hillside, it's a grouping of clapboard houses with wide front porches, porch swings, and hanging baskets of geraniums.

Enchanted, we turned around and drove up and down its few streets, past a church, neatly mowed lawns, and patches of gardens.

Heading home the next day, we routed ourselves on country roads, as we had been advised to do, and good advice it was.

The rolling farmland overlays a valley: row after row of crops, like a chenille bedspread draped across the fields. Route 655 took us through a part of Mifflin County that calls itself Big Valley. No billboards here, but the occasional sign with an inspirational or frankly biblical message.

Our favorite: "Your life is like a ladder. Every step is either up or down."

Development around Lancaster has prompted some western migration among the Amish and Mennonites, which has benefited this area. Small hand-painted signs occasionally announce "Quilts," and we passed at least one roadside stand selling homemade pies.

In Belleville, both the Hill Store and Main Street Antiques were closed, but signs said that they are open on Wednesday, Sunday, or "by appointment." A nearby 125-year-old stone mill is home to Old Woolen Mill Antiques, a collection of antiques dealers open Tuesday through Saturday, except during the winter.

Another stop in Belleville (also on Route 655) was at Brookmere Winery, headquartered in a 19th-century stone-and-wood barn. All of its wines are available for tasting. We had to wait while two couples ahead of us discussed who would and who wouldn't have a mid-afternoon sip, but we tried one red and one white. While neither France nor California need worry about the competition, we bought a bottle of a pleasant, dry white wine for $6.

Our several stops on the way home, we realized, were an attempt to extend our short trip, and we finally decided that, since we really had to get home, it would be better to come back another time. Perhaps even to fly-fish.

Earlier in our visit to Spruce Creek, we had a half-hour conversation with Allen Bright—who owns Spruce Creek Outfitters on the main road of this tiny burg—that convinced us that we should give fly-fishing a try. Bright is a fly-fisherman, but it was only a few years before we met him that he had turned avocation into vocation. For 14 years, he had been director of operations for a small restaurant. He sums up those years in a single word: hectic.

The increasing popularity of fly-fishing, he said, can be attributed to the hectic pace a lot of people endure these days.

"I think, aesthetically, a lot of people prefer [fly-fishing to deep-sea fishing] because of the scenery," Bright said. "It's a very relaxing activity, a very graceful activity. It can be as complex or as simple as you want to make it. I've been doing it over 20 years, and there are times I think I'm just learning.

"I find, more and more, that we're drawing professionals in the 30-and-up range who need an outlet. You just jump in your gear and wade in and watch the water go by."

And, you don't have to be a beleaguered U.S. president to benefit from that.

—Mary Jane Fine

Directions from Philadelphia: Take the Pennsylvania Turnpike west to 522 north. Go about 35 miles to Route 22 north. After about 25 miles, pick up 45 north to Spruce Creek.

For more information, contact the Centre County Visitors Bureau, phone 814-231-1400.

A short trip to Paradise

STRASBURG, PA.

A STREAMLINED PROTOTYPE sizzles down the track at 102 miles per hour, setting the tone for an era of efficient, reliable, and environmentally responsible mass transportation.

The presidentially-endorsed X-2000, Amtrak's high-speed Swedish import, circa 1993? Wrong.

It's the Pennsylvania Railroad's GG-1 electric locomotive, 1935. It's not sizzling down the track anymore, of course. But it looks like it's ready to roll—one of many freshly painted locomotives and restored railroad cars inside the Railroad Museum of Pennsylvania here in Strasburg.

Across the street from the museum is the fully operational Strasburg Rail Road, a short line that runs from here to Paradise—Paradise the village, that is—and back. Traveling closer to 30 mph than 100, the SRR's trains let you experience luxurious turn-of-the-century travel firsthand.

During your ride on the railroad, you'll even pass a curious site where a cluster of 37 refurbished cabooses and two dining cars form one of Lancaster County's more unusual hostelries—the Red Caboose Motel.

The fact is, on a weekend visit to Strasburg, a history-laden town just a few miles southeast of Lancaster, you're going to see trains. In addition to the museum, the railroad, and the aforementioned motel, Strasburg is home to the Toy Train Museum, the Choo Choo Barn, the Depot Attic, the Iron Horse Inn, the Strasburg Train Shop, and the Depot Doll Shop.

Granted, some of these places are as kitschy as their names might suggest. But, as I discovered, if you dig around a bit beneath the layers of tourist clutter and nostalgic debris, you will find plenty of intriguing ruins and well-preserved examples of the huge iron creatures that ruled the continent before the Asphalt Age.

The funny thing is, Strasburg was never really a railroad town. It was settled around 1700 and began to flourish as a convenient stopover for travelers on the Conestoga wagon trail between Philadelphia and Columbia, a trading center farther west on the Susquehanna River.

But then the original Pennsylvania turnpike (of the 1790s) and the Philadelphia-Columbia Railroad (1820s) were built north of here, and Strasburg's future as a major center of commerce was doomed.

The Strasburg Rail Road was chartered in 1832 as a short-line for both freight and passengers between Strasburg and Paradise—and by short, we are talking a round trip of nine miles. And if it weren't for modern tourism, it seems safe to say that this is one railroad that would be long forgotten.

As for Strasburg, instead of withering away, the town seems to have been expertly pickled. It's immaculate. Strolling the length of Main Street—a mile at the most—you notice that most of the houses, which average between 150 and 200 years old, look as if they had been restored and painted in the last month. The corner lampposts look brand new. Even in its heyday, the late 1700s, the place probably never looked quite this good.

One building that is far less than two centuries old is the Railroad Museum of Pennsylvania, just east of Main Street, on Route 741. From the road, it looks more like a water-treatment plant than a museum. Its only remarkable feature is the huge clock that hangs near the building's entrance. The corresponding plaque tells you that the clock, white with elegant, black, Roman numerals, adorned the tower of Philadelphia's Broad Street Station from 1881 until the station was demolished in 1952.

The first exhibit that a visitor sees on entering the museum, "Speed," describes how the railroad industry changed our perception of time. Because of the revolutionary speed with which trains were suddenly able to transport goods and people, Americans stopped thinking of time in terms of seasons, months, and weeks and began thinking in terms of hours, minutes, and seconds. The exhibit attributes the phrase and concept "on time" to the railroad industry.

Another exhibit, "Service," displays a full complement of fine china and sterling silverware used in serving meals on the PRR's sumptuous Pullman dining cars. In the 1920s, the Pullman company said it was the largest hotel chain in the country since, on any given night, approximately 100,000 people were staying in Pullman's 10,000 sleeping cars on trains around the country.

In the third exhibit, "Power," a diagram depicting the inner workings of a steam engine, covers a wall.

But to those of us who have grown up during the last three decades, raised between threads of the interstate highway web that covers the country, the main mystery that the museum solves is this: What happened to the railroads?

Some of their remnants are literally in the next room. Rolling Stock Hall, sort of a modified warehouse, holds 23 of the museum's impressive collection of railroad engines and cars. The stock—including freight cars, dining cars, passenger coaches, sleeping cars, and service cars—rests on four rows of tracks recessed into the concrete floor.

There are small observation decks between and next to most of the cars, so that you can get a good look inside them. After getting a close peek inside the luxurious Pullman Lotos club car on a visit, it was all I could do to refrain from sneaking in through a window to recline on one of the car's plush divans like a cocktail-soaked 1920s fat cat fresh from the Ritz.

Next to a locomotive called the Tahoe—so named because it was built for a Nevada railroad—squats Steinman Station, a replica of a turn-of-the-century station house. The station house was usually home to the town's post office, as well as to Western Union and the railroad telegrapher.

Inside the telegrapher's office, telegraph keys and sounders—the telegraph receivers—clattered away as they once did, sending and receiving the complicated train orders that used to keep the trains on schedule and out of each other's way. In the baggage room, a television plays a corny though very informative promotional black-and-white film about the mighty railroad industry, prepared for the Pennsylvania Railroad in 1946.

Featured upstairs are the railroad paintings of Grif Teller. Teller's paintings were commissioned by the PRR to be released with promotional calendars for most of the years between 1928 and 1952. The calendars are now hot collector's items; one tour guide says that collectors can often be spotted drooling over the museum's paintings.

When, as is likely after a couple of hours in the museum, the history of the place becomes temporarily overwhelming, the perfect antidote is directly across the street: The Strasburg Rail Road, where you can ride one of those trains you've been hearing and reading about.

At East Strasburg Station, tickets to Paradise (and back) are sold, including round-trip tickets for the ornate parlor car "Marian." On the hour, the conductor bawls, "All aboard!" Steam pours from the locomotive, the steam whistle screams, and Number 90's wheels churn to life.

"Please," urges Strasburg Rail Road conductor John McKenzie, "resist the temptation to jump off the train and run ahead."

The train chugs along smoothly between 20 and 30 miles per hour. Cruising along in one of the coach's wide, green velvet seats, surrounded by chandeliers and huge windows, you wonder why, instead of traveling in such comfort, we put up with the expressways, traffic jams, urban parking snafus, and all the pollution that the automobile generates. Certainly, you say to yourself, there must be a perfectly good reason that long-distance interstate rail travel in America is virtually nonexistent when compared to Western Europe.

During the ride to Paradise, McKenzie spices up the trip with well-delivered jokes about the humble origins and size of the railroad. The line became a successful tourist attraction after a group of 24 train buffs bought the company out of impending abandonment in 1958.

When the train reaches Paradise, it grinds to a halt in a bleak switching yard. An Amtrak commuter train rattles past. Our locomotive detaches from the Paradise end of the train and rolls by on its way to link up at the Strasburg end for the haul back to East Strasburg Station.

The trip back from Paradise is a quiet affair. The conductor ceases his humorous banter, leaving the passengers to contemplate in silence the fertile, rolling fields of Lancaster County.

At the Strasburg depot, the Dining Car Restaurant offers hearty local food, with the inevitable shoo-fly pie for dessert. A gift shop holds two floors of railroad-related goods, such as fireman's overalls and books like *The Caboose Who Got Loose*, as well as gift-shop fare: etched crystal, boomerangs, and key chains. All told, the train excursion and a perusal of the gift shop should take a little more than an hour.

For the visitor in search of a country-inn experience, there are plenty of quaint bed-and-breakfast establishments in and around Strasburg. An oval plaque dates the Limestone Inn, at 33 E. Main St., near the center of town, from 1786. Its exterior is white stone with red trim. Other B&Bs include the Strasburg Village Inn and P.J.'s Guest Home, both on Main Street.

But for those who still have trains on their brains, the Red Caboose Restaurant & Motel is just off Route 741, less than a mile east of the museum. It consists of a restaurant, a gift shop, and 37 cabooses, painted various shades of red, which have been converted to motel rooms. The restaurant is composed of two railroad dining cars, which gently rock and bounce to simulate a train's motion. The cavernous gift shop is stuffed with railroad paraphernalia and books about the Amish and other local communities.

My cousin, Jeremy, and I also checked out Traintown, U.S.A., a group of shops just east of town. Sadly, the Choo Choo Barn's 1,700-square-foot model-train layout was temporarily closed.

Railroads aside, one important activity here that should not be missed is a drive through the countryside.

On the way to Strasburg, I was fortunate to get slightly lost just south of Paradise. Amish children were just getting out of school for the day, and the hilly back roads swarmed with bonneted girls zipping along on scooters, and black-suited boys holding their stiff hats in one hand, swinging lunch boxes in the other as they roller-bladed home in formation.

(For a local angle on the countryside, Ed's Buggy Rides 717-687-0360 offers a 30-minute trot through three miles of Amish farmland.)

After stopping in at Patrick McEvoy & Co., purveyors of fine Irish goods, we decided to conduct a survey of Strasburg's shops and watering holes along Main Street.

While Strasburg's main strip has been home, over the years, to at least six taverns, today it's a relatively dry haul. We were informed by a burly young man sweeping gutters that there are only two bars in Strasburg—the Swan Tavern at the west end of Main Street, and the Iron Horse Inn on the east end.

At the Swan Tavern, Vickie Harnish, the barkeep, told us the Swan had been a tavern since 1790, and was itself part of a railroad in the early 1800s—the Underground Railroad that helped bring slaves to freedom in the North. This was definitely a local watering hole. At the bar, two local men discussed the finer points of bachelorhood; one man came in, bought a six-pack to go and left without ever exchanging a word with Harnish. Definitely a local bar.

Of all the houses along Main Street, the most ornate and sprawling is the Gonder Mansion at 130 W. Main, a block east of the Swan. In a pamphlet issued by the Strasburg Heritage Society, the house's style is listed as "Queen Anne–Chateauesque." One of the few Strasburg houses not built flush against the street, it has two spires that feature inlaid glass murals between curved windows.

After lunch, we crossed to the Pequea Trading Company, at 10 E. Main. Previously a Colonial tavern—so was the country store—the Pequea now deals in, among other things, teas from around the world and dried herb and flower bunches. The place is olfactory sensory overload.

Whether walking down Main Street, learning about the railroad culture of pre-1950 America in the Railroad Museum, spending the night in a cozy caboose, or chugging through Amish fields on the Strasburg line, you can—if you pack a little imagination and a sense of humor—ride the town of Strasburg back through history.

—Josh McHugh

Directions from Philadelphia: Take 76, 322, and 30 west to Strasburg, which is southeast of Lancaster.

For more information, contact the Pennsylvania Dutch Convention & Visitors Bureau, 501 Greenfield Rd., Lancaster, Pa. 17601. 717-299-8901.

2

New York City
and New York State

❧

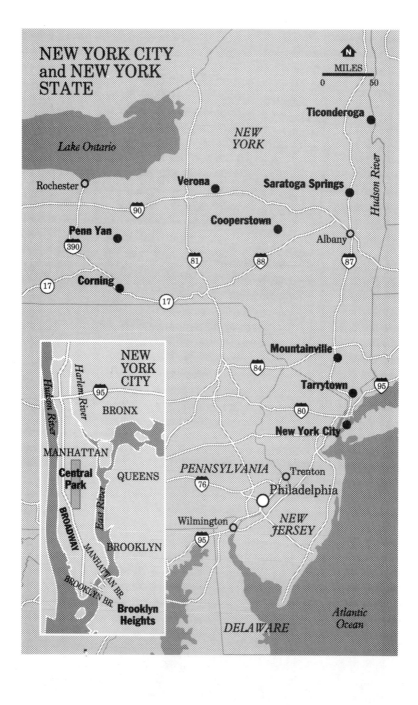

∾

One city, one street

NEW YORK

WE'LL KEEP THIS SIMPLE: one city, one street, one direction. No way to get lost. Exhausted, yes. Impressed and intimidated, yes. But not lost.

We're going to walk what many would say is the most famous street in the world—Broadway—as it runs the length of one of the most famous islands in the world—Manhattan. We already know Broadway for its theaters, but we'll see that there is much more to it than the Great White Way's footlights and opening nights.

We'll walk stretches of Broadway where, if Diogenes were to go looking for an honest man, someone would hit him over the head with his own lantern and steal his toga. But we'll also walk stretches where parks and museums, art and architecture are unexpected treats.

We'll witness a street that struts and stumbles, bullies and beguiles. Often shocking but seldom shocked, often bored but seldom boring, Broadway is ostentatious, chaotic, callous, loud, dangerous. And always fascinating.

From top to bottom, Broadway is 14 miles long, so plan to spend two days, to travel light, and to wear comfortable, sturdy shoes. If you need to spend less time, cut the walk to one day by starting at Columbus Circle at 59th Street and walking south to the Battery.

We begin the full two-day walk on an unremarkable steel bridge over the Harlem River north of 220th Street. This is where Broadway enters Manhattan, rolling unpromisingly out of the inner-city combat zone of the South Bronx near an area that the Dutch settlers called Spuyten Duyvil (in spite of the devil).

In Broadway's first 100 blocks, we pass south through the neighborhoods of Inwood, Washington Heights, and Harlem. Up here, Broadway is unaccustomed to sightseers. If the Times Square district is a million bright lights, these three areas are single 60-watt bulbs.

The street is raucous at times. At others, it's quiet. Clusters of aimless young men loiter on the cracked sidewalks, freely spending what may be the only currency they have—time. Older men shuffle dominoes and pass brown paper bags. Storefronts are shuttered; vacant lots are protected by chain-link fences with barbed wire coiled around the top.

73

And yet, even here, Broadway flashes glimmers of history and fine arts. Inwood Hill Park was once the last refuge of the island's Indians as Europeans began pushing them steadily back. Arrowheads, pottery, and other artifacts have been found in caves. Baker Field, where a young Lou Gehrig once played football, is part of the park.

At 204th Street is Dyckman House, Manhattan's only surviving Dutch Colonial farmhouse, authentically restored and open to the public.

A few blocks below, as we pass Fort Tryon Park, you may think that we have suddenly detoured 3,000 miles and 800 years—to Europe and the Middle Ages. This is the Cloisters—a museum incorporating remnants of five medieval monasteries, stained glass, and the Unicorn Tapestries. Serenity is almost palpable here. The horn of the unicorn replaces the horn of the taxicab; Gregorian chants replace boom-box rap.

As we pass 165th Street, on the left is the Audubon Ballroom, where Malcolm X was assassinated in 1965.

At 156th Street, we can browse a neoclassical group of museums that includes the Museum of the American Indian, the Hispanic Society of America, and the American Numismatic Society.

A block later, Broadway whistles through Trinity Cemetery. Ornithologist John James Audubon is buried on the left, Clement ("A Visit From St. Nicholas") Moore on the right. On Christmas Eve, children gather at Moore's grave to hear a minister read his famous poem.

The tone of the street begins to change at 120th Street as it borders Columbia University. It is quieter here, 27,000 students notwithstanding. Shade trees, stately buildings. Chartered by King George II of England in 1754, Columbia is older than the United States.

At 110th Street, Broadway enters the Upper West Side. This is middle-class Manhattan: tidy apartment buildings, tearooms, delis, chop houses. One business advertises divorces and travel tours. Grocers display their produce in front of their stores, transforming the sidewalk into a Cezanne still life.

Even this far north, the muses sometimes have brightened Broadway: Novelist Damon Runyon lived at 111th Street, Edgar Allan Poe at 84th.

At 80th Street, we can duck into Zabar's gourmet grocery for protein. The store sells 10 tons of cheese a week. Huge wheels of cheese, cheese of every race, creed, and cholesterol level.

At 73rd Street, the Ansonia Hotel (1904) looms like a Beaux Arts dowager. In its salad days, tenants included Enrico Caruso, Babe Ruth,

Flo Ziegfeld, and a pet bear on the roof. More recently, it housed the notorious Plato's Retreat sex club.

Tired? We are only halfway done. As you have seen, Broadway runs down Manhattan like a spine, albeit slightly curved—it bends at 72nd Street and again at 14th. More than 250 streets branch off it like ribs.

Seven ribs farther south, at 65th, is Lincoln Center—home of the Metropolitan Opera and the New York Philharmonic. The cultural center was built on the site of slums where *West Side Story* was filmed, the Sharks and the Jets yielding to the sopranos and the woodwinds.

At 59th Street, Broadway kisses the corner of Central Park. This is Columbus Circle, as in Christopher. Look up. Atop a granite column is a statue of the explorer.

We cross the diamond district at 47th Street. Eighty percent of the country's wholesale diamond business is conducted along these few blocks. Many of the merchants are Hasidic Jews, recognizable by their beards, hats, and black suits.

Here, Broadway also enters the Theater District. But the real show is the street itself. Slick young men run games of three-card monte. Others sell cheap souvenirs to tourists: More than 300 years after an outsider named Peter Minuit traded trinkets to the natives of Manhattan, the natives are getting even, trading them back.

At 43rd, we pass strip joints and the offices of the *New York Times*. All the nudes that's fit to print, you might say.

The next block has one of the most famous intersections in the world—Broadway at 42nd Street. Times Square. This is where America rings in the new year as the illuminated ball descends the tower. Times Square also is a popular speaker's corner for the fringe element. One preacher, protected by four muscular disciples, uses a loudspeaker to rail against social injustices. He singles out people at random in the passing throng and addresses them by some physical feature: "Take heed, Bow Tie. Your time is coming. You and your wife and your children will be enslaved in Palestine, Bow Tie." The preacher is ignored, even by Bow Tie.

At night, this stretch of Broadway is kaleidoscopic, flowing like a neon Nile. Theater marquees, giant illuminated billboards advertising brand names: Camel, TDK, Coke, Jockey. (A huge supine Nadia Comaneci wears nothing but underwear and a come-hither look.)

By now, Broadway is well into the pincushion of Midtown, bristling with skyscrapers. At 34th Street, in the shadow of the Empire State

Building, is Macy's, the world's largest department store. It's worth a quick tour if only to ride the clackety wooden steps of its escalators.

Traffic is hectic at 34th. Drivers caught in an intersection when the light turns red respond impatiently with blaring horns, as if honking hosannas to the great god Gridlock. Getting from one corner to the next is the true miracle on 34th Street.

Stretch limos are parked two deep, idling shoulder to chauffeur; homeless men paw through trash cans or sleep in doorways.

Here, as elsewhere, the two-note warble of police and ambulance sirens is a somber—and too-common—counterpoint to the honking. Remember: Even King Kong didn't get out of this town alive.

At 23rd Street, pointing at us like the prow of a ship, is the Flatiron Building. In 1902, its vertiginous 20 stories made it the city's first skyscraper and the tallest building in the world. The triangular shape of the building (only six feet wide at its apex) created air currents that caused women's skirts to billow, attracting oglers. Police shooed them away, thus, it is said, giving birth to the expression "the 23 skiddoo."

As we walk past Waverly Place, the people on the sidewalks are young. This is Bohemian Broadway—it grazes New York University and separates Greenwich Village from the East Village. Students rollerblade down the middle of the street in heavy traffic. They whiz past wafts of steam that rise from manhole covers, as if the underworld were on fire.

On the sidewalk, we must step around mounds of garbage bags here and there. A handwritten notice on a wall advertises "The Leon Trotsky-Abbie Hoffman-Madonna radical walking tour of the Village."

At Houston Street, we enter artsy SoHo. Along here, no two buildings are alike. Oh, they may have similar and prosaic ground-floor storefronts. But look higher—at the architectural serendipity of the upper stories: Columns and pilasters rise, accentuated by delicate capitals. Ornate keystones crown arches. Gargoyles stare down at us impassively.

At Broome Street, the Haughwout Building (1857), with its colonnaded arches repeated on two sides, stands as an impressive example of early cast-iron architecture. It was also the first building to have an elevator designed for passengers.

At Canal Street, we clearly are in Chinatown—an anthill of a neighborhood where every corner is part melting pot, part bazaar. A man in a turban selling watches off a card table waits on one man in a cowboy hat, another in a yarmulke. Beside them, an Asian woman selling socks off a TV tray waits on a Hispanic man.

Vendors who lack city permits rely on a grapevine to spread an alert when police enter the area. When the single word "Cops!" is relayed down the street, tables are folded, TV trays collapse and vendors fade into the crowd until the all-clear is sounded.

Those police don't have far to travel: At Chambers Street, Broadway enters the Municipal District with its imposing buildings—granite wedding cakes decorated with fluted columns and elaborate pediments. Least imposing of these buildings, in a small park on our left, is City Hall (1811). President Lincoln lay in state here in 1865.

On our right at Park Place is the Woolworth Building (1913). Frank Woolworth built this Gothic monument to free enterprise with profits from his five-and-dime stores. The three-story lobby resembles a cathedral—marble, bronze, carved wood, vaulted glass ceiling. The building cost Woolworth $13.5 million. He paid cash. That's a lot of fives and dimes.

At Vesey Street, looking out of place—and time—with the World Trade Center rising behind it, is St. Paul's Chapel (1766), one of the oldest buildings in New York City. George Washington worshiped here. On this day, a sign on the door reads: "Please keep your belongings with you at all times."

At 160 Broadway is the fanciest McDonald's you are apt to see anywhere. Let's open the polished brass door and, wait, the white-gloved doorman is doing that for us. Ah. Inside are marble tables, fresh flowers, even a pianist. And a stock ticker. This is, after all, the Financial District.

And soon we come to the intersection of Broadway and Wall Street. This, you could say, is where manna meets mammon: Trinity Church on Broadway and the New York Stock Exchange on Wall Street are but a block apart. The island has changed considerably since 1705, when England's Queen Anne granted Trinity Church the right to all unclaimed shipwrecks and beached whales.

Farther south, the prestigious address of 1 Broadway is occupied by Citibank, housed in the United States Lines maritime building (1884). During the Revolution, Gen. Washington lived in a house on the site.

Across the street is little Bowling Green park. This is said to be where Peter Minuit, in 1626, in the real estate coup of all time, bought Manhattan from the Indians for $24 worth of trinkets. Appropriately, perhaps, today it is where Broadway ends, just short of New York Harbor.

After more than 250 blocks, 14 miles, a dozen distinct neighborhoods, and two sore feet, we have walked Broadway (and Manhattan) from top to bottom, trudging between the Duyvil and the deep blue sea. We have seen the magic and the maggots, rubbed elbows with the have-lots and the have-nots.

So, that done, how do we get back uptown?

I vote we take a cab.

—Mike Nichols

Directions from Philadelphia: Take the New Jersey Turnpike north to the Lincoln Tunnel. You'll exit in Midtown Manhattan, west of Broadway. More information is available from the New York Convention & Visitors Bureau, 2 Columbus Circle, New York, N.Y. 10019; phone 212-484-1200.

Beyond Manhattan, to Brooklyn

NEW YORK

I'LL TAKE MANHATTAN. Or I'll leave it. Too congested. Too noisy. Buildings too tall.

So how about on the other side of the East River, in Brooklyn? Most of it is not nearly as congested or noisy, you can find a place to park (you can actually drive around there) and, like Philadelphia, it actually has the feel of a city of neighborhoods (albeit a city with a population of 2.2 million).

Brooklyn has a 52-acre botanic garden, the world's first museum created expressly for children, a world-class art museum, a 526-acre park that was designed by the team that created Central Park, and the best blintzes this side of Kiev. Jackie Robinson played here. (Ebbets Field, where he once roamed, is now the site of a housing project named Jackie Robinson Apartments.) Neil Simon lived here and wrote about it, and so did Barry Manilow.

Brooklyn is a good-size city. If you're dropping by for only a day or two, pick a couple of neighborhoods to explore in depth. Some suggestions:

Dumbo and Brooklyn Heights. If you are coming in from Lower Manhattan, say from near the South Street Seaport, walk or ride over the Brooklyn Bridge, bought and sold many times since its opening in 1883. A few blocks north, the Manhattan Bridge also spans the East River. Between the bridges, the area is known as DUMBO (for Down Under the Manhattan Bridge Overpass). DUMBO features Empire Fulton Ferry State Park (at Dock Street), the scenic and gentrified waterfront, and nice views of Manhattan. If you have children with you, you must visit the Harry Chapin Playground on Columbia Heights near Everit Street.

For fans of alternative art, a few blocks away are the New Waterfront Museum and the AMMO Artists' Exhibition Space on Plymouth Street (phone 718-624-4719). The nearby River Cafe (phone 718-522-5200), at the river and Water Street, is renowned for its food and the celebrities who eat there.

From DUMBO, go a few blocks south to the heart of Brooklyn Heights. The Heights is highly yuppified, tree-lined streets and all. The Wall Streeters who live there wouldn't have it any other way. Stop at Brooklyn's History Museum (718-624-0890) on Pierrepont Street and experience the essence of Brooklyn: stills from the vintage TV comedy "The Honeymooners," photos of the summertime amusements at Coney Island, and memorabilia of the Brooklyn Dodgers.

Montague, Clinton, and Henry streets are excellent for all kinds of shopping—toys, clothing, knickknacks. If a flight of steep metal steps doesn't deter you, go up for lunch at the second-floor Leaf & Bean (718-638-5791) at 136 Montague St., where the eclectic menu lists great soups, salads, and sandwiches and the prices are very reasonable.

East on Montague Street (at Clinton) is St. Ann's and the Holy Trinity Church, where the 150-year-old stained-glass windows—considered by experts to be a national treasure—are being refurbished. Officials at the church will let you watch.

And for transit buffs, the New York Transit Museum (718-330-3060) at Boerum Place and Schermerhorn Street showcases a century of transit lore in an actual 1936 subway station. There are antique turnstiles, a working signal tower, vintage subway maps, and 18 restored subway and elevated trains—and no muggers. A few blocks south, on

Atlantic Avenue, is the Brooklyn Historic Railway Association (718-941-3160). It's in an old tunnel and to get to this attraction, which gives visitors an impression of New York's early mass-transit days, you climb down a ladder in a manhole. The tunnel was built in the mid-1800s, then sealed amid political scandal. It was rediscovered in 1980.

Not far away, at 205 Atlantic St., is the Moroccan Star restaurant (718-643-0800). Despite the geographical confusion, the Moroccan Star serves wonderful Middle Eastern food.

Park Slope. The Park in Park Slope refers to Prospect Park (information: 718-788-0055), designed by Frederick Law Olmsted and Calvert Vaux (the Central Park designers). The "entrance" is the stately Grand Army Plaza on Flatbush Avenue. Prospect Park is more than proof that a tree grows in Brooklyn. The park has foliage, rolling lawns, and much more: cross-country skiing after a snowfall, ice-skating on the pond in the winter, paddle boats in the summer. There is a circa-1912 carousel that has been restored. Lefferts Homestead (718-965-6505), a restored house, depicts life on a Brooklyn farm in the 1820s.

Park Slope, on the west side of Prospect Park, is home to young families who populate the area's well-preserved brownstones. Fifth and Seventh Avenues are the neighborhood's prime shopping streets, with everything from toys to ceramics to furniture.

Cross the Prospect Expressway, find your way to Fifth Avenue at 25th Street, and pay your respects at Green-Wood Cemetery (call 718-788-7850 before you go), a sort of deathstyles of the rich and famous of 19th-century New York. Among the ornate headstones and mausoleums are ones bearing the names of Tiffany, Samuel F.B. Morse of code fame, "Boss" Tweed, and New York governor DeWitt Clinton of Erie Canal fame (or notoriety). If you're up for more memorials, go to Holy Cross Cemetery in East Flatbush, about 20 minutes east, and visit the grave of bank robber Willie Sutton. (Unlike Philadelphia's Eastern State Penitentiary, he never escaped this place.)

On the east side of Prospect Park, near Crown Heights, are attractions that are themselves worth a day or more of your time, the Brooklyn Botanic Gardens at 1000 Washington Ave. and the Brooklyn Museum at 200 Eastern Parkway.

The 52-acre garden (718-622-4433) is best appreciated in the spring, especially in late May, when the cherry blossoms are in bloom. The themed gardens include rose, Japanese (which children love for its winding pathways), herb, and children's.

The world-class Brooklyn Museum (718-638-5000) is a treasure. Walk in and you encounter art, as in water art. Meg Webster's "Running Water" is a waterfall and quite intriguing. There are 28 American period rooms housing an extensive collection.

A bit east, where the Crown Heights and Bedford-Stuyvesant sections meet, is the Brooklyn Children's Museum (718-735-4400) at 145 Brooklyn Ave. It was founded in 1899 and is the world's first museum created expressly for children. As children's museums go, it is not the best. (The ones in Boston and Worcester, Mass., are far, far better.) Some of the Brooklyn Children's Museum's exhibits include "Animals Eats: Different Feasts for Different Beasts" and "Night Journeys," explaining dreams. (And speaking of nightmares, this neighborhood is nasty after dark.)

Brighton Beach and Coney Island. The world that Neil Simon has written about no longer exists. Brighton Beach 40 years ago was a mostly Jewish enclave. It declined to near-slum conditions from the 1950s through the 1970s. When the Soviets loosened their grip on emigration, Brighton Beach became a Soviet emigres' haven. It is far from glamorous but it shows signs of a comeback. Predictably, cyrillic signs fill Brighton Beach Avenue. Supper clubs (yes, they live on here) feature wild tabletop dancing and endless supplies of vodka. The beach is not gorgeous but the famous boardwalk is worth a stroll. This is not Loveladies, by any stretch.

Coney Island, right next door, doesn't really exist either, or at least not as it did four decades ago. The wooden Cyclone roller coaster is still good for a summertime scream. An off-season drive on Surf Avenue is rather dreary, lightened up by Nathan's Famous hot dogs and a long Russian market. The real bright spot is the New York Aquarium (718-265-3400) on Surf Avenue at Eighth Street West, still packing in crowds to see the more than 10,000 specimens of 300 species.

DUMBO, Brooklyn Heights, Park Slope, Coney Island, and Brighton Beach are only a fraction of what Brooklyn has to offer. There is Greenpoint, a western outpost of Poland. There is Fort Greene, home to African-American artists and musicians and the Brooklyn Academy of Music. There is discount clothes shopping in Borough Park.

And because Brooklyn is so extensive and only two hours from Philadelphia, there is good reason to make several weekends' worth of trips.

—Michael Klein

Directions from Philadelphia: Take the New Jersey Turnpike north to Exit 13 and Interstate 278 east across Staten Island, over the Verrazano-Narrows Bridge, and into the Bay Ridge section of Brooklyn. Stay on 278 and it will feed you onto the Brooklyn Queens Expressway. Follow it to Atlantic Avenue in Brooklyn Heights.

If you plan to stay overnight, look into a bed-and-breakfast because hotel rooms in Brooklyn are scant. B&B services can help. Some of the larger ones—all Manhattan-based—are Urban Ventures (212-594-5650), Bed & Breakfast of New York Inc. (800-900-8134) and City Lights Bed & Breakfast Ltd. (212-737-7049).

Brooklyn is for eaters. Brighton Beach has fabulous Russian specialties. Bay Ridge has excellent Scandinavian. Carroll Gardens is Old World Italian. Flatbush is known for its Caribbean foods. Half the fun is exploring.

For more information, The Fund for the Borough of Brooklyn (718-855-7882) has maps and all kinds of valuable reading material. And because all those so-called New York guidebooks virtually ignore Brooklyn, do yourself a favor and pick up a copy of Brooklyn: Where to Go, What to Do, How to Get There by Ellen Freudenheim with Daniel P. Wiener (St. Martin's Press).

Adrift in Central Park

NEW YORK

I SUPPOSE I SHOULD BE making use of the rest of Central Park instead of just drifting here in this little rowboat on this lake under this big sky.

But it's just so satisfying to float here on the water, nudged this way and that by an occasional gypsy breeze. It is especially satisfying, somehow, to be inactive, if for only an hour, in this most active of cities.

If daily life in Manhattan is a storm, Central Park is the eye of the storm, and this little lake is the pupil of the eye. From the vantage point of this lake, America's biggest, brashest, most congested city looks more like Thoreau's Walden Pond than Havoc on the Hudson.

And yet this lake is just a small part of a park that on weekends beckons work-weary Manhattanites by the tens of thousands. But because the park covers 840 acres, there is room for everyone. There are even pockets of privacy. Central Park is where Manhattanites go to be alone together.

It is where they unwind and unclench. To paraphrase Voltaire, if Central Park did not exist, it would be necessary to invent it.

And that's just what two pioneer urban designers—Frederick Olmsted and Calvert Vaux—did in the 1860s. As I look around me, this lake and this park appear very random, as if nature had created them.

But the random appearance is the result of decidedly unrandom landscaping. Central Park opened in 1876 after workers spent 20 years moving (or removing) millions of tons of earth and rock, draining swamps, planting trees and shrubs and flowers, and building fountains, bridges, and shelter houses.

Today, because Central Park is only a half-mile wide, Manhattan madness is never more than a quarter-mile away. And yet, from this lake, rimmed by trees that baffle street noise, the city might as well be a hundred miles and a hundred decibels away.

Honking horns on Broadway? I can't hear them. Domestic violence on the Upper West Side? Not that I'm aware of. Jackhammers on Fifth Avenue? That's news to me. All I can hear is the water lapping at the boat's hull, a man blowing a doleful sax on the shore, and two seagulls squawking as they hover over me like irascible angels.

Now and then, more energetic boaters row past me. Couples, families. Perhaps they have places to go and things to do: Maybe to play on the tennis courts, or to ponder the hieroglyphics on Cleopatra's Needle—the 3,500-year-old granite obelisk given to the city by Egypt in 1869—or to stop and smell the roses at the Conservatory Garden.

Or maybe their itinerary includes the Sheep Meadow south of me. It's a vast green expanse, a fitting place to fly a kite, throw a Frisbee, tone, tan, or take a catnap. It's a place to spread a picnic blanket, a place for babies to take their first steps, stumbling toward the outstretched arms of mom and dad. The Sheep Meadow is a veritable showroom of family values.

I could go join them. But why rock the boat?

To the north, I can see some bird-watchers on the edge of the Ramble—more than 30 wild acres of tree and boulder and brook laced with unpaved paths that are cushioned by leaves of a dozen autumns. I could join the birders in their quest for some ornithological grail.

Near the lake's southern shore, I can see some people exercising at Bethesda Terrace, picturesque with its biblical Angel of the Waters fountain. I could join them for a few push-ups on the terrace's red brick herringbone pavement.

But it's easier to stay right here and exercise my right to relax.

I could mosey up north of the Ramble to the Great Lawn and get in on a game of football or soccer. It's just a pass, punt, and kick away. Or I could get in a quieter game at the Chess and Checkers House, just a hop, skip, and a jump away.

Or I could go over to the zoo—renovated to be less zoolike—and talk to the animals.

But I am content to drift here and do little. In the distance, I can see the tops of the tall buildings. Luxury hotels and apartment buildings muscle up to the edge of the park on all sides and peek over the treeline, as if coveting all this undeveloped, unrented space. It is appropriate that Central Park is green and rectangular—the color and shape of a dollar bill—because surely these 840 acres in the midst of Manhattan are among the most valuable on Earth.

One building that is in Central Park is the Metropolitan Museum of Art. I could take a few hours (or a few days) to explore it. The Met looks more like some country's Capitol Building than a mere museum. But then, it's not a mere museum, is it? It's the biggest art museum in the United States.

Or I could stroll through Shakespeare's Garden, which grows only those plants mentioned in the Bard's writings. Or, nearer, a garden commemorating another British poet—Strawberry Fields, which honors John Lennon, who lived and died at the Dakota Apartments across the street.

But I've got a ticket to ride this little rowboat.

When I get hungry, I could go eat a bite at the Tavern on the Green—once a sheepfold, now a trendy restaurant. Or I could dine at the restaurant at the Loeb Boathouse—home port for this humble little vessel.

Or I could join those men who are fishing over there on the shore. They may have baited their hooks for perch, but they're catching a few minutes of peace.

But I have more important fish to fry: Suddenly, a rain shower comes up, so I row my boat under the lake's gently arched, cast-iron bridge. The lake is shaped like a rather ragged bow tie; the bridge cinches the two halves in the middle. The rain lasts only a minute and does little more than sprinkle goose bumps on the water.

I could go on a statuary tour, wandering from Alice in Wonderland (always animated with children scrambling over her), to Columbus to Balto the dog to Mother Goose to the Still Hunt—a bronze cougar forever crouched to pounce on passers-by from atop a huge boulder.

I could mosey down the Mall past statues situated beneath trees that form a leafy tunnel: Robert Burns, Walter Scott, Shakespeare, Schiller, Beethoven. Pigeons have soiled the shoulders of composer Victor Herbert.

I could join the impromptu audiences that gather to enjoy the performances of amateur mimes, comics, acrobats, jugglers and magicians, or musicians (their instrument cases opened to receive pocket change) playing everything from keyboards to clarinets.

But I prefer to drift here and listen to woodwinds of another kind—a stand of cane in the lake that rustles as the breeze plays it *sotto voce*.

I could saunter over to the Conservatory Water and cheer on the radio-controlled scale-model boats as they jostle port to starboard for position in the miniature regattas.

But I think I'll just drift here, sitting on my own stern. As I drift, a group of mallards suddenly lifts off the lake as if at some signal from its squadron leader. Even ducks have more get-up-and-go than I do.

I could go play croquet or bocce. Or I could saddle up and go horseback riding on the bridle paths, or take a ride in one of the horse-drawn carriages parked on 59th Street at the bottom of the park.

I could play miniature golf at Wollman Rink, go skating at Lasker Rink. I could rent a bicycle, being careful to stay out of the way of the roving packs of roller-bladers. Or I could join the joggers as they run the park's streets, their bodies bent in italics as they conquer the hills.

Yes, I suppose I really should bestir myself, grab these oars, row back to shore, and partake of some of these other possibilities of Central Park.

Naaaah.

—Mike Nichols

Directions from Philadelphia: Take the New Jersey Turnpike north to the Lincoln Tunnel. You'll exit in Manhattan, west and south of Central Park. Head uptown and east. For more information, contact the New York Convention & Visitors Bureau, 2 Columbus Circle, New York, N.Y. 10019; phone 212-484-1200.

A West Side story

NEW YORK

MILESTONES IN A CONNECTICUT childhood, within commuting distance of New York:

First career goal: to be a Rockette.

First motto: East is east and West is west.

Regarding the latter, I speak not of coasts but of sides. There are the East Side and the West Side, and, although the twain meet at Fifth Avenue, loyalties are fierce.

Until my husband and I spent a long weekend in the Upper West Side apartment of vacationing friends, we had minimal experience with the avenues west of Fifth. Meet at a restaurant in the West 80s? Nah, Midtown's more convenient.

A friend rented on Amsterdam Avenue? Poor thing probably couldn't find anything more central.

This East Side orientation—nay, prejudice—was nothing I learned at my parents' knees. Depression newlyweds, their first apartment was on West 74th Street. "Just off Central Park West," my father said, when I called from a pay phone at Park Avenue and 33rd Street. He described the route, and the building, as if he'd been there just yesterday.

We found the place, a five-story brownstone on an attractive, tree-lined street that, I would guess, has changed little since they moved in. Doubtless the Murphy bed that they wrestled nightly from the wall has been retired, but otherwise, I could easily picture my parents—young and excited to be starting their lives together—striding down the streets of their new neighborhood.

So, that was one of our reasons for liking the Upper West Side. But there were others: Zabar's, Shakespeare & Co., Murray's Sturgeon Shop, the Cat Store, Welcome Home Antiques, La Belle Gourmet Delicatessen, and the Cafe in the Bakery, to mention a few.

Like so much of New York, the Upper West Side is a place for walking, and we walked for miles. We would set out in the morning, no particular destination in mind, and simply explore one block after another.

The Upper West Side—essentially 72nd to 116th Streets between the Hudson River and Central Park—was practically country not too very long ago, still farmland when Midtown was already a bustling city.

The first luxury apartment house built in the area was the Dakota, which for an entire generation attained near-shrine status as the place where John Lennon lived—and in front of which, died. Built for Singer sewing machine heir Edward Clark in the early 1880s, its location was considered as remote as "Dakota in Indian territory." It soon became, and remains, a prestigious address—72nd Street, overlooking Central Park—that also has been home to the likes of Lauren Bacall and Leonard Bernstein.

Nearby, and also fronting on the park, is the American Museum of Natural History, which shortly before our visit had become a target of New York's tabloid press over the barosaurus skeleton that rears five stories high in its rotunda. The creature was certain to be, said New York *Newsday*, "the largest displayed dinosaur in the world and the most controversial." Fueling the controversy: whether the beast's upright posture was authentic or mere dramatic license, given its monstrous proportions.

Either way, we decided, it's a handsome beast.

Finding ourselves once again at Central Park, we decided to stroll through it. A lovely idea, as it turned out. We walked along 72nd Street, which bisects the park. The sky was bright blue, the air mildly crisp.

Midway through, we heard music and followed it. A Spanish guitarist, outfitted in formal dress including tails, had situated himself at pond's edge in the plaza, where he had attracted an appreciative crowd: lunch-hour folks dressed for the office, parents with young children, idlers such as ourselves. For a backdrop, it would be hard to beat the formation of ducks gliding across the pond behind willow trees gone gold and green with autumn.

It was the pastoral splendor of the park one day, the sidewalks of New York the next.

On the Upper West Side, those sidewalks pass by an eclectic array of shops, whose variety delighted us. Even my husband—hardly the inveterate shopper that I am—found the mix intriguing.

From our friends' apartment on 87th Street, we struck out toward the river, then turned north or south to meander along Broadway and Amsterdam Avenue. One of our first finds was the Cat Store, at 562 Amsterdam Ave., a small shop with a clutter of cat *tchatchkas*—calendars, ceramic cups, greeting cards, jewelry, figurines, socks, all imprinted with pussycats. Also a delightful assortment of stuffed cats and their jungle cousins, lions and tigers.

Over on Broadway at 88th, we wandered into La Belle Gourmet, at 2393 Broadway, and envied those who live near a store that carries two dozen varieties of mustard, almost as many kinds of olives, cans of plum pudding, jars of artichoke relish, and the kind of marzipan candies (shaped as tiny peaches and apples and bunches of grapes) that I loved as a child.

Outside, a sidewalk display of tulips looked like a new box of crayons brought to life.

Farther down Broadway, we entered West Side Judaica, 2412 Broadway, whose window display of menorahs included one unique for its blend of cultures: The base was a silver reindeer, its antlers balancing brass candleholders.

Inside were both bookstore and gift shop, the books ranging from *Warrior—the Life of Moshe Dayan* and *Chutzpah* by high-profile New York lawyer Alan Dershowitz to *A Photographic Portrait of Jewish Life in Central Europe Since the Holocaust* and academic tomes on Judaism.

What can one say about Zabar's, at 2245 Broadway, the store that is a New York legend, occupying the same corner since 1940? My parents shopped at Zabar's, albeit a far smaller version than the block-long emporium it has become, and I shop there now. Be warned that weekend mornings are a shopper's bedlam, but the lox and sturgeon, the rye and pumpernickel, the bagels and everything are worth it.

Worth mentioning, too, among our favorite neighborhood finds is Shakespeare & Co., 2259 Broadway, a wonderful bookstore where they still have wooden ladders that slide along the floor to give access to upper shelves, the kind of serious bookstore where an hour passes too quickly. And Welcome Home Antiques, home to two dogs and some handsome (and fairly priced) Mission furniture, among other things.

Restaurants? You want restaurants? Here, too, the Upper West Side offers choices enough to make the choosing difficult.

After several days of pure enjoyment, it seemed only fitting that we be jolted back into the reality of New York's darker side before leaving town.

Suitcases in hand, we were walking east on 87th toward the subway when we saw it: a mural painted on the side of a building. "In memory of Hector," it said. "Missed by your wife and kids and friends." The mural had gone up overnight. The dates of Hector's birth and death—along with a pair of dice and a painted hand of cards—completed it. He had died, less than a week earlier, at the age of 24. Someone, or many someones, had lighted candles on the ground beneath the mural, giving it the appearance of a shrine.

As we stood there, trying to absorb the tragedy so newly chronicled on a rowhouse wall, three men stopped as well.

"He looked a little like that," said one of them, indicating the face card, the king, in the ace-high hand. To us, the man explained that Hector had died of a beating "in the projects on 90th Street."

"He wasn't a crazy," the man said, to us and to his friends. "He had two kids."

It altered our view, reminding us that this was much more than a place where people wandered around. They lived and died here also. This was a real neighborhood. A real place.

—Mary Jane Fine

Directions from Philadelphia: Take the New Jersey Turnpike north to the Lincoln Tunnel. You'll exit the tunnel on the West Side of Manhattan, though downtown.

They built it, they came

COOPERSTOWN, N.Y.

CONTRARY TO POPULAR BELIEF, and with apologies to the late, great Abner Doubleday, the national pastime did not begin in a cow pasture here. Nor did Mr. Doubleday invent the game.

But this small, picturesque lakeside town has become its shrine nevertheless—the mecca for more than a quarter-million fans each year.

Cooperstown, as any baseball fanatic knows, is home to the National Baseball Hall of Fame and Museum—at once a most likely and unlikely location for a museum dedicated to such a popular and culturally ingrained sport.

Unlikely because Cooperstown is quintessential small-town America, far removed from the nation's power and population centers, and distant not just from major league baseball, but also from the big money and celebrity status that the game has come to represent.

Probably because the tree-shaded streets and 19th-century atmosphere of Cooperstown evoke a sense that this is the kind of town where baseball should have been invented—a little burg not unlike many thousands of others across America, where small boys (and girls, too) still gather at ball diamonds to play out their dreams.

Those same small boys—and, again, some girls—can be seen trooping around Cooperstown and the museum almost any time of year, accompanied more often than not by their fathers—men of a certain age who have come not so much to dream of the future, perhaps, as to recall the past.

The Hall of Fame and Museum is really about heroes, so it serves both sexes and all ages. But it seems to speak best to those who love the game and can recall a time when it was just that, instead of a unique big business where both the owners and the employees are millionaires.

My wife and I came here on a weekend with the boys—Dave, 17, and Ben, 16, both fans and card collectors and Ben an accomplished practitioner of the sport. They breezed through the place in two hours —with a "wow" here and a "look at this" or "did you see that?" there— and then wanted to go find the batting cages outside town before lunch. I hadn't even made it to the third floor.

"Well, what did you guys think of the place?" I asked.

"Intellectually and spiritually challenging," joked Dave.

"Great," said Ben. "Can we go find the batting cages now?"

"What was the most interesting thing—the thing you'll remember the most?" I asked.

"The girls," said Dave, and I don't think he was joking this time.

"Everything," said Ben. "Can we go find the batting cages now?"

So they went looking for the batting cages with their mother.

I couldn't blame them. The truth of the National Baseball Hall of Fame and Museum, as heretical as it may be, is that while you could easily spend a few days here, a few hours is quite enough, thanks. You can see only so many signed baseballs and bats, gloves, uniforms, and other memorabilia, you can absorb only so many statistics, before over-dosing. It's a good museum, a great museum for baseball fans, yet it is still a museum for a game that's played—a passive look at an active sport.

To digress for just a moment, it should be noted that Cooperstown made the literary map even before baseball was invented. The town was founded in 1786 by William Cooper, whose son was the novelist James Fenimore Cooper, which explains why there is a Natty Bumppo's Tavern, a Leatherstocking Gallery, and a Glimmerglass Restaurant in town.

Just outside town is the Fenimore House, a folk-art museum that sits on part of the old Cooper farm and was the mansion earlier in this century of Edward S. Clark, heir to the Singer sewing machine fortune. It was the Clark money, more than Abner Doubleday, that placed the museum in Cooperstown and opened it in 1939.

Across the road, on the grounds of the old Clark estate, is yet another museum, the Farmers' Museum, which we were wise enough to visit the afternoon before we went to the Baseball Hall of Fame. (Imagine trying to get two teenage boys from the Big City to come to a farmers' museum after the Hall of Fame.) The museum has a good collection of 19th-century farm implements and various restored, historic buildings moved here and arranged in a "village" where crafts and trades—printer, blacksmith, tinsmith, woodcarver—are demonstrated.

But the most memorable part is probably the Cardiff Giant, a bigger-than-life stone statue, secretly carved in 1868 for a Binghamton cigar manufacturer, who then dumped sulfuric acid on it to make it look old and buried it on a farm outside the town of Cardiff. A year later, in 1869, he called in workmen to dig a well and—guess what?—they discovered a "petrified man." In less than a week, up to 500 people a day were paying 50 cents apiece to see the Cardiff Giant. The hoax was discovered before long, but the Cardiff Giant still traveled the sideshow circuit for decades, arriving at the Farmers' Museum in 1948.

I couldn't help thinking he'd make a fine first baseman, which brings us back to Main Street in Cooperstown and the Baseball Hall of Fame and Museum.

All the famous names are here: Ted Williams, Babe Ruth, Jackie Robinson, Hank Aaron, Joe DiMaggio, Alexander Cartwright.

Alexander Cartwright?

The museum gives its due to claims that Doubleday invented the game, noting that a commission in 1907 reported the first scheme for playing baseball, according to the best evidence obtainable to date, was devised by Abner Doubleday at Cooperstown, N.Y., in 1839. But Alexander Cartwright, a New York City fireman, is credited with creating the first set of playing rules—including such basic stuff as the number of innings, the number of players on a team, and the length of the baselines—and forming the first organized team. And Cartwright, not Doubleday, is in the Hall of Fame.

Kids do love this place, but it takes men and women of a certain age to really appreciate it.

"We were fortunate to live in an era that will never come again," said Hank Silverman, a Valley Stream, L.I., furniture salesman who grew up in Brooklyn and was touring the museum with his wife, Gail.

"You had to have lived it day by day," said Silverman, 57, a fan of the old Brooklyn Dodgers. "There was a thrill inside your body. People ate, drank, and died baseball. Three teams in town [the Giants, the Dodgers, and the Yankees], and they were blood enemies. For big games, they even had the radios on in the schools."

And not just for the Dodgers.

"In our family, you only talked about the Yankees," said Gail, a piano teacher and the mother of three grown children. "So, can you imagine: a Dodger fan marrying a Yankee fan? Raising three little Mets?"

Although we'd grown up in different worlds—I on a small farm 200 miles and at least one light-year west of Brooklyn—the Silvermans and I shared a love for that baseball era that made conversation easy. Our memories included not just the greats—Jackie at second and Pee Wee at short, the Duke in center, and Campy behind the plate—but also the lesser-knowns and near-forgottens—the great pinch hitter George "Shotgun" Shuba, for example—and even Ralph Branca, who—the world may forgive but never forget—served up the home run ball to Bobby Thomson that gave the Giants the pennant in '51.

It's all recalled here, not just with the Hall of Fame, but with a film presentation, with video displays, with replicas of ballparks, with baseball cards, and with seemingly endless displays that evoke the great players and the great moments of the game.

Phillies fans suffering through the agonies and ecstasies of the 1993 season can take themselves back to another pennant drive more than 40 years before (1950, to be exact), when a guy named Robin Roberts was throwing fastballs past a lot of hitters, and another young fellow named Richie Ashburn was dashing around center field. Roberts made the Hall of Fame. Ashburn never did, but because he later turned to sportscasting, he's known to a new generation of fans who wouldn't know Robin Roberts from Bobby Shantz.

There's an exhibit on women in baseball. There's another on the old Negro Leagues that recalls the relatively recent past when segregation barred blacks from the major leagues and reviews the post-World War II integration of the majors, led by Jackie Robinson playing for the Brooklyn Dodgers.

I can still recall coming in from hoeing rows of vegetables on a hot summer day to crouch beside the radio and listen to the Old Redhead, Red Barber: "Robinson's dancing off third. He wants to go. But will he? Maglie gets the sign. He watches. Now he starts the delivery. And here comes Robinson!"

For the legions of unfortunate fans whose memories include only a team called the Los Angeles Dodgers, this museum reminds us that the Brooklyn Dodgers captured seven National League titles (but, painfully, only one World Series) in the 10 years between 1947 and 1956.

And for those equally sad souls who know Phil Rizzuto only for his "Money Store" ads on television, this museum also recalls Rizzuto the shortstop, and other men named Whitey Ford, Billy Martin, Allie Reynolds, and a couple of sluggers named Maris and Mantle. And a New York Yankee dynasty that accounted for 15 American League pennants in 18 years.

Silverman and I—men of a certain age—talked of that Yankee-Dodger rivalry, and a few of its greatest moments.

"Being a Dodger fan meant a lot of heartbreak, didn't it?" he asked.

"Yeah, because the Yankees always won," said his wife.

—Mike Shoup

Directions from Philadelphia: Take the Northeast Extension of the Pennsylvania Turnpike north to Interstate 81, and take I-81 north to Interstate 88, outside Binghamton. Follow I-88 northeast past Oneonta to the Cooperstown exit, and take Route 28 north into Cooperstown.

The National Baseball Hall of Fame and Museum is open every day except Thanksgiving, Christmas, and New Year's Day. Hours are 9 a.m. to 9 p.m. May 1 to October 31 and 9 a.m. to 5 p.m. the rest of the year. At presstime, admission was $8 for adults and $3 for children ages 7 to 12.

For a local guide that includes accommodations, call the Cooperstown Chamber of Commerce, 607-547-9983.

ow

The glass factory

CORNING, N.Y.

IN THE BLUE-ORANGE FLARE of his torch, John Hargrave deftly fashions a tiny buffalo from rods of glowing glass. With one tool, he levels the hooves. With another, he crimps the end of the tail, and with still another, he applies texture to the hump.

For a moment, he pauses to inspect his work. Then, acknowledging the tourists who have been watching him, he grins broadly and exclaims, "I can't believe they pay me to do this!"

Hargrave demonstrates his craft, called lampworking, in the Hall of Science and Industry at the Corning Glass Center, a complex that includes the Corning Museum of Glass and the Steuben crystal factory.

A few months before this day, Hargrave was a cleaner in the Glass Center. And two months after he began training as a lampworker, his one-year apprenticeship was cut short. His knack for sculpting lifelike figures in glass had earned him journeyman status.

"The funny thing," he said, "is that I can't even draw."

Hargrave's pride in his craft and his excitement about glass and its possibilities were reflected again and again in people my wife, Jamie, and I met during a two-day visit to this town of 12,000 that is home to the world's leading glass museum.

In addition to the museum and the Steuben (pronounced Stoo-BEN) factory, where teams of crafts workers create fabulously expensive crystal, the town of Corning features small glass-blowing shops run by independent artists, an outstanding museum of American western art, and a nonprofit studio where for $35 you can make your own glass paperweight.

The town also has several good, informal restaurants, an 1890s-style ice cream parlor, antiques shops, and a number of factory outlets, not only for Corning Glass Co.'s Corningware and Pyrex products, but also for shirts, coats, and shoes.

(Don't expect to find outlet prices for Steuben crystal. The company sells no seconds. Rejects are destroyed. Items in the Steuben Shop at the Glass Center range from small glass animals for $150 up to sculptures that sell for the price of a good used car.)

Corning's restored Market Street, which is lined with turn-of-the-century red-brick buildings, gives the town a pleasant Victorian feel.

This ambience was amplified in the bed and breakfast we chose randomly from a list in a Chamber of Commerce brochure. The Rosewood Inn, an 1855 house three blocks from the heart of Corning, was a warm cocoon of late-19th-century luxury. After a wonderful night and breakfast, we went out into the cold and headed across the Chemung River to the Glass Center.

The Corning Museum of Glass, the first stop at the Glass Center, is a spectacular building designed by Gunnar Birkerts and is made, naturally, mostly of glass. The irregular shape of smooth curves and sharp angles suggests the petals of a flower.

The museum's collection is encyclopedic and overwhelming—more than 17,000 objects tracing the history and development of glass from Mesopotamia in 1500 B.C. to now. Methods of making and decorating glass are described and sometimes shown in short movies.

The lore of glass and its uses is also illustrated in quotations printed on the exhibit cases.

One noteworthy quotation, from a 1702 *Brewer's Guide*, is on a case displaying English drinking glasses:

"To make strong ale: Thames-Water taken up about Greenwich at low-water, when it is free from all brackishness of the sea, and has in it all the Fat and Sullage from this Great City of London, makes very Strong Drink. It will of itself ferment wonderfully and after its due purgations and three times stinking it will be so strong that several Sea Commanders have told me that it has often fuddled their Murriners."

The galleries in the museum are arranged chronologically, allowing visitors to trace both the artistic and technical evolution of glass. The path through the museum is along a main circular corridor. On the right, at the center of the building, is the Rakow Library, containing written works on the history of glass. To the left are the galleries in which most of the glass objects are displayed.

We worked our way through all the galleries, a daunting two-hour trek. Somewhere, probably about the 16th century, all glass—no matter how important or elegantly fashioned—began to look to us like all other glass. The displays were just too much to absorb in one visit.

After the museum comes the Hall of Science and Industry, where the properties and uses of glass are demonstrated. Here there are opportunities to fiddle with lasers and prisms, to view the first casting of the 200-inch mirror made for the Mount Palomar (California) telescope, and to see large sheets of glass flex and bend like plastic.

It was at one end of the hall that lampworker John Hargrave was demonstrating his craft. (Later, through the gift shop at the Glass Center exit, we bought the clear-glass buffalo that we watched him make.)

The last stop before the shops is the Steuben Factory. Here visitors can sit in a tiered gallery, like spectators at a basketball game, and watch the glassblowers work. While we were there, a team was making footed crystal bowls. The artisans' moves were perfectly timed and delicately choreographed.

One worker blew the sphere that would be cut to form the bowl itself. Another formed the base, and a third worked with the others to assemble the parts, and then did the final molding and shaping. A fourth worker kept busy with a variety of tasks, providing an extra pair of skilled hands wherever needed.

The process took place wordlessly and with absolute precision.

The glass, which first comes from the kiln at the consistency of honey, cools to hardness in about 40 seconds. While it is hot, it must be kept spinning or it will slump. Each time it cools, it must be returned to the kiln via a "glory hole" to be reheated. When two pieces are fused, they must be turning at the same speed, perfectly aligned and hot at the same time. One artisan making a simple blown vessel is craftsmanship. Four or five artisans making a complex vessel is industrial ballet.

The apprenticeship period for these workers, who are called gaffers, is seven years.

From the glassblowing area, the visitors' corridor leads into the gift shops, which offer a dazzling display of glass items, ranging from the mundane to the sublime and sublimely expensive.

There is an outlet store with Corningware dishes and Pyrex cookware, and there is a black-walled Steuben showroom where $150 paperweights and $4,000 art objects are displayed with reverence usually reserved for crown jewels.

In between these two shops are counters featuring glass from around the world, the works of individual Americans, and the little glass animals created by John Hargrave and his fellow lampworkers. Unless your heart is set on Steuben, you can pick up elegantly made gifts and souvenirs for as little as $5.

Hargrave's buffalo cost a little less than $25.

As extensive as the Glass Center is, it does not tell the whole story about glass in Corning. There is still another museum with an outstanding collection of glass art and, along the west end of Market Street in the rambling old Hawkes Crystal Building, there are three studios where you can watch glassblowers at work.

(At the independent studios, glass blowing can be seen Monday through Friday, but not on Wednesday afternoon. At the Steuben Factory, glassblowing can be seen seven days a week, 9 a.m. until 5 p.m. The level of activity in the factory, however, varies widely from day to day, depending on what is being made.)

At studios on Market Street, the artisans work in colored glass (Steuben crystal is pure and clear); their products range from knickknacks to impressive sculptures.

In each of the shops, Vitrex, Alex Brand, and Noslo, the kilns and work areas are adjacent to the galleries and are open for viewing. The atmosphere is informal, and the glassblowers, if they are not too busy, are willing to explain what they are doing and why.

At Studio Access to Glass, Corning's only noncommercial glass studio, we made an appointment with director Rodi Rovner to come back the next day for a half-hour lesson in hot-glass work and a chance to make our own paperweights.

Then we were ready for a change of pace—and a change of subject.

Fortunately, Corning has just the place for that in the Rockwell Museum, a huge red Romanesque former city hall, jail, and firehouse that now houses an outstanding collection of American Western Art.

To answer the obvious question, the Rockwell Museum has nothing to do with Norman Rockwell, the artist.

It has everything to do with the pioneer artists who brought back images of the untamed American West and fired the imaginations and the expansionist yearnings of the folks back East.

The Rockwell collection was amassed by Robert F. and Hertha Rockwell, whose family fortune came from a small chain of department stores in the Corning area. The museum building was purchased by Corning Glass Works from the town in 1980 for $1. After restoration of the exterior and remodeling of the interior, the museum was opened in 1982.

Even here, though, you can't get away from glass.

Robert Rockwell was a friend and golfing buddy of Frederick Carder, co-founder of Steuben Glass Works and one of the greatest and most prolific glass designers of all time. Carder, who retired in 1959 at 96 and died four years later, is virtually a deity in Corning. More than 2,000 pieces of Steuben glass produced under his direction are on display on the second floor of the Rockwell Museum.

The third floor, however, is all Western art.

There are grand landscapes by Thomas Moran and Albert Bierstadt that reflect the impact of the artists' encounters with natural wonders on a scale unseen by Easterners. It is easy to imagine how these scenes, so otherworldly and so idealized, were a part of the powerful magnet drawing people out of their dirty cities and cramped farms and onto the trail west.

There are paintings of American Indians, some realistic, some romanticized, many patronizing. And there are displays of weavings, pottery, and other artifacts produced by Indians themselves.

Most compelling, however, are the vivid, kinetic paintings and sculptures by Frederic Remington and Charles M. Russell, the Rembrandt and Van Gogh of cowboy art, with their focus on hard riders and fast horses, guns, and action.

On Saturday, the final day of our visit, we were more than ready for our appointments with Rodi Rovner. After seeing so much glass and talking to so many people who were excited about what could be done with it, we were eager to try our hand.

Studio Access to Glass is part of Corning's One Seventy One Cedar Arts Center, but it is at a separate site, an old garage near a railroad overpass at 161 Baker St. Here, classes in glassblowing, engraving, and other skills are taught by master artisans, many of whom work at Steuben or at one of the independent glass shops. In addition, studio time can be rented by independent artists and demonstrations, and classes are available for children's groups.

For $35, each of us had a half-hour with Rovner, making a paperweight by shaping molten glass. Rovner proved to be an excellent teacher, allowing us to do enough to get the feel of working with glass and to claim ownership of our paperweights, but assisting to the point that we neither set ourselves afire nor screwed up the project.

After Rovner loaded the end of our pipes with molten glass, we picked up nuggets of colored glass from a warming table. Then she added layers of clear hot glass, and we rolled and shaped the glass in dripping-wet wooden molds.

With a hiss of steam, the molds dried in seconds and, at Rovner's coaching, we quickly plunged them back into a bucket of water, keeping the glass turning all the while. Jamie chose to twist her paperweight's colors into a swirl design. I left my colors in distinct blobs and used a piercing tool to create a decorative bubble near its top.

Finally, we used giant tweezers called jacks to make a groove where the finished paperweight could be broken off from the pipe. The actual breaking, tapping the pipe while the glass rests against a wet paper pad, was a satisfying moment of truth.

Our conclusion: We see how hot-glass work is done and why people love to do it. We also see why it takes years of practice to get it right.

Rovner carefully placed our paperweights into an annealing oven to cool overnight. A few days later, they were delivered to our door in Philadelphia. They still looked pretty good—not Steuben quality, but, thanks to Rovner, they have our names engraved on the bottoms.

Our adventure in glassmaking, which we followed with a round of hot fudge sundaes served in Pyrex measuring cups at the Ice Cream Works on Market Street, was a fitting conclusion to our visit to Corning.

—William H. Stroud

Directions from Philadelphia: Take the Northeast Extension of the Pennsylvania Turnpike to Interstate 81 north to Binghamton, N.Y., and pick up New York Route 17 west to Corning. The drive will take about 4½ hours.

For information, contact the Greater Corning Area Chamber of Commerce, 42 E. Market St., Corning, N.Y. 14830, 607-936-4686.

The Corning Glass Center, 607-974-8271, is open 9 a.m. to 5 p.m. daily; until 8 p.m. in July and August. Admission at presstime was $7 for adults, $6 for seniors, $5 for children 6 to 17, free for children under 6, $16 for families.

Studio Access to Glass, 261 Baker St., charges $35 for a half-hour lesson, by reservation. Call before noon for same-day reservation, 607-962-3044.

The Rockwell Museum, 607-937-5386, 111 Cedar St., is open Monday through Saturday, 9 a.m. to 5 p.m.; Sunday, noon to 5 p.m. Admission $4, $3.60 for seniors, $2 for children 6 to 17, $10 for families.

An historic fort

TICONDEROGA, N.Y.

THE DRUM MAJOR SIGNALS with his spontoon, and the fife and drum corps marches up the parade ground playing "Hey! Jonnie Cope are Ye a Wauken Yet?" Your adrenalin is pumping, and you're ready to grab a musket and follow these lads right through the gates of hell.

At least I was. Martial music gets me every time. If I hear a bagpipe skirling "Scotland the Brave" or the Marine Band playing "Semper Fidelis," I'm on a natural high.

My companions think I've made this autumn weekend trek north to see the fall foliage. That's all they know. The fort and its environs hold enough fascination for me to fill more than a few days. Leaf-peeping can wait; right now, there's this wonderful music.

These lads are good. The Fort Ticonderoga Corps of Drums, the official name of the group, made its first guest appearance at the 1939 World's Fair in New York. Since then, it has marched across the ice to open the 1980 Winter Olympic Games at Lake Placid and played at the christening of the guided-missile cruiser *Ticonderoga*.

Here at this 226-year-old fort—the finest example of a Colonial fort in the country—the corps parades several times a day during the summer and on weekends in the fall. The commanding officer, Michael Edson, himself a drummer in the corps for 18 years, rehearses these high schoolers once a week throughout the winter.

The 15 corps members wear coats of red with blue facing, the uniform of musicians of the First New York Regiment, Continental Line, which served in these parts during the Revolution. They memorize more than 100 18th-century tunes, including such choice ones as "Oyster River Hornpipe," "Soldier's Wedding," and "La Belle Catherine." Corps members also entertain visitors by re-enacting a Colonial court-martial and the firing of the old cannon and mortars.

We stopped here on our way to Vermont. The foliage here is beautiful, too, but we are brand-conscious. We insist on Vermont foliage, just as we insist on Vermont maple syrup. The fort is convenient if you are entering Vermont at Fair Haven, which is the easiest way to the northern section of the Green Mountain National Forest, a particularly fine spot to view the foliage.

To reach Vermont from the fort, take the dirt road to the bottom of the hill and the ferry across the southern tail of Lake Champlain, a five-minute ride at most. The ferry was started by Lord Jeffrey Amherst in 1759 and has been in operation ever since.

If you're a history buff like I am, a stop at Ticonderoga is worth the trip all by itself. If you're not, it's an enjoyable break in a long drive to view the glories of foliage season in Vermont.

And we found other interesting things to do around here. We took a 90-minute excursion on the vintage wooden tour boat *Carillon*, which ties up near the fort and is a pleasant way to explore the lower end of Lake Champlain.

The fort has special events throughout the season: muzzle-loading rifle shoots in early May and mid-September, re-enactments of the Grand Encampment of the French and Indian War in late June, a Scottish gathering and military tattoo in early July, and a muster of fife and drum corps in late July.

A guide in period costume took us on a tour of the fort. I had seen the fort years before, as a Vermont schoolboy. Although it's just barely over the line in New York, Fort Ticonderoga is sort of sacred to Vermonters. On May 10, 1775, three weeks after the fighting at Lexington and Concord, Ethan Allen and his Green Mountain Boys surprised the sleeping garrison and captured the fort.

Asked by what authority he was demanding surrender, Allen replied, "In the name of the great Jehovah, and the Continental Congress." It was the first American victory of the Revolution. The following winter, Col. Henry Knox dragged many of the fort's cannon over the snow on sledges to Boston, where Gen. George Washington's army was besieging the British.

On this visit, I particularly enjoyed the museum, which houses an outstanding collection of military memorabilia, paintings, and articles of the daily life of the soldiers garrisoned here. Among its treasures: a silver case, shaped like a bullet, that was carried by a British spy, who delivered it by mistake to American General George Clinton instead of British General John Burgoyne; miniature toy soldiers that French General Louis de Montcalm played with as a boy; Gen. Philip John Schuyler's flag, possibly made by Betsy Ross, with 13 stars in a circle on a blue canton, and the knapsack carried in the Revolution by Benjamin Warner, who bequeathed it to his descendants with the admonition that "whilst one shred of it shall remane never surrender your libertys to a foren envador or an aspiring demegog."

The fort, as the guide explained, dates from an earlier conflict. In the early 1700s, France and England were struggling for domination of the New World. The Ticonderoga peninsula here, which the French called Carillon (pronounced Car-ee-OWN), lay at the southern edge of the French empire. (Ticonderoga is a corruption of an Indian word meaning "land between the waters.") To the south was a chain of British forts along the Hudson River. In those days, forts dotted the landscape around here like pepper on a fried egg.

During the French and Indian War, the French began building this fort where it could command either invasion route the British might take—down Lake Champlain or over the two-mile portage from the outlet of Lake George.

In 1758, the Marquis de Montcalm's small garrison repelled a large British force, nearly annihilating the 42nd Highland Black Watch regiment. Entering the fort grounds today, you can see the old French earthworks where the Scottish regiment was defeated.

The next year, Lord Jeffrey Amherst led a powerful assault on Fort Carillon, and the French abandoned it after blowing up the powder magazine. The British rebuilt the fort, renamed it Ticonderoga, and held it until Ethan Allen and the boys arrived.

The Americans built up the garrison to 10,000 troops, fortified the nearby hill called Mount Independence, and linked it to the fort by a floating bridge. They neglected to fortify Mount Defiance, however, thinking it was too steep. When Burgoyne got his cannon up there, Gen. Arthur St. Clair abandoned the fort to the British. Burgoyne had a simple philosophy: "Wherever goats can go, soldiers can go. And where soldiers can go they can drag cannon."

After Burgoyne's surrender at Saratoga, the British abandoned the fort and burned the barracks. Later, settlers in the area scavenged the ruins for materials to build their own houses. Paintings in the museum show its ghostly remains.

To see what the fort looked like then, drive about 10 miles north to the west end of the Lake Champlain bridge and visit the ruins of Ticonderoga's sister fort at Crown Point. It still has that lovely eerie quality.

It probably was that beauty that prompted William Ferris Pell, a New York merchant, in 1812 to buy the land where the old fort stood. Nearly a century later, a descendant, Stephen Pell, began the formidable task of reconstructing the fort.

In 1909, on the occasion of the tricentennial of Samuel de Champlain's discovery of the lake, President William Howard Taft came here to open Fort Ticonderoga to the public.

Since then, the fort has welcomed more than 15 million visitors. Restoration has been completed, and the Pell family has acquired adjacent land, including Mount Independence. The family in 1931 created a nonprofit educational corporation to run the fort, and in 1966 it was declared a national historical landmark.

I had studied the history of the fort in my school days, but there was one question that nagged me. On the tour I put the question to our guide.

"What about Ticonderoga pencils? Were they made here?"

"Not the pencils, but the lead in the pencils," she explained. "One of the largest graphite mines in the country is right outside town."

That made my trip. No more wondering about pencils. Now I knew, and now I was happy.

—Chuck Lawliss

Directions from Philadelphia: Take the New Jersey Turnpike to the Garden State Parkway exit; the parkway to Interstates 87-287 (the New York Thruway) north to Albany at Exit 24. Continue on 87 north (the Adirondack Northway) to the Lake George exit. Take Route 9N to the town of Ticonderoga. The fort is two miles east on Route 74.

Fort Ticonderoga is open 9 a.m. to 5 p.m. daily from mid-May to mid-October, except July and August, when hours continue to 6 p.m. The fort is wheelchair-accessible. Admission at presstime was $7 for those 13 and over, $5 for those 10 to 13, and free for those under 10. Tours, the fife and drum music and the cannon- and mortar-firing are held daily in July and August, weekends in the spring and fall. For further information, write to Fort Ticonderoga, Box 390, Fort Road, Ticonderoga, N.Y. 12883, or phone 518-585-2821.

Crown Point State Historic Site is open Monday and Tuesday, 8 a.m. to 4:30 p.m. and Wednesday through Sunday, 8 a.m. to 7 p.m. (or sunset), from May through October. Handicapped-accessible. Phone 518-597-3666.

For information about accommodations, call the Chamber of Commerce at 518-585-6619. Especially for Vermont during foliage season, make reservations well in advance.

A visit to the Finger Lakes

PENN YAN, N.Y.

ON SEEING THE FINGER LAKES region for the first time, my husband did a double take:

"Wow, what a gorgeous area," was his first reaction. And as we drove along, gazing at the dazzling blue lakes and vineyard-studded hills, his second reaction registered:

"Where," he demanded to know, "are all the tourists?"

And where were the schlocky billboards, the neon-lit motels, the fast-food joints?

The Finger Lakes are one of New York State's top three tourist destinations, but you'd never know it from visiting. Although it's the largest wine-making region in the eastern United States and a year-round mecca for outdoors enthusiasts, this part of west-central New York remains surprisingly rural and unspoiled—uncrowded, even in summer. Yet, the region offers plenty of accommodations, restaurants, and recreational attractions for visitors of all ages and interests.

Although we had visited the Finger Lakes several times, this trip was special: It would be our first vacation with our 11-month-old daughter. Eager to initiate her into the region's abundant outdoor activities, we planned to bicycle around (with her in our trusty carrier) and hike along one of the area's spectacular gorges. The only hitch, we figured, was that our traveling tot might get too fussy to enjoy the fun.

As it turned out, her disposition stayed bright and sunny. But the weather was another story. A cold, foggy, and persistent downpour canceled most of our outdoor plans. Luckily, the Finger Lakes surprised us again: Water sports, cycling, and hiking may be primary reasons for a visit here, but we discovered plenty of indoor adventures, from winery tours and tastings to offbeat museums and historic landmarks.

In good weather, a car drive is an easy way to get acquainted with the region and enjoy its stunning views. The 11 long, slender lakes that make up the region look like giant blue ribbons and range from the westernmost lake of Conesus to Otisco Lake in the east, a distance of about 80 miles.

Eons ago, the lakes were gouged out by Ice Age glaciers so powerful that the bottom of the deepest lake, Seneca, is 632 feet below the surface. Between the lakes lies a patchwork quilt of forests, farms, quiet hamlets, and occasional gorges with rushing waterfalls.

It's hard to get lost in the Finger Lakes, even when you're distracted by a demanding infant. If you lose your bearings, just head for the top of the nearest hill and look for a lake. Because the lakes lie in north-south valleys, they provide an instant fix on your position. What's more, even obscure country roads are well-marked—a pleasant surprise for city folks.

A five- to six-hour drive from Philadelphia, the Finger Lakes are best visited over a long weekend. We stayed a week and didn't begin to run low on things to do. What's more, our trip was low-cost as well as low-key. For a modest price, we stayed at the Viking Inn (315-536-7061), a pleasant but unpretentious resort on the eastern shore of pretty Keuka Lake. Our two-room suite wasn't posh, but it had everything we needed: a kitchenette, dining area, deck overlooking the lake, and separate bedroom for the baby. The hospitality wasn't bad either. When my husband asked our friendly Norwegian-American innkeeper to recommend a place to buy beer, he surprised us with six free bottles, left by a previous guest.

We sipped our first beer aboard the *Viking Spirit*, the resort's party and tour boat that cruises Keuka Lake. Public cruises are offered on most of the larger lakes, including Cayuga, Seneca, and Canandaigua. You can go out for an hour, as we did, to enjoy a close-up view of the snug cottages nestled on the shores, or you can sail on one of the many brunch or dinner cruises. On Skaneateles Lake, you can accompany the mailboat on its rounds. On one of the few remaining water-borne U.S. postal routes, the boat delivers the mail dockside, Mondays through Saturdays during July and August, to cottagers around that 16-mile-long lake.

Whether you're floating atop Keuka Lake or driving around it, the views are magnificent. Unique among the Finger Lakes, Keuka (pronounced CUE-ka) is shaped like a Y with a main body of water that splits into two branches. Between the branches is a high, rounded peninsula known as the bluff. One of our favorite rides (by bike or car) is along the peninsula's quiet shoreline.

Penn Yan, the village at the northern tip of Keuka Lake, also is worth checking out—if only because it has the only combination pool hall/coffee shop we've ever seen. Actually, Penn Yan is best known as the home of Birkett Mills, the world's largest producer of buckwheat products. You can stop in, as we did, and buy buckwheat flour to take home. Or, if you go in September, you can feast on buckwheat ice cream and pancakes at the town's annual Buckwheat Festival.

From Penn Yan, it's an easy shot into wine country. If you go south on Route 54A, you'll see signs for the Keuka Lake Winery Route, which covers seven wineries open for tours and tastings. The route provides a good cross-section of the region's varied viniculture, from the giant Taylor Wine Co. in Hammondsport to the small-scale "boutique" wineries on back roads. In all, about 40 wineries are scattered about the Finger Lakes, most of them on the slopes above Keuka, Cayuga, and Seneca lakes.

For a truly different tour, don't miss Bully Hill Vineyards. (From Hammondsport, take Route 54A north and turn left at the sign for Bully Hill.) Bully Hill is owned by Walter S. Taylor, a flamboyant entrepreneur and grandson of the founder of Taylor Wine Co. After a long legal wrangle with Coca-Cola, which bought Taylor Wine in 1977, Walter Taylor lost the right to use his last name as a trademark.

A savvy promoter, he began referring to himself on his wine labels as "Walter S——" Other such eccentricities, plus his wild paintings hanging on the winery's walls, make this a one-of-a-kind tour. The funky winery complex includes a museum of antique winemaking equipment, a bed-and-breakfast inn, a restaurant, and a gift shop.

About two miles north of Bully Hill—and a million miles away in atmosphere—is Heron Hill Vineyards. Its Swiss chalet-style tasting room gives it a classy, European feel. Its dry white wines are well-regarded and reasonably priced, so we headed straight for the tasting room. If you dismiss New York wines as grapey stuff, try some of Heron Hill's chardonnays and Rieslings. And if you go, take your camera. Perched near the top of a steep hill, the winery commands a spectacular view of Keuka Lake and Bluff Point.

You also can sample Finger Lakes wines in many local restaurants. For nondrinkers, Widmer Wine Cellars and others make a variety of nonalcoholic sparkling grape juices. We enjoyed some of those at Fred's Family Restaurant, which serves homemade soups and good roast chicken, on Route 54 south of Hammondsport.

With our tiny, food-throwing maniac along, our dining was necessarily casual. But had we been planning a romantic dinner, we would have gone to Geneva, at the northern tip of Seneca Lake. Geneva has two stunning inns, both with elegant restaurants. The first is Belhurst Castle (315-781-0201), on the western shore of Seneca Lake. The sight of this turreted redstone mansion—a riot of architectural excess—is staggering. We stopped in for drinks and dessert, just to ogle the gorgeous hand-carved woodwork, stained glass and antiques. We also tried the spigot on the second-floor landing, which dispenses free wine to overnight guests. (It worked.)

Practically next door is Geneva on the Lake (315-789-7190), another estate-turned-inn. Built as a replica of a 16th-century Italian villa, the hotel overlooks a large terrace, exquisite formal gardens and a 70-foot swimming pool bordered by tall Greek columns. We ended our trip with a stay here. The place was breathtaking, but then so were the prices: $200 a night for our two-room suite, which included a small kitchen.

If luxury inns are too rich for your blood, you can camp for a small fee in most of the region's 25 state parks. Many parks also offer swimming, boating, and fishing, as well as hiking and cross-country ski trails. In Taughannock Falls State Park in Trumansburg, you can hike to and around the highest straight-drop waterfall in the eastern United States. The 215-foot Taughannock Falls, higher than Niagara, plunge into a rocky gorge.

For a different form of exercise, you can shop till you drop at the Windmill Farm & Craft Market on Route 14A between Penn Yan and Dundee. Open only on Saturdays and holidays from May to mid-December, the Windmill is crammed with 300 vendors, who sell everything from farm-fresh produce and baked goods to antiques and knickknacks galore. This is a good place to shop for quilts and local crafts, some of them bargains. I spotted a nicely priced handcrafted cedar chest.

In Geneva, we explored some of the region's history—or more apt, herstory. The northern Finger Lakes are the cradle of the women's suffrage movement and a historic springboard for several remarkable women. For example, a plaque on South Main Street marks the spot where Elizabeth Blackwell became the first woman to graduate from an American medical school. According to our guidebook, the all-male school (which eventually became Hobart and William Smith Colleges) admitted her only because her application was considered a joke. When she arrived, the faculty advised her to leave. But she persevered, and when she graduated two years later, in 1849, she ranked first in her class.

Nearby Seneca Falls is known as the birthplace of American feminism. There, we visited the Women's Rights National Historic Park, which traces the history of the women's suffrage movement. Guess what, guys: It all started at a tea party. That's where Elizabeth Cady Stanton supposedly first vented her discontent about women's lot to several other women. That, we are told, led to the first Women's Rights Convention in 1848 in Seneca Falls, and its radical declaration that women deserved equal rights, including the right to vote.

Coincidentally, another early feminist, Susan B. Anthony, was arrested and jailed in nearby Canandaigua in 1872, when she attempted to vote in a regional election. You can visit her home, now a National Historic Landmark, in Rochester, about an hour's drive northwest.

Also in Seneca Falls, in a nondescript former bank building, is the National Women's Hall of Fame. Most Hall-of-Famers are well-known, such as Emily Dickinson, Helen Keller, and Billie Jean King. But we were more struck by the overlooked achievers, such as Florence Seibert, a medical researcher who was subsequently inducted. (Seibert worked for many years at the University of Pennsylvania School of Medicine, where she developed the skin test that is used today worldwide to diagnose tuberculosis.)

Elsewhere, in Hammondsport, older children and aviation buffs might enjoy the Curtiss Museum, which features vintage airplanes and motorcycles. Also worth visits are Sonnenberg Gardens and Mansion in Canandaigua and Rose Hill Mansion, east of Geneva; both are on the National Register of Historic Places.

If a day of museums and wineries leaves you a bit dazed, there's nothing like touring a working pig farm to clear your senses. On a rainy Saturday, we went to Misty Meadows Farm in Romulus, on Cayuga Lake's western shore, where the Sepe family raises as many as 1,200 pigs a year. The family started the tours to help make ends meet. We learned a lot about the "other white meat" as we toured the farrowing barn, breeding pens, and the finishing barn.

But the high point of the tour came when visitors were given wiggling, squealing piglets to cuddle. (Don't wear your designer duds here—these babies aren't in diapers.)

After the tour, my husband and I got in the spirit of the place and pigged out on pork-barbecue sandwiches, served in the farm's restaurant that overlooks Cayuga Lake. Our little porker smacked her lips as she devoured her juice-soaked roll. The waitresses were so nice they didn't say a word about the pile of food scraps she tossed under her highchair. As we drove away, the three of us were practically oinking ourselves.

—Jean Wallace

Directions from Philadelphia: Take the Northeast Extension of the Pennsylvania Turnpike to Interstate 81 north to Binghamton, N.Y., and pick up New York Route 17 west to 14. Follow 54 west to Penn Yan.

For more information, contact the Finger Lakes Association, 309 Lake St., Penn Yan, N.Y. 14527, or call 800-548-4386 or 315-536-7488.

The town with the one-track mind

SARATOGA SPRINGS, N.Y.

FORGET BRIGADOON. Every August, this sleepy town magically materializes as it was a century ago—the glittering late-summer playground of the rich and famous (and the people who like to rub elbows with the rich and famous).

Not to be seen in Saratoga in August is as bad as not going to the Academy Ball in Philadelphia.

Social suicide.

Socialites wouldn't dream of missing Marylou Whitney's soirée at the Canfield Casino, where she makes her entrance in a horse-drawn carriage. Or the other notable galas and balls of August—all charity functions that would cost a couple thousand a pop, if you could wangle an invitation.

If society balls bore you, join the rich and famous at the Fasig-Tipton thoroughbred auctions. But they're also hard to get into, and you might absentmindedly scratch your head and find that you've just bought a $40,000 filly.

Not to worry. For a pittance, you can mingle with the swells at the Saratoga Race Track. After all, the track—which says it is the oldest in the country—is the reason so many people come to Saratoga in August anyway, and everything here revolves around it. In Saratoga in August, everyone is a racing fan, just as during the World Series everyone is a baseball fan.

Saratoga in August also means Philadelphia Orchestra. The orchestra has been spending time at the Saratoga Performing Arts Center since 1966. Music lovers will also want to note that Tanglewood is less than two hours away in the Berkshires of western Massachusetts.

And, good news for those who absolutely can't do Saratoga in August: It's a great weekend destination any time of the summer. The New York City Opera comes to the Performing Arts Center in June and the New York City Ballet in July. Saratoga Raceway (near the race track) has harness racing most months of the year—including all summer—and a racing museum and hall of fame are nearby.

But if your goal is Saratoga in August, remember this: You'll want to reserve a hotel room very early, and be prepared to pay top dollar for it. Even if you plan to go in June or July, it's advisable to make early reservations.

That said, let's talk racing for a minute. The first race meeting was held here in 1864, a month after the Battle of Gettysburg, and the annual $1 million-added Travers Stakes dates from that time. Over the years it has attracted the finest three-year-olds, including such legends as Man O' War, Exterminator, Whirlaway, Kelso, and Forego. The mile-and-a-half Travers hasn't always been kind to Triple Crown winners. The great Secretariat lost here in 1973; Affirmed lost to his arch-rival, Alydar, on a disqualification in 1978.

Like much of the town, the track is beautiful—all gingerbread and towering oaks and white pines. And unlike some tracks, it isn't intimidatingly big with a serious, betting-only feel to it. You don't need a winning day to have a good time here, although it surely helps. The track has a touch of garden party and a dab of country fair.

My secret for having a great day at the track in Saratoga is to start off by watching the horses work out while breakfasting at the clubhouse's open-air restaurant. The workouts are from 7 to 9:30; get there early because you'll have a lot of company.

After you've accomplished this, stop by the National Museum of Racing and Hall of Fame, across Nelson Street from the track's parking lot. The museum got a $6.6 million rejuvenation in the early 1990s, and it was money well spent. If you like the Sport of Kings, you'll have a grand time here. On the lawn in front is the eighth pole that Secretariat flew by, leading by 28 lengths, on his way to winning the Belmont in 1973.

Inside, a starting gate leads to dozens of exhibits of racing paraphernalia. In the Hall of Fame, you can punch up film clips of your favorite champion. The collection of silver racing trophies would make Bailey, Banks & Biddle green with envy. A 15-minute multiscreen movie, "Racing America," captures the flavor of horse racing, from a moving scene of a foaling to a bettor tossing his losing tickets into the air.

The museum also has displays on the resort's fascinating history. A canny visionary named John Morrissey opened the first gambling rooms here in 1861, and the race course was built in 1863. For those who needed more excuses to come here, there were mineral springs, cool weather, and a nearby lake. Soon, steamboats were bringing visitors up the Hudson River from New York City.

By the 1890s, Saratoga was at its peak of prosperity and enjoying a reputation for impropriety. Nelly Bly, newspaper writer and world traveler, called it "our wickedest summer resort." Then as now, Saratoga was known for its liberality, a place where the humble could mix with the grand. If you had gone to the track in those days, you would have seen such celebrities as Mark Twain, Lily Langtry, Lillian Russell, Diamond Jim Brady, Enrico Caruso, and Flo Ziegfeld getting bets down with bookmakers.

The chill wind of reform blew through Saratoga from time to time. The track was shut down in 1911 and 1912, and the casino fell victim to Sen. Estes Kefauver's anti-gambling crusade in the early 1950s. The track was taken over by the New York Racing Association in 1953, however, and has been on a roll ever since. Attendance now tops 50,000 on major stakes days.

You will want to be at the track well before the first race at 1 o'clock to study the morning line in the Racing Form. The best place to do this is in the Turf Terrace restaurant, at a table as close to the rail as possible. Make a reservation, and tip the maitre d' appropriately. You will have a delicious lunch, and your table will be your base of operations; the betting windows and paddock are steps away, and drinks will appear with a wave of your hand.

Saratoga is dressy, at least in the clubhouse, and that's part of its charm. Novelist Henry James once wrote, "Saratoga is . . . where the greatest amount of dressing may be seen by the greatest number of people. At any hour . . . you may see a hundred rustling beauties whose rustle is their sole occupation." Things haven't changed all that much. Ladies now wear colorful silk dresses and picture hats; gentlemen, sporty jackets and ties. (In the restaurant, a jacket is required, and jeans are forbidden.)

One of the things I enjoy most at Saratoga is watching the horses being saddled in the shade of the trees in the paddock behind the clubhouse, just before a race. Few tracks give you such a close look at the horses and their jockeys. To see thoroughbreds just before a race is to agree with horse breeder George Pratt, who once observed, "The horse that walks around, eats grass, looks at the view, and gives every appearance of tranquillity was, in fact, designed by God to explode." In the paddock, some are nervous, and some are calm, but all give you the sense that if they aren't turned loose soon they surely will explode.

The outriders come and lead the horses onto the track and to the starting gate. The horn player in the traditional red coat blows the call for the race. Bettors scurry to the windows to get down their last-minute bets. God's in his heaven and all's right with the world.

My companion, Margo, and I enjoy going to the track, but we both lack the handicapping skill and/or luck to make it a profitable enterprise. Perhaps Lady Luck is bored by small, conservative bettors like us. I tend to bet a horse whose looks and paddock demeanor appeal to me, particularly if its jockey is enjoying a good meet.

I assume Margo has a system, but I don't know what it is. We both left the track modest losers. We empathize with Joe E. Lewis, the old comedian and inveterate horse player, who, when asked how he had fared at the track, replied, "I broke even, and I can sure use the money."

Serious bettors grab a quick bite to eat and head for Saratoga Raceway, the harness track near the race track, where trotters and pacers hold forth all summer. But if Lady Luck couldn't find us on a sunny afternoon, she probably wouldn't find us in the evening either.

Besides, there's a lot to do in Saratoga besides playing the horses.

You might enjoy a leisurely sweat and massage at the Roosevelt or

Lincoln Baths. Or pack an elegant picnic and watch top international players at the polo field. History buffs enjoy walking around the Saratoga National Historical Park, where American General Horatio Gates walloped Britain's John Burgoyne, bringing France into the Revolutionary War on our side. Bottle collectors find nirvana at the National Bottle Museum.

Everyone, however, should take a stroll downtown to experience the charm of Saratoga.

Small but cosmopolitan, Saratoga is the home of Skidmore College and has about 24,000 year-round residents. It's determinedly Victorian in character—red brick and white gingerbread, shaded by stately elms and ideal for strolling. In Congress Park, in the center of town, is a reminder of Saratoga's naughty days, the casino, where the nabobs played games of chance. It is now a museum, with exhibits depicting the town's history.

An early dinner at Siro's is a Saratoga tradition. Siro's, long a popular stop for the racing fraternity, is a short walk from the clubhouse. An outside tent contains "the world's largest cocktail party" in the early evening. We feasted on roast rack of Vermont lamb while seeing who could spot celebrities faster.

At dusk, we were off to visit the Philadelphia Orchestra, at the nearby Performing Arts Center, a facility that always makes us even more unhappy with the Mann Music Center in Philadelphia's Fairmount Park. It is architecturally attractive, the parking is plentiful, the acoustics are excellent, and all the concertgoers on the lawn can see the orchestra.

As the orchestra members tuned up, we tried to guess who among them had had a good day at the track. Concertmaster Norman Carroll was as inscrutable as ever, but one of the de Pasquale brothers had a smile that suggested at least an Exacta hit.

On the lawn at intermission, we were enjoying a moon the size of a dinner plate when, suddenly, a trumpet sounded, playing the race call. This time, however, it was a signal to the audience that the concert was about to resume.

Everything at Saratoga truly does revolve around the track.

—Chuck Lawliss

Directions from Philadelphia: Take the New Jersey Turnpike to the Garden State Parkway, to the New York State Thruway (Interstate 87). Follow I-87 north to Exit 24 in Albany, and continue north on I-87 (the Adirondack Northway) to Exit 14. The drive will take about five hours.

Saratoga Race Track (in town on Nelson Avenue just south of Union Avenue; telephone 518-584-6200) opens at 11 a.m., and the first race is at 1 p.m. Admission at presstime was $2 for the grandstand, $5 for the clubhouse (no shorts or T-shirts allowed). The Turf Restaurant opens at 11 a.m. Breakfast is served during the workouts from 7 to 9:30 a.m. All windows at the track pay off on winning tickets and book bets of various sizes and types. The track is accessible to wheelchairs.

The National Museum of Racing and Hall of Fame (across Union Avenue from the track; 518-584-0400) is open Tuesday through Saturday from 10 a.m. to 4:30 p.m. and Sunday from noon to 4:30. Admission was $3, $2 for senior citizens and students, free for children under 5.

The Saratoga Raceway (near the race track on Nelson Avenue; 518-584-2110) presents harness racing every month of the year except December. During August, races start at 7:45 p.m. every day except Sunday. Admission was $3 to the clubhouse, $1.75 to the grandstand.

The Saratoga Performing Arts Center (off Ballston Avenue just southwest of town in Saratoga Spa State Park; 518-587-3330) has covered seating for 5,100 and a lawn area that will accommodate 25,000 more. The New York City Opera comes in June, the New York City Ballet in July, and the Philadelphia Orchestra in August. Admission ranged from $6 and $13 on the lawn to $42 for covered seating.

∾

Sculpture centers

MOUNTAINVILLE, N.Y.

HERE IN THE HUDSON VALLEY lie two of the most remarkable—
even astonishing—outdoor "museums" anywhere, places to experience
works of sculpture that can only be called heroic.

The Storm King Art Center occupies 400 acres of carefully tended,
rolling fields and woodlands outside this town, 60 miles north of New
York. More than 100 sculptures, many of them massive, by distinguished modern sculptors from around the world are brilliantly placed
in the landscape, so that a stroll through the trees and over the hills
becomes a series of delightful surprises.

And just about 50 miles north of Mountainville is Opus 40, an astonishing sculptural achievement created by one man over 37 years. It
is a monumental "environmental sculpture," rising out of an abandoned bluestone quarry near the town of Saugerties, N.Y., and consisting of thousands of tons of finely fitted stones.

Both sites are in the Hudson Valley which, with its charming small
towns, historic attractions, and wineries, is a near-perfect weekend destination from Philadelphia.

A short distance east of Storm King, for instance, are West Point and
the West Point Museum, which has one of the largest collections of
military artifacts in the world. And midway between Storm King and
Opus 40 is Hyde Park, home of Franklin D. Roosevelt and site of the
Roosevelt Library and Museum and the Eleanor Roosevelt national historic site.

A good place to set up weekend headquarters is New Paltz, about
halfway between Mountainville and Saugerties. New Paltz is just off the
New York Thruway. It's a college town with a couple of interesting
bookstores and a good array of restaurants.

For your trip to the sculptural attractions, you can put together a
powerful picnic by purchasing wine at the Adair Winery and picking
up food at one of the greatest delicatessens anywhere, Toscani & Sons.
The wonderfully aromatic deli on Main Street in New Paltz features
homemade Italian specialties, pasta, cheeses and great, great pickles.

You have to leave town to reach the winery. Take Route 32 south to All-husen Road. It's in a 200-year-old red barn and is open from noon to 6 p.m. from April to November.

There is a picnic area near the main building at the Storm King Art Center, which is named for the nearby Storm King Mountains. You follow the signs to center headquarters, which is also an indoor museum with permanent and changing exhibitions. The center building is a Normandy-style chateau built in 1935. Here you can pick up information about the sculpture and a map of the grounds. There is also a small gift shop.

It is impossible to describe the impact of the striking, soaring, and often monumental works here. They appear suddenly or emerge gradually from their lovely, pristine surroundings.

The balance between nature and sculpture is carefully maintained. There are cool, quiet areas of formal plantings with sculptures neatly enclosed, and there are vast expanses of greensward transformed by the presence of post-1945 sculpture.

Among the artists represented are Alexander Calder, Louise Bourgeois, Henry Moore, Louise Nevelson, David Smith, Barbara Hepworth, and Mark di Suvero.

Particularly impressive are Calder's "Five Grand Stabiles" and David Smith's metal abstractions.

The placing of the works allows the visitor to see them from different angles, surrounded by hills and trees or framed by the sky.

Although the center covers 400 acres, a great many of the works are within easy walking distance of the headquarters building. It's a good idea, however, to allow lots of time for ambling through the extensive grounds, exploring the neat paths and peeking into clusters of shrubbery to find works of art. The broad fields and woodlands would make for a pleasant hike, even without the added attraction of the sculpture.

The works' titles are placed at a distance from them, so that visitors can form their own ideas about the works before being influenced by the artists' titles.

There is one sculpture—and only one—that may be touched and even sat on. It is Isamu Noguchi's "Momo Toro," which is based on the story of a Japanese folk hero who emerged from the split halves of a peach pit. Sitting on one of the large granite "peach" pieces on a hill created to the artist's specifications, visitors get a grand view of the art center and the surrounding art-spangled landscape.

Every year, a new major exhibition is installed in the indoor and outdoor galleries.

Admission at presstime was $5 for adults and $3 for seniors, students and children. Those under 5 are admitted free. There are guided tours at 2 p.m. It is open from 11 a.m. to 5:30 p.m., April through November.

On Route 32 near the center is a remarkable Japanese restaurant, Gasho. It is housed in a 16th-century Japanese farmhouse that was dismantled, shipped, and reassembled here. The name means "praying hands" and refers to an architectural style characterized by a triangular roof.

But if you are looking for something less dramatic at lunchtime, try the Open Pantry on Main Street in nearby Cornwall-on-Hudson. It features modestly priced homemade salads, quiches and gourmet sandwiches.

It is just an hour's drive north on the New York Thruway (Interstate 87) from Mountainville to Saugerties and Opus 40, a genuinely astonishing sculptural achievement. Sculptor Harvey Fite purchased an unused quarry site in 1938. An art professor at Bard College, he began working there in his spare time.

The environmental sculpture that exists there now began as background and pedestals for his statuary, but he soon began to see it as a separate work that ought to stand on its own.

He began to construct sweeping terraces with accents on steps and ramps and pools. He used only turn-of-the-century quarry tools, many of which are on display in the Quarryman Museum nearby. In the museum is a slide show about Opus 40 and a small gallery exhibition of Fite carvings.

Fite worked alone and used dry-key construction, which relies on fitting stone upon stone in such a way that mortar is not needed. Thus, frost and erosion have little effect, and the work theoretically could stand for centuries.

On the site, he found a nine-ton pillar of stone and made this craggy monolith the centerpiece of his six-acre construction.

Whereas the Storm King Art Center offers modern art, Opus 40 is closer to the monumental stone works of the ancients.

Fite called the work Opus 40 because he calculated that it would take 40 years to complete. He had been working on it 37 years when, in 1976, he was killed in a fall from the artwork to which he had devoted so much of his life. He was 72.

His family decided not to attempt to finish the work. You see an unfinished wall here, a pile of blue stones there. It is as if they were waiting for the hand of the artist who will never return.

There are ramps leading to high, level places and cool, narrow passageways in low areas. The passageways and other details remind you of the stone creations of the ancient Mayans.

In the land around the quarry, you come upon some of Fite's carvings—mainly stone statuary nestled neatly in rustic corners. There are paths for strolling and grassy spots for picnicking. Some of the paths must have been carved out by Fite himself as he carried or dragged stones to incorporate into Opus 40. As you walk these paths, you see the work from various angles, and your admiration and wonder only increase.

Opus 40 and the Quarryman's Museum are open noon to 5 p.m. on Friday, Saturday and Sunday from May 25 to October 27. Admission was $5 for adults and $4 for seniors and children. Some Saturdays may be reserved for special events, so it is best to call ahead. The number is 914-246-3400.

—John Corr and Marjorie Matthews Corr

Directions from Philadelphia: Take the Garden State Parkway north to I-87 (the New York Thruway) to Exit 16. Pick up 32 north and follow to Storm King.

The Washington Irving home

TARRYTOWN, N.Y.

"GOOD DAY. WELCOME TO SUNNYSIDE," said a smiling Thomas, the coachman, as we crunched up the gravel path on a bright April day toward the picturesque red-roofed house that stood on the brow of a bluff overlooking the Hudson River.

"Mr. Irving is at home today," he said as he ushered us through a wisteria-covered entryway into the vestibule. "It's his birthday, you know, his 71st, as sure as the year is 1854."

With that, he opened the door to the study and we came face to face with Washington Irving, who, we recollected, was the first home-grown American writer to win international acclaim. The author (expertly played by retired local businessman Charles Duda) greeted us and pointed out the shelves that held his library of 2,000 volumes and the desk where he wrote. A whale-oil lamp stood atop the desk he told us was a gift from his publisher, George R. Putnam.

Early morning, he remarked, is the best time for writing, adding that a cup or two of hot chocolate helps to get his creative juices flowing. He confided with a twinkle in his eye that he sleeps in the same room, on a divan in an alcove in the rear, "because my brother Ebenezer and his five daughters live here with me and they need all the bedrooms!"

For our part, we felt a bit like Rip Van Winkle, one of Irving's own characters, when Rip stumbled back into town after his 20-year sleep in the mountains. As "Washington Irving" talked about his narratives, we could almost visualize Ichabod Crane fleeing the headless horseman of Sleepy Hollow and Katrina Van Tassel flirting with her country swains.

For on this sparkling spring day in the lower Hudson Valley, Sunnyside came to life as it was a century and a half ago, when Irving, brother Ebenezer, and his nieces—all played in costume by local history buffs—showed us through the house that Irving once characterized as "as full of angles and corners as an old crooked hat." The author had converted a 1680 Dutch farmhouse into a country retreat and here he lived for the last 24 years of his life.

It is easy to step into the past in Sleepy Hollow country, the lower

Hudson Valley, where the history and folklore of the early Dutch settlers inspired much of Irving's writings. The region lies 120 miles from
Philadelphia, near where the New York Thruway crosses the Hudson
River on the curving Tappan Zee Bridge. On the east side of the river,
the 30-mile stretch from Tarrytown to Peekskill still bears reminders
of the days when hard-working Dutch patroons built extensive estates
along the river, purchasing land from the Indians and organizing
profitable enterprises based on fur trade, lumbering, agriculture, and
livestock.

Fortunately, several examples of this Dutch heritage on the Hudson
have been saved and now coexist with the villages, residential developments, motels, and gas stations that came along later.

We were surprised to learn that for the privilege of seeing this slice
of Dutch Colonial life in America, we have the late John D. Rockefeller,
Jr., to thank, the same wealthy conservationist who in the 1930s gave
the public Colonial Williamsburg in Virginia. As three of the most
significant homesteads in the area were offered to developers, Rockefeller interceded each time and purchased them so they could be preserved and operated for the public's education and enjoyment.

In so doing, he preserved for all of us the historical heritage that lay
literally at his own doorstep—he had built a mansion for himself on
his estate in Pocantico Hills near Tarrytown. During the three days we
spent in Sleepy Hollow country, we would see the evidence of the far-
reaching preservation efforts put forth by this heir to the Standard Oil
fortune.

Sunnyside was his first success. When, in 1945, a descendant of Irving's offered to sell Sunnyside, Rockefeller bought it and organized a
nonprofit group called Sleepy Hollow Restorations (later renamed Historic Hudson Valley) to maintain it and interpret it to the public.

At the northern edge of Tarrytown, along U.S. Route 9, which runs
through Sleepy Hollow country, we found another testament to Rockefeller's preservation legacy. Philipsburg Manor, the oldest of the preserved Dutch manors along the river, was established by Vredryck Fly-
psen (later Anglicized to Frederick Philipse), a one-time carpenter who
came to America in 1647 to work for the Dutch West India Company.

After prospering as an entrepreneur in New Amsterdam (New York
City), he turned his attention upriver, purchasing 52,000 acres, where
he grew wheat and built a gristmill to grind his grain and that of other
farmers. His son, Adolph, turned the gristmill and farm into an even
more profitable operation.

Three centuries melt away when you walk across the dam that backs up a pond used to produce waterpower for the gristmill. A costumed guide leads visitors past the mill to the plain, rectangular building that doubled as a warehouse, office, and manor house for the Philipses.

Inside, you stoop to walk through doors cut low to conserve heat, a scarce commodity when a wood fire in the fireplace was all you had to heat each room. Our guide explained that Dutch doors, with their two horizontally hinged sections, were kept closed at the bottom to keep animals out and children in but kept open above to let light in during temperate months. A Dutch door also saved on taxes, she said, because the tax collector assessed the real estate tax on the number of windows in a house.

We quickly got the idea that 17th-century life was not easy. Rugs, considered a luxury, covered the tables while clean sand carpeted the floor. Even the lord of the manor slept on a bed consisting of straw ticking on a lattice of rope instead of springs. Curtains encircled the bed to hold the warmth.

The genial miller greeted us at the mill's doorway when we came to see the heart of the enterprise at Philipsburg Manor. He demonstrated how water power translated into energy that turned two sets of carefully adjusted millstones to grind wheat, corn, oats, and barley into flour or meal.

After leaving the mill, the children in our tour group ran for the nearby barn and fields to see the oxen, sheep, cows, and chickens. If you visit Philipsburg in early spring as we did, you will see the living-history farmer and his helpers shearing the sheep. They show you how the wool is combed, spun, dyed, and woven into warm wool clothing.

Four miles north on Route 9 is Van Cortlandt Manor, the last Dutch spread saved from a developer's bulldozer by Rockefeller. To see the estate, we had the assistance of Jan Horton, one of Historic Hudson Valley's corps of knowledgeable guides. As we walked across the original 300-year-old flooring and admired the mansion's extensive collection of Queen Anne, Chippendale, and Federal furnishings, Horton told us the story of one of the outstanding families of New York.

Oloff Van Cortlandt, the progenitor of this family of Dutch patroons, came to America in 1638 as a soldier with the Dutch West India Company, which had a charter to colonize along the Hudson River. After he completed his hitch as a soldier, Van Cortlandt built a fortune in fur trading, milling, and brewing and became one of New Amsterdam's leading citizens. His son, Stephanus, as astute a businessman as his father, purchased the land from the Indians and erected Van Cortlandt Manor at the end of the 17th century.

The family maintained possession of the property for three full centuries until Rockefeller intervened and restored it with the help of a team of experts he brought from Williamsburg. As a consequence, you may now experience what it was like to live the life of a patroon in those early times.

A distinctive feature at Van Cortlandt is a 750-foot brick pathway that leads from the main house to the Ferry House, a fully restored tavern that once served horseback and stage-coach passengers traveling the Post Road from New York City to the capital of Albany. A small ferry carried passengers and coaches across the Croton River to the tavern. In May, the Long Walk is brightened by hundreds of tulips, the trademark flower of the Dutch.

Many years after the Dutch patroons carved out their productive manors, another breed of entrepreneur found his way to the steep-sided shores of the Hudson. New Yorkers, newly enriched from 19th-century shipping, railroads, oil, and banking, built showplace mansions along the river as palatial retreats from their homes and offices in the city.

One such gothic showplace is Lyndhurst, once the country estate of financier Jay Gould, who controlled at one time Western Union Telegraph, New York City's elevated railway, and the Union Pacific Railroad. Since few ordinary homeowners today could afford even the heating bill for the huge mansion, Lyndhurst is preserved and operated by the National Trust for Historic Preservation. The entrance fee, $6 for our visit, goes to help pay the bills (trust members get in free).

A well-informed volunteer guide led us through the ornately furnished rooms, relating stories about the Goulds and the mansion's earlier owners.

Nearby, the National Trust also preserves part of another famous estate, the Rockefeller compound at Pocantico Hills. The mansion, completed in 1908 for John D. Rockefeller, Sr., was later radically altered and occupied by his son John D., Jr., and even later by his grandson, Nelson Rockefeller, who served as New York's governor and as vice president of the United States.

Visitors are guided by bus through the grounds and tour the handsome Georgian mansion with its numerous works of art and priceless ceramic pieces. They stroll through the gardens, designed in a combination of Italian, French, and English styles, past sculptures collected by Nelson Rockefeller. In a gallery under the mansion, they can see the outstanding collection of abstract-expressionist canvases and modernist sculpture works acquired by Nelson Rockefeller.

If all this traipsing through the homes of history's rich and famous has given you an appetite and a yearning for a comfortable bed, have no concern. Several chain hotels and motels offer accommodations in Tarrytown and nearby Elmsford, White Plains, and Hawthorne.

Before we left the area, we wanted to see one other feature offered by Sleepy Hollow country—stained-glass windows created by two of the world's finest artists. The luminous windows are in a small stone church in Pocantico Hills, the chapel attended by the Rockefeller family. Commissioned by the Rockefellers, the windows represent the last work to be completed by Henri Matisse before his death in 1954 and the only cycle of church windows created by Marc Chagall in the United States. Even in the fading light of an afternoon sun, we found the windows glowed brightly.

The church and its windows were the perfect reintroduction to the 20th century for our trip home.

—Arthur Miller and Marjorie Miller

Directions from Philadelphia: Take the New Jersey Turnpike north to Exit 18. Follow U.S. 46 east to Fort Lee. Follow the signs to Palisades Interstate Parkway and take it north to Exit 4, Route 9W. From 9W, follow signs to the New York Thruway east, which will take you across the Tappan Zee Bridge. Immediately after the bridge, take Exit 9 and follow signs to Tarrytown. To get to Lyndhurst and Sunnyside, go south on Route 9 one mile. Philipsburg Manor is two miles north of Tarrytown, also on Route 9.

Sunnyside, Philipsburg Manor, and Van Cortlandt Manor are open 10 a.m. to 5 p.m. daily, except Tuesdays, March through December; weekends only in January and February. Lyndhurst is closed Mondays. At press time, admission to each site was: $6 for adults, $5 for senior citizens, $3 for juniors 6 to 17. There are numerous seasonal special events.

For more information, contact Historic Hudson Valley, 150 White Plains Rd., Tarrytown, N.Y. 10591 (914-631-8200). Ask for calendar of events and accommodation and restaurant guides.

～

A quiet casino

VERONA, N.Y.

NOT ALL CASINOS SOUND ALIKE.

In the temples of chance in Atlantic City and Las Vegas, or on the riverboats and barges in Iowa, Illinois, and Mississippi, there is the cacophony of machine gambling. It is the slots that draw the masses—people who either do not understand the odds or just don't care that they're being parted from their money as quickly as the law allows.

The din created by a thousand or more of these one-armed bandits operating at once—the bells, the sirens, the clank of coins into slots, and the clink-clink-clink of payouts—makes conversation impossible.

And when the casino lounges are in full swing and there is the constant blare of musicians who confuse volume with skill, the level of noise dulls the mind as well.

Turning Stone is different. Here, about 30 miles east of Syracuse, is a casino that is almost silent.

An evening in the Empire State's first legal casino is not quite the same as one spent fly fishing on a stream deep in the Catskills. But it is relatively peaceful—a tranquillity that Turning Stone's owners, the Oneida Nation of Indians, have purposely created.

And that means gambling at Turning Stone, especially for those who enjoy the mental skill of blackjack, is unlike playing at any other casino in America. Here is a place where you can concentrate on the game with few distractions. If you like to try keeping count of the cards, this is one casino where your mind is not constantly inundated by an aural storm front, its flotsam and jetsam interrupting or spoiling your short-term memory.

There are no gambling machines here—neither the mechanical contraptions of the Industrial Era nor the computerized one-armed bandits of our Infotechnic Age. Only cards and dice and roulette wheels.

On one evening of our visit—save for the adrenalin-charged shouts from a craps table where a smiling man in a green Bally's sweatshirt was playing with purple ($500) chips and making his points on throw after throw after throw—the casino was hardly much louder than a university library filled with junior scholars rustling papers and whispering advice to one another.

And when the band played, it was with the volume control set to pleasant.

Truly, Turning Stone is something really new in casino gambling. It has been open since July 1993, and it's about a five-hour drive from Center City Philadelphia.

We found that getting within a few thousand feet of Turning Stone was easy. But just as you could drive along Pacific Avenue in Atlantic City searching in vain for the old Playboy-Atlantis, the inattentive can drive right past Turning Stone.

Traveling east on the New York Thruway, you take Exit 33. Leaving the toll booth you will notice that the road forks. Go left. At the traffic light turn left and, once your turn is completed, look out the driver's side window. That large concrete bunker half rising from a manmade hill off in the distance is Turning Stone.

And that is another pleasant oddity about Turning Stone.

Las Vegas reveals itself in the distance as a bright spot in the desert night, glowing ever brighter until the stars fade from the heavens, replaced by a neon forest that is the gambling world's tree of life. Atlantic City, on the many nights when low clouds hang over Absecon Island, creates the misleading impression of existing beneath a halo.

But Turning Stone looks more like a modest shopping mall, without even the usual giant plastic signs where the parking lot meets the road.

Instead, there is an eight-foot menhir, a faux stone obelisk that rotates on a base. To the left is a giant oak with a sign warning that hunting and trapping are strictly forbidden.

Parking is free.

The casino entry is as plain as plain can be, starting with a bubbling pond outside that serves as a catch basin when rains flood the parking lot. The walkway is concrete, a bare gray slab on the left, a rock garden on the right, and, overhead, arched steel with glass to hold back rain and snow.

Inside is another faux stone slowly rotating on its base. The visual theme is built around motifs drawn from the creeks and rivers that flow through the forests of upstate New York, not the ersatz Tahiti of Steve Wynn's Mirage or the hot pink mausoleum of Donald Trump's Taj Mahal.

The lobby is simply an open room. But the natural-shapes theme is apparent at once in the sign for the coat room and all other signs. They look like black rock, worn by millennia of rushing water, with the words in bright blue.

Ahead are three places to eat: A snack shop with sturdy, art-deco chairs and tables made of aluminum, a cafeteria, and a restaurant with tablecloths and moderately priced fare. The latter is closed Mondays and Tuesdays.

To the right is a barrel-vaulted ceiling filled not with chandeliers, but with the rays of the sun. At night, the ceiling is a canopy of black or, when the weather is clear, a vista of the moon and sky.

This is also the spine of a giant room, more than an acre in size, with gaming tables down the center and off to either side.

The carpets are subtle, unlike the riots of color in most casinos. The expanses are designed to recall the blue waters of Lake Ontario or Lake Oneida, dotted with large, irregular black shapes suggesting stones here and there. Much of the carpet is simply gray, like a cloudy sky.

A deck of gargantuan cards appears to be fanned along the right wall, each revealing just the suit and rank. On closer inspection, it is a trompe l'oeil, an undulating white wall on whose curves the edges of giant playing cards have been expertly painted. We suspected that the curves had a secondary effect of helping to dampen noise and contribute to the tranquillity of the casino.

The casino cage was across the room, only it wasn't a cage—no bars or inch-thick glass. Instead customers cashing in chips stepped up to a large counter, like a hotel reservation desk.

The bar, a rich, faux mahogany, ran for perhaps 50 feet along one wall, and behind it, on a blue background, was another wall of cards. These were all face cards, done in fluorescents that were as engaging from far across the room as from immediately across the bar. It was the only decoration that even hinted of Atlantic City or Las Vegas, but was so relatively low-key and artful that it would be lost in the glitter of casinos there.

The bar stools were giant black springs capped with red Naugahyde —stable, surprisingly comfortable, and one of the few reminders that this was, after all, a casino. The ceiling was partly open, the ducts and steel supports painted cloud white.

You can order a margarita or a daiquiri at the bar, and bottles of wine and beer are lined up behind it. But the drinks are all virgins.

The Oneida do not serve alcohol, unlike the gambling joints on the Jersey Shore and Nevada desert. They know—and don't we all, when we're sober—that alcohol clouds judgment, helping to convince a player that his luck is about to take a turn for the better while, in fact, his skill deteriorates. They are satisfied with just the odds, in other words—odds that in all casinos favor the house anyway.

The Oneida have publicly predicted that their casino will win $500 million a year, though that seems as far-out a fantasy as the mega-resorts on the Vegas Strip, the biggest and busiest of which have yet to reach that figure. But even if they win just one-fifth of that, they should prosper because their costs are so low.

It cost a billion dollars and a trip through bankruptcy court, for example, for Atlantic City's Taj Mahal, which still struggles. Turning Stone, the Oneida say, was built for just $10 million, a figure that virtually guarantees the Indians a torrent of profits.

With clear heads, we went in search of a low-stakes blackjack game. There were plenty of $5 tables, a few at $10 and $15, and one at $25. Over in the far corner there was also something that passed for a high-roller pit, but the walls were maple, not marble. Inside was a Rochester man who, dealers told us, had blown $85,000—hardly enough to get noticed in Atlantic City.

Eventually, we found a blackjack table with a $3 minimum bet. Unfortunately, not only were all seven spots taken but the table was two deep with waiting gamblers. So we settled on a $5 table with no players and a friendly dealer busy fanning his cards while waiting.

We bought in for $60 and by the second round, when we were down $15, the table had begun to fill with others. One appeared to be a college student, barely old enough to shave, and a girlfriend who also looked to be in her late teens. They were soon joined by a buddy in a Syracuse University sweatshirt.

No surprise. The legal age to gamble here is 18, three years younger than on the Boardwalk or the Vegas Strip. Indeed, among 2,000 or so people spread around the casino, several hundred appeared to be of college age. And, here and there, a few looked not quite ready for the high school junior prom.

When daughter Amy, 21, came in, she said she felt that she was among peers. But it was the white walls, the sunlight and, as night came, the bright lights that struck her.

"It's not like Atlantic City," she said. "It's so clean."

A surprise came when one of us had a 10 and a jack, and motioned for a card—one of our ways of testing how casinos treat players. The dealer paused.

"Sir, you have 20—are you sure?"

On the Boardwalk and the Strip, a 21 player with 20 who asks for a card usually gets treated like a chump—the card is dealt.

At Turning Stone, players are quietly and politely asked to reconsider.

Given the chance, we did just that—we waved him off.

And won. The dealer had 19.

—David Johnston and Jennifer Leonard

Directions from Philadelphia: Take the Northeast Extension of Pennsylvania Turnpike to the end, then switch to I-81 north to Syracuse. Go east on New York Thruway to Exit 33. After the toll booth, bear left to the traffic light. Turn left onto Route 365; after a few hundred feet, at next light, turn left onto Patrick Road. The casino, which is open 24 hours a day, is the only big structure.

For more information, including information about accommodations or the Syracuse area, phone the Syracuse Convention and Visitors Bureau at 800-234-4797. For information about the casino, write to Box 126, Verona, N.Y. 13478, or phone 315-361-7711.

3

New England

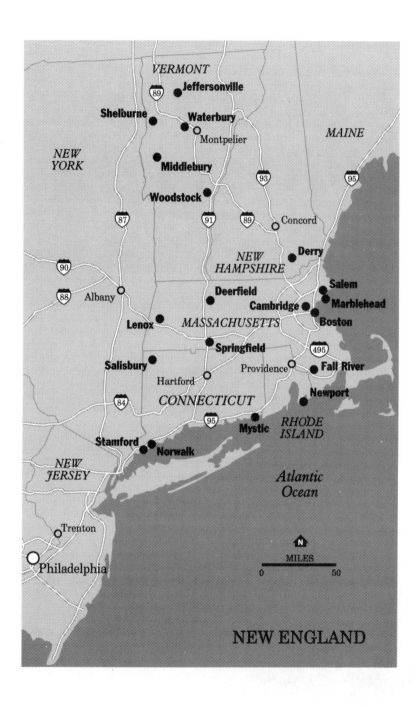

VERMONT

Jeffersonville

89

Shelburne

Waterbury

Montpelier

NEW
YORK

Middlebury

MAINE

93

95

Woodstock

87

91

89

Concord

Derry

NEW
HAMPSHIRE

90

Deerfield

Salem

88

Albany

Cambridge

Marblehead

Lenox

MASSACHUSETTS

Boston

Springfield

495

Salisbury

Providence

Fall River

Hartford

Newport

CONNECTICUT

84

95

Mystic

RHODE
ISLAND

Stamford

Norwalk

NEW
JERSEY

Atlantic
Ocean

Trenton

N

○ **Philadelphia**

MILES

0   50

NEW ENGLAND

❧

Harvard Square

CAMBRIDGE, MASS.

IN ALL THE WORLD, there is surely no other place that's even remotely like Harvard Square. Actually, the world probably could not handle two Harvard Squares. One is quite enough, thank you. But one is essential, and a weekend is barely enough time to explore its assets. Harvard Square is the intellectual, cultural, and fantastical heart of Cambridge, a city of 95,000 people that is home to Harvard University and one that is often referred to as "a city surrounded on four sides by reality."

Geographically, only the Charles River separates Cambridge from its larger, more reality-based next-door neighbor, Boston. Spiritually, however, the two cities are planets apart. And right in the center of Cambridge is this bustling hodgepodge called Harvard Square.

I like to arrive mid-morning, pick up a newspaper, coffee, and a muffin, and head for the center of the square. In warm weather, its big open plaza is an absolute must for visitors who want to get their bearings and do an initial survey of the scene. If the day is blustery, they'll all be inside warming up with coffee.

By mid-morning, things are rolling pretty well. A few Harvard or Radcliffe professors are working on their papers, visiting scientists are perusing the *Times*, *Le Figaro*, or the *Moscow News*, and students are chatting excitedly. Poets are writing, musicians are composing, and the chess games are beginning.

From a good seat in the plaza, I can watch the taxis, the buses, the bicycles, ambulances, roller-bladers, skateboarders, grocery carters, the purple-haired, the sidewalk artists, marching poets, Asian women in emerald satin, and Indians in purple saris. It's fun to spot the parents of a Harvard freshman. The looks on their faces say it all, "Honey, our daughter is living here."

But wait a minute. There is more to Cambridge than cappuccino and people-watching. How about the oldest college in America, more bookstores per capita than in any city in the country, world-famous coffeehouses, Henry Wadsworth Longfellow's home, art museums and architectural wonders, historic cemeteries, and the site where George

Washington first took command of the Continental Army and from which he directed the siege of Boston?

And how about great restaurants and jazz clubs, theaters, eclectic shopping, historic movie houses, and fine old mansions?

Enough of coffee and muffins. It's time to check out the rest of the square.

The place to start is "the bellybutton," or Omphalus, a distinctive marble and metal sculpture at the point of the concrete peninsula that juts out into the middle of traffic at Harvard Square's very heart. The Omphalus, by sculptor Dmitri Hadzi, marks Harvard Square as the "Center of the Universe." But of course.

The bellybutton shares the peninsula with such notable wonders as the Punk Pit (the place to be seen if you're sporting fuchsia hair or a shaved head, spikes, kilts, and 26 earrings and are generally disaffected), the Red Line subway station, the Cambridge information kiosk, street preachers, Peruvian drummers, and Out-of-Town News.

If you're looking for a copy of the *Sydney* (Australia) *Herald*, a French *Playboy*, or the *Asahi Shimbun*, Out-of-Town News is the place to go. It hums from 5 a.m. till midnight, seven days a week.

Across from Out-of-Town is another major newsstand—Nini's Corner. French and British fashion mags are a specialty.

Shopping at Harvard Square is not exactly like a trip to the local mall. The Harvard Cooperative Society, known locally as "The Coop," is a large, old department store right in the heart of the square, where Eliot Street and J.F. Kennedy Boulevard branch out from the bend in Massachusetts Avenue.

The front entrance to The Coop is part of the scene. Of all the spots in Harvard Square where street musicians perform, The Coop's doorway is prime territory. This is where pop folk singer Tracy Chapman and other notables have gotten their starts.

Walking through the front door of The Coop is like walking in the front door of that old downtown department store my grandmother used to take me to when I was a kid in Cincinnati. You know—high ceilings with big old posts, and creaky wooden floors, and elevators that go "Ding." They have tables full of wonderful, colorful wool sweaters, a big candy counter filled with assorted chocolate truffles, and a whole room full of tablets and pencils and little leather memo books.

Nowadays, of course, The Coop also carries computers, electronics, and a huge assortment of CDs and tapes, posters, art prints, and books, along with anything and everything with "Harvard" emblazoned upon it.

The Coop is only the beginning. All along the streets of the square, shop after shop unfolds with wonder upon wonder. It's fun to just browse the square—you never know what may turn up. There are shops that feature individually designed jewelry, Indian clothing, unusual games and puzzles, fantastic flowers, Russian beads and crafts, chocolates, tobaccos, maps and globes, crystals and mystical accessories, quilts, leather bags, caviar, and fine wines.

Then there are the art galleries. Many feature regional artists, and the Cambridge Artists' Cooperative at 59-A Church St. displays jewelry, ceramics, glass, fiber, leather, wood, and graphic work of more than 100 American artists and artisans. A visit to the Artist's Co-op is as interesting and enjoyable as a visit to a museum. Browsing is free and a purchase is a reasonably priced, one-of-a-kind gift that helps support an artist at work.

Bookstore browsing at Harvard Square is an art in itself. Cambridge boasts about 32 bookstores, 25 of them in the Harvard Square area. Most have interesting and knowledgeable proprietors, jazz or classical music playing, a full complement of browsers, and maybe a cat or two. Many are open until midnight, making bookstore shopping a popular after-the-theater pastime.

The bookstores of Harvard Square have their own brochure, which you can pick up at the information kiosk. There are stores that specialize in Asian books, antiquarian books, art, philosophy, foreign language, black studies, or scholarly texts.

Grolier Book Shop, 6 Plympton St. off Mass. Ave., has been specializing in poetry since 1927. Schoenhof's, at 76-A Mt. Auburn St., carries foreign-language books and has 160 languages in its reference section. Marxism and third-world culture are the order of the day at Revolution Books, 38 J.F. Kennedy Blvd.

If all the browsing, shopping, and walking have given you a pair of sore dogs, you won't have to look far for a place to rest and refresh.

Grendel's at 89 Winthrop St., in the Pi Eta Club House, is a great place to pause, and perhaps have lunch or dinner. It's where the old grads go when they come back to town, it's where the "in" crowd shares tales and a few beers, it's where I go to laugh with friends or family over a late-afternoon lunch.

In summer, we dine out on the front porch, enjoying a Greek salad or light seafood dish. On a cold, snowy afternoon, we gather inside by the roaring fire with all the other regulars to share a pot of cheese fondue and a bottle of burgundy. Moussaka, chicken shish kebab, broiled scrod, and spinach pie are but a few of the hearty specialties, which are priced amazingly low.

Another special place for kicking back and relaxing is the Algiers Coffee House on Brattle Street. During its 21 years at Harvard Square, the Algiers has become a favorite haunt of professors, students, writers, and artists, travelers, and visitors from every state and continent.

There are enough restaurants around the square to keep a person eating full time for several weeks, rarely repeating a similar cuisine. Explore. Enjoy.

It's really tough to decide if Harvard Square is more fun in the daytime or at night. For all its carnival atmosphere and myriad of worlds by day, the magic of Harvard Square when the lights come on is, in some ways, even more special. During "the Season," from the first warm evening in early spring until fingers grow too cold to pick guitar strings late in autumn, the streets and plazas of Harvard Square hum and hop with street performances.

If it's chilly outside, you might want to check out some of the square's indoor nightlife. For jazz, no spot in Cambridge or Boston can top the Regattabar at the Charles Hotel (reservations suggested).

For folk acoustic music and coffee, the place to go is Passim's at 47 Palmer St. Tom Waits, Suzanne Vega, Bonnie Raitt, Shawn Colvin—they're just a few of the folks who started out here. Who will be the next star to rise from Passim's?

Theater—live or on film—is big in Harvard Square. The American Repertory Theatre (A.R.T.) presents a full season of plays at the Loeb Drama Center, 64 Brattle St.

The old Brattle Theatre, downstairs from the Algiers, is famous for vintage and foreign films and creative programming.

Of course, day or night, winter or summer, there is the wonderful oasis of serenity in the middle of Harvard Square—the reason it all started, Harvard University.

Museums abound at Harvard. The Fogg Art Museum is one of my favorites. Two floors of galleries surrounding an Italian-Renaissance courtyard feature an amazing collection of Van Goghs, Cezannes, Fra Angelicos, Pollocks, and more. The Sackler Museum houses the school's collection of Oriental, ancient, and Islamic art, and four natural-history museums boast a wide range of important and unusual collections.

The history buff could easily spend a month exploring Harvard Square. Cambridge Common, the city's central park, is the site where freedom of speech was declared in 1637, and freedom of religion in 1740. The Blacksmith House, where Longfellow's "Village Smithy" once stood, now houses a bakery and café, and the poet's home is a short stroll out "Tory Row" on Brattle Street. A month, a semester there seems never enough time to take in all the square has to offer. A weekend is plenty, though, to get a sample—and the basis for a return visit.

—Barbara Claire Kasselmann

Directions from Philadelphia: Take the Garden State Parkway north to the New York Thruway (I-287). Follow 287 east across the Tappan Zee Bridge to I-684. Take 684 to I-84 northeast to the Massachusetts Turnpike. Follow to the Boston area and Cambridge.

Drifting through time

DEERFIELD, MASS.

THE DAY IS DYING, the hills are darkening.

We're on a long drive from northern Vermont to southern Pennsylvania.

In north-central Massachusetts, reality is coming into focus a bit too suddenly—like a TV set being turned on after days of silence. The four-lane interstate is becoming crowded as we approach the complex of colleges near Amherst.

We're losing the sense of countryside, the gift that days in rural Vermont have given.

So at Greenfield, we skip off the interstate. And within minutes, we're back into the comfort of countryside.

We're 300 years back, in Deerfield—a quiet place to return to, a place to drift back into history some slow weekend.

The kids jump out of the backseat and something like "neat" is all they can say, into the gathering dark. The village seems little more than one solitary street, set out near farmland, near marshland, near a slow stream.

A village.

Speckled with the sorts of homes that one can imagine Indians found when they came here to massacre in 1704. If you can stomach massacre sites, this is worth a taste—the last place in New England, historians say, where a massacre took place.

Today, it consists of the boarding school known as Deerfield Academy, the white-clapboard Deerfield Inn, a tiny gift shop between school and inn, a museum and shop . . . and homes from the 1700s and 1800s, most of which folks still live in, some of which are silent, silent but for the murmur and tread of tourists.

Silent.

No grocery store. No laundromat. No necessities. (Well, a gas station had recently reopened on the two-lane highway to Amherst.) No video arcade. No bowling alley. No tavern. None of the soiled fringes of tattered towns.

Only the school, the inn.

Only the houses from bygone days.

And on this late afternoon, only the silence.

We park in front of the inn and cross the empty road to a dark clapboard house with creaking plank floors—the information center.

It's near the 4:30 p.m. closing, but a straight-backed, gray-haired gentleman, properly dressed in tie and coat as all good gentlemen should be, suggests that we watch an eight-minute video about the village.

We are the only ones there. He could just as well have shut the door and said: Come back another day.

But he seems keen about the place. So though the house tours are done for the day, we take a taste.

He leads us into another low-ceilinged room full of dark wood. And, miracle of miracles, after sitting in the car for the last four hours, the kids sit again, for eight minutes.

The video tells of a couple from Greenwich, Conn.—Helen and Henry Flynt—whose son began his studies at Deerfield Academy in September 1936, in the midst of the Great Depression.

"They [the Flynts] fell in love with the village," explained Grace Friary, public relations officer for Historic Deerfield Inc. "Houses were crumbling, the village was right on the edge (of ruin). Their entrance could not have been more fortuitous. They saw the need to preserve and restore, rather than to re-create."

By the 1940s, the Flynts had begun buying up houses. Their efforts led to formation of Historic Deerfield Inc., which marked its 40th anniversary in 1992. The nonprofit organization now owns 54 houses, 13 of them open to the public as historic museums.

Only one building dates to the massacre. Most were built between 1725 and 1850. The last restoration was completed in the late 1960s, but the latest purchase—of an 1848 house and nine acres of pasture running to the river—took place on the last day of 1990.

The entire mile-long street is on the National Register of Historic Places. So are meadows to the north and south of the village.

The 20th century intrudes on the main street, slightly. Deerfield Academy built three dormitories on this avenue—simply called The Street—in the 20th century. "But," said Friary, "they look so old you wouldn't be able to tell."

I had been here before and walked through a couple of the historic houses on a guided tour—something any visitor here should do.

Creaking planked floors. Low ceilings. Comforting period furniture, surrounded by austere walls and plain windows.

A Historic Deerfield annual report tells how the houses have been furnished with gifts: "Quilts that had descended in her family were given in memory of Florence Chase Bartlett. A clock by Nathan Storrs of Northampton was presented by Kenneth D. Roberts. . . ."

Very nice.

But I've also found the insides of these houses frightening.

They give me the spooky feeling that I've been carried back 200 years and suddenly everybody has died and I'm the only one left in the house and there's no way out. It's a smothering sensation.

But if you get that smothering feeling, I suggest you still try the town.

I love to walk its sidewalks and sense its past, living in the present. The village is a terribly old grandfather, speaking of a terribly distant past, and speaking vigorously, persuasively.

On this day, in the gathering dark, we scoot across the street to the gift shop, before its 4:30 closing time. And we find that the shop is the antithesis of every trashy emporium polluting these United States.

Silverware. Needlework. Writings.

I pick up a small handbook and open to an early page.

"Bundling. A man and a woman lying on the same bed with their clothes on; an expedient practiced in America on a scarcity of beds, where, on such occasions, husbands and parents frequently permitted travelers to bundle with their wives and daughters."

Yipes! Hide the kids!

It's a reprint—from Globe Pequot Press in Chester, Conn.—of a thin 1871 book, *Bundling: Its Origin, Progress & Decline in America.*

Well, somebody running the shop has a pretty good sense of humor.

Where else could I have come upon such an oddball—and nicely historic—item? It's a lovely discovery: and an immediate gift purchase.

On a visit the year before, I'd come across another thin volume, a long essay on Emily Dickinson, who lived down the road in Amherst. It was an essay not on her poetry but on her cookery—with a bunch of her own recipes. After sitting on my sideboard for a year, it went out as a gift.

Heck, I would have jumped off the interstate just to pick up such stuff at the gift shop. I could stay all night here. But in the midst of browsing, the young son of my friend needs to go talk to a man about a horse. So we walk next door to the inn, ask permission at the desk, and he heads toward the gents' room.

When he comes back, we stand ourselves before the roaring fire in the main sitting room and warm our backsides. In a country inn, what the heck else is a roaring fire for, but to get the chill out?

And as we stand there, in one of the inn's three sitting rooms, I recall how Deerfield first warmed me.

In 1986, I came to town for a conference on Shays' Rebellion, sponsored by Historic Deerfield and Amherst College nearby. It attracted 250 historians from across the nation who were interested in the 1786–827 uprising—an uprising of farmers in western Massachusetts that helped stiffen the writing of the U.S. Constitution in Philadelphia in the summer of 1787.

Deerfield is a good place to drop your rucksack and wander off to some of the scenes detailed in a book prominent at that conference: *Shays' Rebellion: The Making of an Agrarian Insurrection* by David P. Szatmary, published in 1980 by the University of Massachusetts Press.

When I returned here in 1990, I came not for history but for refuge.

And after walking in the late afternoon on the chill streets and running on the track at the vacation-emptied academy and hearing the rifle-cracks of deer hunters off across the fields, I went to my room and showered and changed into tie and jacket.

And in the candlelit dining room, I warmed myself with a dinner of corn chowder and venison and Indian pudding.

And in one of the sitting rooms after, I sat within sight of a fireplace fire and read and let the silence warm me—like an old lap blanket.

—Walter F. Naedele

Directions from Philadelphia: Deerfield is about a five-hour drive from the Philadelphia region. Take the New Jersey Turnpike to the George Washington Bridge, the Cross Bronx Expressway, and Interstate 95 to New Haven, where I-91 heads north through Connecticut and into Massachusetts. Take I-91 north past Amherst, and exit onto Route 5, which runs past Deerfield.

For information about lodging, contact the Deerfield Inn, 800-926-3865; for information about the town, call Historic Deerfield, 413-774-5581.

ॐ

New Hampshire's Merrimack Valley

DERRY, N.H.

ON A TYPICAL SUMMER WEEKEND, the traffic from Boston and its suburbs, about 35 miles south, whizzes past on Interstate 93 en route to the resorts of the Lakes Region to the north and the White Mountains beyond.

It is a safe bet that, as they adjust their speed controls to New Hampshire's 65-m.p.h. limit, most drivers are oblivious to the jewel of a historic site that sits just off Exit 4.

The Robert Frost farm, one-time home of the poet who in his lifetime was one of America's best-loved, most-revered literary figures, sits beside Route 28, just south of this small town. It would be understandable if someone, driving along the two-lane road, unwittingly passed right by the site. The unimposing, two-story, white-clapboard house and connecting barn is so typical of New England farmsteads that, were it not for a couple of small signs along the road, the place would stand in anonymity.

The farm is assuredly not the only reason to visit this oft-overlooked part of New Hampshire. The serious weekend explorer of the Merrimack Valley will include such nearby attractions as the Christa McAuliffe Planetarium in Concord, Canterbury Shaker Village in Canterbury, the renowned Currier Gallery of Art in Manchester, and the many state parks and riverside swimming and picnic areas along the Merrimack River.

The Frost farm is worth a visit for reasons other than that the esteemed poet lived and farmed there while he taught at Pinkerton Academy, two miles up the road in Derry, between 1900 and 1909. The 100-acre site was, in fact, the inspiration for some of Frost's most important early works.

"Forty-three of his most famous poems were centered on the farm," said Claire Ternan, manager of the state historic site.

And the sources of that inspiration are still here, readily accessible to visitors guided by the farm's Nature/Poetry Walk brochure. One can stroll beside the wall immortalized in the poem "Mending Wall," in which Frost recounts how, each spring, he and his neighbor would "walk the line" replacing the stones that the ravages of a New England winter had dislodged; how he, remarking that they do not need a wall to separate his apple orchard from his neighbor's pines, receives the laconic reply: "Good fences make good neighbors."

Also to be found on the Nature/Poetry Walk are features of the property that helped beget such poems as "Birches," "Hyla Brook," "After Apple Picking," and "Mowing."

A visit to the farm begins in the barn, now a mini-museum of Frost memorabilia, where two short videos—one featuring Frost's oldest daughter, Leslie—highlight the poet's life and times.

After the barn presentation, Ternan, or docent Kate Bruno, leads visitors on a tour of the house, explaining how the Frost family used the various rooms—the first-floor bedroom, the library, the dining room with its round table arrayed with china, silver, and glassware for five. The furnishings are of the period but did not belong to Frost. It is a tastefully decorated home, which, in its elegant simplicity, reflects the poet's work (although some of Frost's poems, while seeming simple and straightforward, have been described by critics as some of the most intricate in the language).

After the house tour, you should take the Nature/Poetry Walk. Ternan says she tells visitors to figure on about 1 1/2 hours at the farm, a half-hour each for the barn, the house, and the walk. But there is a serenity about the place that makes one want to tarry, maybe to enjoy a picnic lunch on a blanket spread in the expansive pasture directly behind the house, to contemplate again the effects of this pastoral setting on the poet's work.

In a long life (1874–1963), Frost's stay at the farm was rather brief. He sold the place in 1912 and moved his family to England for a three-year stay, during which he wrote the important poems inspired by his years on the farm.

When he returned to this country, he lived in places that became better-known as Frost's homes—Franconia, N.H., and South Shaftsbury and Ripton, Vt. In Ripton, he lived in a log cabin while lecturing at nearby Middlebury College, which now owns the cabin.

In fact, according to Ternan, the small farm outside Derry might have languished in anonymity had it not been for President John F. Kennedy's secretary of the interior, Stewart Udall. Udall discovered that the farm had become a repository for junked autos. While plans were underway to make it a national site, the state of New Hampshire snapped up the property, made it a state historic site, and restored it to its present condition.

Beyond Derry, in Concord, about 40 miles north, the Christa McAuliffe Planetarium—dedicated to the memory of its namesake, the first teacher in space, who died in the fiery explosion of the Challenger space shuttle on January 28, 1986—is a state-of-the-art facility offering a wide range of informative and entertaining programs.

Many of the programs are interactive, allowing viewers to participate in the presentations via electronic control panels in the auditorium seats.

In addition to the shows, there are exhibits and hands-on displays to keep adults and children busy between performances.

About 10 miles north of Derry on I-93 is Manchester, home of the Currier Gallery of Art. The permanent collection of this diminutive institution stretches well beyond what one might expect when first seeing the building housing it.

Picasso, Matisse, Gilbert Stuart, and a host of other major painters spanning six centuries are represented. A fine sampling of American furniture and decorative arts is also on display.

A special feature offered by the Currier is a tour of a home designed by Frank Lloyd Wright. The nearby Zimmerman House, bequeathed to the museum by Isadore and Lucille Zimmerman, is one of Wright's

"Usonian" designs, created in the 1930s to satisfy a Depression-spawned need for low-cost housing.

Wright designed not only the house but also the furniture and fabrics in it. (Tours are available Thursday through Sunday; call for required reservations, 603-669-6144.)

As clean and simple as the lines of Wright's design are, they are no match for the purity of the Shaker designs on display at Canterbury Shaker Village. The village, about a dozen miles north of Concord, just off Exit 18 of I-93, was one of several New England centers established by the religious community of celibate isolationists who pursued a quiet dedication of their lives to the glory of their Creator.

Five village houses are open to the public, and some of the finest examples of the Shakers' elegant design in buildings, furniture, and utilitarian arts are on view. There is also a gift shop, where Shaker crafts are available for purchase.

Throughout the Merrimack Valley, there are dozens of other historic sites and commercial attractions, ranging from a tour of a Budweiser brewery complete with Clydesdales (in Merrimack) to "America's Stonehenge," an assemblage of stones thought to have been built by neolithic peoples 4,000 years ago.

And, of course, away from the major cities and highways of the valley, there are wonderful woods and streams and country lanes to explore at leisure. It is these elements of the valley that Robert Frost loved most and that provided his inspiration.

Those who blow by on I-93 may never know what they've missed.

—Jack Severson

Directions from Philadelphia: It's about six to seven hours from the Philadelphia area to the Merrimack Valley. Take the New Jersey Turnpike north to the George Washington Bridge. Cross the bridge and follow Interstate 95 north to New Haven, Conn., to I-91. Take I-91 north to Hartford. There, take I-84 north to the Massachusetts Turnpike; go east to I-495 north and on to I-93 north.

The Robert Frost farm is open daily, 10 a.m. to 6 p.m. until Labor Day. From Labor Day through Columbus Day, it is open those same hours, but only on weekends. Information: 603-432-3091.

The hours for the Christa McAuliffe Planetarium vary with the show times. Call for information and show-ticket reservations (a must): 603-271-7827.

The Currier Gallery of Art in Manchester is open Tuesday through Saturday, 10 a.m. to 4 p.m. (until 9 p.m. on Thursday) and on Sunday from 1 to 5 p.m.

The Canterbury Shaker Village is open daily May through October, 10 a.m. to 5 p.m.; and Friday through Sunday in April, November, and December, 10 a.m. to 5 p.m. It is closed from January through March. Information: 603-783-9511.

For information on accommodations and other attractions in the area, contact the New Hampshire Office of Travel and Tourism Development, Box 856, Concord, N.H. 03302; phone 603-271-2343.

The home of Lizzie Borden

FALL RIVER, MASS.

I MUST ADMIT that my first visit to Fall River was out of morbid curiosity: I wanted to see where Lizzie Borden was buried.

Could a woman who supposedly chopped up her parents with 81 whacks of the ax really rest in peace? Or would the ground around her grave quake ever so slightly?

But the turf surrounding the small headstone in Oak Grove Cemetery —marked oh, so coyly, "Lizbeth," and bedecked with a few pink and lavender posies—was quite still. Nearby, two other small stones, marked "A.J.B." and "A.D.B.," sent out not a quiver. Mom and Pop—Andrew Jackson Borden and Abby Durfee Borden—were apparently resting well, too.

I later learned that Lizzie Borden's grave doesn't quake because she's actually walking the halls of a home near where she once lived in Fall River's fashionable Highlands section. Her ghost, resplendent in Victorian gown, supposedly stalks a halfway house for mental patients, across the street from Maplecroft, her former home on the hill.

Take that for what it's worth. But this much is certain: Fall River is much more than the macabre.

I was amazed to find I had discovered a little mini-vacation treasure along the water, pretty much due east of Cape Cod, and sandwiched between New Bedford, Mass., and Providence, R.I. This city of 92,000 has a textile past that lures visitors with its history and museums and a textile present that pulls them in for shopping (Fall River is perhaps best known for its outlets).

Personally, I can do without the shopping, although it's here in abundance for anybody who wants it. For me, Fall River has become an occasional retreat from Boston, a place where I can get away from the big city.

Fall River is where I go to dine on stuffed quahogs (fat Atlantic clams to the uninitiated) and fisherman's chowder, to drive up and down hilly old streets lined with magnificent Victorian mansions and old-fashioned flower gardens, to ride the 1920 carousel and to consider the days when this was known as Spindle City, U.S.A. Sometimes, in midafternoon, I take coffee and pastry up to Bicentennial Park and sit on the grass, watching white sails fill the huge and brilliantly blue Mount Hope Bay.

Almost everything about Fall River, including its name, is connected to the abundance of water surrounding the city. The name itself comes from the Indian word Quequechan, meaning falling water. Water from the Quequechan River, falling from large Watuppa Pond into Mount Hope Bay, has long been prized for its power.

First, there was a gristmill at the falls during the Revolution. Then, early in the 19th century, cotton mills—built from granite quarried in the area—sprang up to take advantage of the abundant water power, and to launch Fall River on its journey to destiny as a major milling center. By 1875, Fall River had become what was said to be the nation's leading textile producer, with 120 mills and four million spindles and a national reputation as "Spindle City."

The history of this era is everywhere evident today, from names on streets, schools, and tombstones to factory outlet shopping in some of the old mill buildings. Borden, Durfee, Buffington, and DeFlint were among the most prominent mill-owning families, and monuments bearing their names dominate row upon row of Oak Grove Cemetery, surrounding Lizzie Borden and her parents.

Some of these gravesites are quite interesting. Cotton mill owner

Foster H. Stafford, for example, hoping to have his role in the city's development remembered long beyond his death, had his granite grave marker carved to look like a miniature mill, complete with windows and doors and a peaked roof. (Cemetery enthusiasts—or Lizzie Borden historians—can find this graceful and historic Victorian cemetery at the head of Prospect Street, east off Robeson Street.)

Blessed with natural beauty and abundant water and power, Fall River has nevertheless suffered more than its share of major traumas: Disastrous fires, depression, bankruptcy, serious labor problems, a major hurricane in 1938, and rising transportation costs all worked together to bring the textile kingdom tumbling down.

Tough Yankee ingenuity, however, has always come through to save the day. One hundred-twenty idle mills seemed to industrious Fall Riverites to be 120 opportunities for the outlet heaven of any shopper's dream.

Voilà! Wicker, wigs, and Calvin Klein for a song! All sold from those same old, magnificent granite mills. Plus window curtains, silverware, mattresses, sheets, luggage, jewelry, candy, books, toys, bags, designer clothes, and much more, a lot of it at 50 percent off, or more.

An additional attraction is that the state some residents call "Taxachusetts" has a soft spot for clothing and shoes—no tax. At today's prices, that adds up.

The outlets are easy to spot: Just look down from expressways and ramps for huge granite-block mill buildings with spacious parking lots. When your eye catches such a combination, get off at the next exit and follow the tour buses.

Fall River Heritage State Park is the place to learn what Fall River was like before the outlets. There are fascinating exhibits telling how the cloth was woven, including an old working loom and legendary photographs by Lewis Hine, known for his studies of turn-of-the-century working-class Americans. It's worth the 66-stair climb to the top of the museum's bell tower for a spectacular view of Mount Hope Bay and Fall River.

Heritage Park is actually only part of a bigger water complex. Lining the shore are a historic carousel and a marine museum and railroad museum, and floating out on the water in Battleship Cove is a big tourist attraction—a collection of U.S. naval vessels.

The classic 1920 carousel has 48 beautiful horses with flowing silver manes, shiny black harnesses and collars, and glorious saddles encrusted with dazzling arrays of what might easily seem to a child the hugest of emeralds, sapphires, diamonds, and rubies. The music goes round and round, and in the summertime you have to be prepared to wait your turn. But it's worth it.

The star of Battleship Cove is the battleship *Massachusetts*. "Big Mamie" is longer than two football fields and as tall as a nine-story building. Kids and adults can climb inside huge gun turrets, see the engine room, tour all nine decks, and, of course, buy battleship souvenir sweatshirts, books, games, and flags.

On display also are two PT boats—the destroyer *Joseph P. Kennedy Jr.* and a World War II attack submarine. Visitors can tour most of the boats.

Next door to the battleships is a grouping of old railroad cars that house the Old Colony and Fall River Railroad Museum. You can tour the old cars, watch railroad movies, and, in general, just enjoy reliving the railroads' glorious past. Interactive displays allow visitors to operate a switchstand, ring an old steam locomotive bell, and even play engineer of an operating model railroad.

Nearby at the Marine Museum—in an old mill, of course—you can study the history of steamboats and great ocean liners and view the museum's most popular exhibit, a lighted 28-foot model of the *Titanic*. Created in 1952 by Twentieth Century Fox for its film about the sinking of the "unsinkable" ship, this amazingly accurate one-ton replica is just part of an exhibit about the famous vessel and its tragic fate.

The museum also houses an ambitious display of lithographs, paintings, and photographs and claims to have one of the world's most impressive collection of steamship models. Franklin D. Roosevelt, King Frederick IX of Denmark, Emperor Hirohito of Japan, and other historic figures are among those who have donated some of the more than 150 models, which range from a half-inch in size to 28 feet.

If you've seen where Lizzie Borden and her parents were buried and still have a hankering for more, how about a visit to where they lived? The murder house isn't tough to find, although the resident at the time of my visit isn't exactly crazy about having his house and printing shop listed on tour brochures. (It's at 92 Second St.; don't knock, the owner doesn't welcome visitors.)

It's a strange feeling to stand across the street, look at the rather ordinary house with the printing shop in front, and contemplate the brutality of what went on within those walls on a hot August morning in 1892.

At the time of the bloody ax-murders, Lizzie, a 32-year-old Sunday school teacher, lived there with her wealthy but somewhat miserly parents. Although she was acquitted of the crime and the slayings were never solved, townspeople then and now deemed her guilty, giving rise to the famous little ditty:

> Lizzie Borden took an ax,
> And gave her mother 40 whacks.
> When she saw what she had done,
> She gave her father 41.

With her parents out of the way, Lizzie took her sizable inheritance and moved up the hill to the Maplecroft mansion. Maplecroft, at 306 French St., is in an area still filled with beautiful, old Victorian mansions, with marvelous gardens and magnificent views of the city and the blue waters of Mount Hope Bay. But, again, it's private.

Then there is the library. I found it quite by accident, and even though I didn't have a card, just touring the handsome Italian Renaissance building was a thrill.

The exterior of the library, which opened in 1899, is of Fall River granite. The vestibule off the main entrance at 104 N. Main St. is finished in white Vermont marble with delicate green veins and is lighted by a central skylight. The dramatic dome is supported by 10 marble columns rising from a pink Tennessee marble base. Elaborate marble mosaic floors, marble-and-iron staircases and rippled silver glass skylights make the Fall River library an architecturally noteworthy stop.

The Fall River Historical Society, housed in an imposing 1843 Greek Revival-style mansion at 451 Rock St. in the Highlands, is another must-stop for history and architecture buffs. Also built of Fall River granite, the 16-room house has a fascinating history all its own.

An early Quaker owner, William Hill, used the house as a station on the Underground Railroad for escaped slaves in the years before the Civil War. A wealthy businessman purchased the house in 1869 and had it dismantled and moved higher on the hill, to a more prestigious location, where it has remained.

The mansion's beautifully restored and furnished rooms are open to the public, as are the historical society's collections of old dolls, toys, china, glassware, and elegant Victorian costumes. And, of course, the museum houses the world's largest collection of artifacts relating to the Borden murder, including rare photographs and a handleless ax said to be the murder weapon.

The gift shop is the place to purchase your Lizzie Borden souvenir sweatshirt, T-shirt, stationery, or tote bag.

For more serious students of the case, there are books, transcripts of the courtroom testimony and reproductions of photographs and newspaper accounts of the trial.

—Barbara Claire Kasselmann

Directions from Philadelphia: Fall River has about 100 outlets in five major malls, plus 50 more scattered about. To get to the heart of the outlets, take Exit 8A from eastbound Interstate 195 and follow Route 24 south a short distance to Exit 2. Take that, and go left on Brayton, then take the first right on Jefferson, which becomes Quequechan (pronounced Quickeshan). The Big Red Q at 638 Quequechan stands for Quality Factory Outlets. There are 40 of them there, plus a big parking lot, a color-coded map, and a free shuttle bus to other Fall River outlets. If you're driving around Fall River, just look for the blue "Outlet District" signs.

For more information on outlets and other attractions, contact the Bristol County Convention and Visitors Bureau, 800-288-6263 or 508-997-1250. Other numbers: Fall River Chamber of Commerce, 508-676-8226; New Bedford Chamber of Commerce, 508-999-5231; Taunton Chamber of Commerce, 508-824-4068.

A New England bicycle tour

JEFFERSONVILLE, VT.

WE WERE 15 MIDDLE-AGED BICYCLISTS, dripping in sweat and aching with hunger, who trickled gratefully into the picnic spot—a grassy cemetery in northern Vermont.

There, sitting amid the white, weathered tombstones, we piled bean sprouts, avocado, and local Cheddar cheese atop oatmeal bread and guzzled gallons of juice. But lunch, it turned out, was not the main attraction of this, the first day of an inn-to-inn bike trip.

It was the cemetery's neighbor, 69-year-old Buck Heath—a Vah-mont original, whose quick wit and raunchy language would have made him a comedy club sellout. Instead, he was regaling us bikers with stories of his pitched battle against those . . ."unfair" taxes, the . . . wife who "cleaned me out," and his "woman" who worked down in Stowe.

But what brought the most laughs was Heath's description of his first (and last) experience on a bicycle a few years back—a graphic story of the saddle sores a too-hard seat can cause.

That was a complaint few of us on the five-day tour, organized by Vermont Bicycle Touring, were willing to admit. After all, any pain we felt was self-inflicted, either because we weren't in shape or because we'd chosen to chew up too many miles that day.

The choice of distances—a mileage menu of sorts—was, in fact, what had attracted our friends Phil and Essie Goldsmith and my husband, Larry, and me, all from the Philadelphia area, to pick an organized bicycle trip.

On any given day, the men, who'd been working out for years on bicycles, could challenge their macho selves with demanding routes ranging from 50 to 70 miles, while Essie and I could tool along for about half those distances, take in a little shopping and local color and still meet up with them for lunch.

The trip we selected was among the more challenging five-day "vagabonds" run by VBT, with five nights spent at three different inns in northern Vermont. The challenge, of course, wasn't the inns but the rides between them, ranging from 19 to 71 miles a day depending on whether you followed the direct route or a looping one.

But VBT, and other companies like it, also offer easier jaunts. Many of the two- and three-day weekend getaways, for instance, have mileage starting as low as 10 miles per day.

In some ways, riding the different distances was like taking separate vacations together. The trick, we discovered, was admitting that—and enjoying it.

The first hint we had that togetherness wouldn't be the order of the week came our first evening, when the group, ranging in age from 32 to 47, gathered in the lounge of the spartan Red Fox Alpine Lodge in Jeffersonville, just the other side of the mountain from Stowe.

We approached evening warily. The ski-dorm-type accommodations with one shower per floor were a bit of a shock; we had expected New England Charming. VBT, we learned, had made this one-night compromise for the sake of the central location and a spacious parking lot where we could leave our cars for the week.

But the fabulous food almost made up for the rooms. The French chef produced perfect poached salmon and fresh blueberries in a puff pastry. And the easy camaraderie of people who like biking made it clear that the week would be special.

The one area of potential conflict involved the tension of trying to ride with someone, particularly a spouse, who kept a different pace.

"It can be very frustrating to keep stopping for someone who is biking slowly," said one of our VBT leaders, Suzan Hall.

"I think it's even worse for the person who's behind and biking like crazy to try to keep up," added our other leader, Bob Munstock.

At that, Judy Mishkin of Marblehead, Mass., observed: "I came here knowing I wouldn't be biking with Billy, and that's fine."

After an enormous breakfast of pancakes and fresh melons and berries, we spun out of the driveway of the Red Fox. By the time we returned on Friday, I would have ridden 185 miles; Larry, by taking extra loops, would have accomplished nearly 300—about as many miles as we'd driven from Philadelphia.

The range of ability on our trip was extraordinary. Judy Mishkin, it turned out, was no slouch. She had run the Boston Marathon in 1988, and her lean, muscled body made me feel like a marshmallow. Still, she was slower than her husband, Billy, and several others on the trip, including Jill McCutcheon of Huntsville, Ala., a woman so dedicated to exercise that she'd jog before breakfast, then bike the longest route so fast that she'd still arrive at lunch an hour ahead of anyone else.

In the middle somewhere were Phil and Larry. And then came turtle-paced Essie and me.

That lunch in the cemetery was my first rendezvous with my husband since breakfast. And I wouldn't see him again until about 5 p.m. when we rolled into the Gables Inn in Stowe.

But both of us were happy with our separate experiences. By the end of the day, Larry had pedaled 50 miles and spent hours chatting with new friends who were, you might say, about his speed. Essie and I could boast about our 40-mile push, not to mention some great shopping at the Johnson Woolen outlet in Johnson, Vt. (I bought a jacket, she bought a blanket; we had them shipped.)

Mostly, though, it was the gorgeous expanse of Vermont scenery that sated our eyes all day and blotted out the city clutter of our minds: The fields of tall green corn set against plum-colored mountains; the quaint houses with a touch of artistry in front of each, be it flowers in a wagon wheel or lush hanging plants; freshly painted barns and charming villages, each with a commons and country store.

It was a no-hassles experience. We didn't have to worry about carrying luggage or food, getting overtired, or what to do in the event of a flat tire, which was lucky because Essie had three flats that first day. Our security blanket was the well-stocked "sag wagon," the VBT van that carried our picnic in coolers, and our luggage, and did the "sweep" of our routes in search of anyone having trouble on the way to the next inn.

At Stowe, the Gables Inn was waiting for us, the sole guests that night. On the porch was a punch bowl of iced tea, sliced apples and oranges, Vermont smoked Cheddar cheese and crackers. The rooms had white eyelet curtains, sloped dormer ceilings, and quilted bedspreads. Yes! This was just what we'd expected.

Dinner was at small tables set out on the lawn—something missed by the many skiers who come to this charming village in winter. Interestingly, Stowe has become even more popular in summer.

Feeling no guilt (how many calories had we burned off?), we indulged in a buffet of ribs, quiche, zucchini croissants, and chocolate cake with puréed blackberries on top. To top it off, we took a walk down the road and ate some more at the local TCBY yogurt place.

By 10 p.m., Larry and I had tumbled heavily into bed, noticing each other about as much as two logs on a bed of pine needles.

Our second day dawned warm and sunny and I woke up with a great sense of relief. In a dream, I'd given myself permission to do the shortest route. "I know which one I'm going on," I announced to Larry. "The 24-mile."

Said Larry, "I know which I'm doing—the 58."

As it turned out, Judy and Billy were ready for a short day (Billy wanted to get in a round of golf in the afternoon and claim the distinction of being one of the few bikers on a VBT trip to play golf as well.) So they joined Essie and me on the short loop, straight down Route 100 to the second most visited place in Vermont after the Shelburne Museum—the Ben and Jerry's ice cream factory in Waterbury.

The museum enshrines the kind of spunk and humor that have made Ben and Jerry not only an instant commercial success, but a hit with both its workers and Wall Street.

For $1 (half of which goes to a charity selected by B&J workers), you get a movie, a tour, and a guide who launches the program with "Everyone for the 11 o'clock tour, mo-o-o-o-ve along." (Cows, of course, being crucial to the product.)

The movie recounts the saga of Ben Cohen and Jerry Greenfield, chubby teenagers who met in seventh-grade gym class in Merrick, Long Island. Eventually they would take a Penn State extension course on making ice cream, and the rest is history.

Down on the factory floor, where workers pack ice cream to music and get periodic massages, a new, politically correct flavor was in production: Rain Forest Crunch, full of cashews and Brazil nuts grown in the Amazon on trees that are not being cut down. Only Ben and Jerry can turn eating ice cream into an act of conscience. "Caring capitalism," they call it.

After loading our bellies with ice cream samples and our bike bags with T-shirts saying "one percent for peace," we headed back to Stowe on a dirt country road that went unrelentingly uphill for about two miles.

Essie and I happily talked our way through "granny stops,"riding a little and stopping a little, a method of ascending hills that supposedly gets you to the top faster than walking the bike, and at the same time builds some muscle.

The exhilaration of the long, fast downhill into Stowe was easily worth the exertion. And we were back in Stowe in time for a lunch of homemade tomato basil soup at Mom's Bakery and, of all things, an afternoon nap at the Gables.

Meanwhile, 30 miles or more farther south, rain was closing in on Phil and Larry and the rest of the gang. And by the time they hit that mammoth up-and-downhill several hours after us, they were exhausted. Dinner conversation was full of talk about that last stretch and the dangers of wet roads—and a bit of jealousy over the easy day that Essie and I had given ourselves.

Still, some found the energy to go to the 10 p.m. showing of *Presumed Innocent*, joking that by morning they themselves might be Presumed Dead.

By day three, as we set off for our last inn, something had happened to the 15 of us and our leaders, Bob and Suzan. We had gone beyond the discussions of what it's like being a professor of philosophy in Houston or a Jersey electrician who commutes 60 miles each way to New York City. We had coalesced into a family, watching out for one another.

When Miamian Burt Wolfson, a physical therapist who was so driven that he wouldn't let himself rest on the hills, admitted to feeling weak-kneed, his riding group quietly came up with ruses to get him to stop.

At the top of one hill, Larry said he needed a rest. At the next, Phil had to make a nature stop. Then Bill Nelson of Houston announced he wanted to check out some wildflower blooms in the little book he carried. And Gail Byrnes, a teacher from Branford, Conn., insisted on stopping to take a photograph.

By the time the VBT van pulled up, Burt Wolfson was in the home stretch and feeling well enough to pedal back in time for the surprise bachelor party we threw for him.

Our last two nights were at the Black Lantern Inn in the village of Montgomery. In the summer, this lovely hostelry is like a stagecoach stop for bicyclists. We shared the inn—and a gorgeous swimming hole and waterfall nearby—with two men and a woman who, having biked for a week in Vermont, were heading home to Montreal.

Two other men, one of whom was 74, were pedaling about 75 to 80 miles a day—with gear. We were impressed.

To our delight, our room turned out to be a small suite, with a small sitting room and, best of all, a Jacuzzi in the bathroom.

After a dinner of the quality and quantity we'd come to take for granted, a group of us took a sunset walk down the road to the old covered bridge, then climbed the hill beyond it as the stars began emerging against the darkening sky. The landscape's peace seemed to mirror our own inner contentment.

Our last two days were spent from our base at the Black Lantern in a part of Vermont that flattens out a bit into rolling hills—which means you pedal like crazy down one hill in the hope that your speed will carry you to the top of the next.

For those, like Larry and Phil, who craved extra pedaling, there was the option of a 15-mile loop into Canada (on top of 57 miles for the day). Never mind that there was nothing to see except U.S. and Canadian Customs houses; hey, it makes for a great story, not to mention a photograph for the scrapbook.

Of course, Essie and I never saw Canada.

It was on our last day, as we were pedaling back to the starting point in Jeffersonville, that Larry decided to bike with me.

He had stopped for some maple syrup and carelessly stood in the middle of the road, packing it up. When I did my motherly thing and warned him to get out of traffic, he replied:

"When I ride with Phil, he doesn't tell me what to do!"

But a little while later, I got even when he demanded that I stop and smile for a photograph:

"Essie," I said, "doesn't tell me what to do."

—Dorothy Brown

VBT is one of several organizations offering inn-to-inn bike tours—in Vermont and elsewhere in New England. Call for rates, directions to your starting point, and other information.

Vermont Bicycle Touring, Box 711, Bristol, Vt. 05443, 802-453-4811; VCC Four Seasons Cycling, Box 145, Waterbury Center, Vt. 05677, 802-453-4811; Bike Vermont, Box 207, Woodstock, Vt. 05091, 802-457-3553.

Literary New England

LENOX, MASS.

STANDING ON THE BROAD TERRACE of The Mount, the former Berkshires home of writer Edith Wharton, you see the glimmer of a lake through the tall pines, you breathe in the fresh mountain air and wonder: Well, who wouldn't be inspired to write the Great American Novel in this setting?

Yet standing in the small, austere upstairs bedroom of Louisa May Alcott's house outside Boston, you feel cramped. You wonder where you'd put the typewriter, how cold you'd be in the winter. Inspiration here could be long in coming.

A weekend tour of New England authors' homes is more than just a visit to the shrines of American literature. It is a quest for the source of the Muse among the everyday hardships of 19th-century life, when few authors could support themselves in the grand lifestyle of an Edith Wharton.

It is also an interesting way to learn more about an author whose work may be only a hazy memory from a high school anthology.

Driving northeast from New York along interstates 684 and 84 takes you right into downtown Hartford, Conn., and into the neighborhood quaintly known as Nook Farm. Once a select writing colony overlooking the scenic countryside, Nook Farm now sits on a busy Hartford street, just a few blocks from the roar of I-84 traffic. It was here that Samuel Clemens (better known as Mark Twain) and Harriet Beecher Stowe, two of the best-known writers of the 19th century, were neighbors—with a good rapport—for more than 20 years, beginning in the mid-1870s.

Voted by readers of a local newspaper in an annual poll as the best place to take visiting relatives, Mark Twain's home reflects the opulent lifestyle of one of the era's wealthiest authors. He and his wife, Livvy, entertained such guests as *Atlantic Monthly* editor William Dean Howells and Gen. William Tecumseh Sherman at lavish dinner parties.

On the house's completion in 1874, the *Hartford Times* wrote, "The novelty displayed in the architecture . . . the oddity of its internal arrangements, and the fame of the owner will all conspire to make it a house of note for a long time to come." It was indeed an accurate prophecy, as anyone seeing the house for the first time will agree. Designed by architect Edward Tuckerman Potter, the large, richly detailed brick house has projecting balconies, gables, and chimneys, and is painted orange and black with contrasting red trim and railings. An article aptly described it as looking like a combination "steamship, church, and cuckoo clock."

Inside as well as out, a tour of Twain's house evokes the elaborateness of the Gilded Age in all its ornamental splendor. The 19 rooms feature extensive hand-stenciling, original Tiffany windows, and an abundance of carved wood moldings. The house is furnished with many of the original pieces, some from the Twains' frequent trips to Europe.

But it's still the fame of the owner and his eccentric sense of humor that makes a visit here particularly entertaining. His sensibility is still in evidence throughout the house—as in the phone closet, where his weekly "report card" to the phone company on its service remains posted. His crooked cue rests on the pool table in his third-floor combination study and billiard room, where he shot rigged games with his cronies until the wee hours—when he wasn't writing such classics there as The Adventures of Tom Sawyer and The Adventures of Huckleberry Finn.

When the Twains left after a beloved daughter's death in 1896, the home went through a series of lives as a branch of the local library, a wartime storage place for coal, and an apartment house for "young ladies of good reputation," before extensive restoration began in the early 1970s to turn it into a Mark Twain Memorial.

Today, more than 60,000 visitors a year tour the house, including the basement, which features interesting exhibits on Victorian life and an array of Twain-related relics.

The Stowe house next door is a much more modest example of Victorian living and makes for an interesting contrast. Harriet Beecher Stowe, best-known for the anti-slavery epic Uncle Tom's Cabin, moved into the house with her husband and grown twin daughters in 1873, after rearing seven children and completing the bulk of her 30 books.

The house is designed in traditional Victorian style and has many of the original furnishings. Stowe's own paintings hang on the walls, and the china she designed is in the dining room.

The one nontraditional room is the kitchen. Considered quite modern for its time, it reflects the author's passionate beliefs on the importance of a comfortable, well-run kitchen to the health and welfare of a household, as described in American Woman's Home, a book she wrote with her sister, the educator Catherine Beecher.

Stowe's kitchen features plenty of light and "good ventilation," shallow shelves for easy access, compact storage, and a central work area. The kitchen was intrinsic to Stowe's busy life, not only as a 19th-century mother and homemaker, but as a writer; despite the presence of her own separate study, she continued to write almost all of her work on the kitchen table.

The 90-minute tour of both the Stowe and Twain homes is conducted by guides who furnish many interesting and humorous anecdotes. The homes at Nook Farm are open to the public year round.

The image of Emily Dickinson, dressed in white, alone in her attic, secretly scribbling poetry, has captured the public's fancy since her trunk of poems was discovered after her death in 1886. Her home, known as the Dickinson Homestead, is on Main Street in Amherst, Mass., about an hour's drive from Hartford north on Interstate 91. The Federal-style house is now the property of Amherst College and is used as a faculty residence, but enough of it remains open to the public so that visitors can get a good sense of the life of one of America's best-known poets.

On a visit to the Dickinson Homestead, one can almost sense her presence. It is here that "Aunt Emily" lived for more than 40 years, tending to sick relatives, baking her famous gingerbread, and writing a total of 1,775 poems in her spare time.

Tours, which are given by appointment only, May through October, begin in the living room. On a visit, we sat in a circle with our guide, who offered a general discussion of Dickinson, her life and work, while passing around photographs and other artifacts. The tour then proceeded upstairs to Dickinson's bedroom. Numerous family portraits line the hallway, and the bedroom itself features her original sleigh bed, her white dress, and the small table and chair where she wrote.

Although most of Dickinson's manuscripts and other important possessions (such as the trunk in which she stored her poems) are now at the Harvard and Amherst university libraries and are used primarily for scholarly study, the Jones Public Library in Amherst has a smaller array of Dickinson-related memorabilia and a fine selection of her books. The cemetery in which the Dickinson family is buried is also nearby.

Amherst, as well as the neighboring college town of Northampton, are delightful places to pass an afternoon, with numerous bookshops and other interesting stores, as well as restaurants and cafés. One can get a second wind there before heading west on the Massachusetts Turnpike to the Berkshires and Edith Wharton's home in Lenox, which is north off the Lee exit on Route 20.

A century ago, the Berkshire Mountain area of western Massachusetts formed a hub for artists and intellectuals, as well as a retreat for the wealthy who scattered huge castlelike homes among the foothills and lakes.

Wharton belonged to both groups. As the author of more than 41 books, including such novels as *Ethan Frome* and *The House of Mirth*, she proved herself a talented writer worthy of the Pulitzer Prize (for *The Age of Innocence* in 1920).

As the daughter of a wealthy New York family, she was able to design and build an architecturally magnificent home called The Mount in the resort town of Lenox. Wharton lived at The Mount most of the year, with her husband, Teddy, between 1902 and 1912, leaving behind the bitter Berkshire winters for her homes in New York and France.

Because of its sheer size and scope, The Mount has not fared well over the years. Its primary function until 1976 was as a dormitory for a girls' boarding school. Since then, it has been kept from the hands of developers and is now being slowly restored to its original condition, right down to the contents of the bookshelves in the library.

But the impact of The Mount—both as a representative of a bygone lifestyle and as a departure from the popular Victorian style of the time—is far from lost. Seated on 50 of the property's original 130 acres, the white-stuccoed house rises majestically on a hill, its large windows and wide terrace allowing stunning views of the nearby mountains, meadows, and lake. Although grand with a ballroom, servants' quarters and gallery entryway, The Mount is considered small in an area where many estates have 50 or more rooms.

Wharton, who co-wrote the popular *Decoration of Houses* in 1901, had very determined ideas about the functional design of homes. And with the help of architect Ogden Codman, Jr., she put many of them to work at The Mount. Every aspect of the interior is purposefully designed, with a minimum of the cramped space or clutter characteristic of the Victorian style Wharton was reared with and so detested. Having traveled extensively through Europe since her childhood, Wharton was influenced by the classical 18th-century style of design that emphasized small detail and the illusion of spaciousness. This is evident throughout The Mount, in its barrel-arched entryway ceiling and matched carved moldings in the drawing room and library.

The three main downstairs rooms open onto a large terrace that is linked to the gardens below by an impressive double staircase. Wharton, whose passion for design was matched by her love of gardens, created a terraced formal garden with her niece, the noted landscape artist Beatrix Farrand, that slopes down naturally through a meadow of pines toward Laurel Lake.

The Mount is open for tours Tuesday through Sunday from Memorial Day through Labor Day. From Sept. 5 through Oct. 27, the schedule is Thursday through Sunday.

If you have extra time on your weekend tour, double back east to the town of Concord, Mass. Not only is Concord a paradigm of New England towns; it is a treasure-trove of literary sites.

Home to the 19th-century philosophical movement known as American transcendentalism, Concord and its surroundings were the setting for the works of many writers, including Henry David Thoreau (*Walden Pond*) and Ralph Waldo Emerson (*Nature, Self-Reliance*). Transcendentalists searched for life's meaning and self-knowledge through communion with nature and shunned the trappings of urban society.

In addition to Emerson and Thoreau, Concord was also the home of Nathaniel Hawthorne (*The House of the Seven Gables, The Scarlet Letter*), and Louisa May Alcott (*Little Women*). They frequented each other's homes for debate and conversation, and tales of their discussions, as related by tour guides, make for interesting anecdotes.

Tours are offered at Orchard House, which was home to Alcott and her family. Her father, the famous educator Bronson Alcott, borrowed $500 from Emerson in 1857 to purchase what was then two houses and 40 apple trees on 12 acres. Orchard House was the setting for *Little Women:* Beth's piano and Amy's paintings figure prominently in the furnishings.

Emerson's house, and Hawthorne's two homes—Old Manse and Wayside House—also offer tours. Because of the cost of staffing and upkeep, the tours are offered only irregularly, so it is best to call first. Sleepy Hollow Cemetery, a few hundred yards up Bedford Street from the town center, features Author's Ridge, where Hawthorne, Thoreau, Emerson, and the Alcotts are buried. The Museum of the Concord Antiquarian Society, next to Orchard House, offers a further look into the lives of the famous Concordians.

In addition, the Thoreau Lyceum in Concord offers scholarly lectures, programs, and nature walks for educators and students. It also has an extensive public exhibit of both Concord history and Thoreau manuscripts and memorabilia.

The original site of Thoreau's cabin at Walden Pond is a few miles south of Concord on Route 20 and is a great place for hiking, canoeing, fishing, and picnicking—any of them a welcome diversion at the end of a weekend tour through literary New England.

—Kim Moon

Accommodations near all sites are plentiful, but advance reservations are recommended. Local chambers of commerce and visitors bureaus can provide information on hotels, motels, bed-and-breakfast inns, and the houses: Greater Hartford Convention and Visitor's Bureau, phone 203-728-6789. Amherst Chamber of Commerce, phone 413-253-0700. Berkshire Visitors Bureau, phone 413-443-9186. Concord Chamber of Commerce, phone 508-369-3120.

☙

A fishing town

MARBLEHEAD, MASS.

ONE OF THE BEST TIMES of the year to visit Marblehead is the winter. When the snow settles in the eaves of the Colonial-and-Federal-era houses, and the light slants on the harbor in a certain austere way, you'd swear you were back in the 1700s. Or that you were the main character in an Emily Dickinson poem.

Marblehead, a Yankee coastal town 35 miles north of Boston, is a place of narrow, winding streets and clapboard houses. It was established in 1629 and looks very much like an old Cornwall, England, fishing village. In fact, Marblehead's original settlers were Cornish fishermen.

In the early mornings, down at the State Street Wharf, lobster boats and small and large fishing boats head out for their daily catch. Sitting on the wooden benches that front the harbor is a favorite Marblehead activity in clement weather.

The town quiets down during the winter, with none of the feverish tourist hustle and bustle of July and August.

Marblehead harbor is known all over the world for its sailing activities. More than 4,000 sailboats berth in town during the season, and 20 fleets compete in races conducted on weekends, starting Memorial Day.

But once the crew shirts and Topsiders are stashed away and the weather turns cool and gray, Marblehead becomes a slower-paced, more attractive destination for a long-winter-weekend visit.

Sightseeing in Old Town, a roughly eight-mile area, is easy. You just start at Abbot Hall, the town hall. Built in 1876, it has a huge clock tower, which can be seen all over Old Town and makes a handy point of reference for those strolling Old Town. Abbot Hall is open year-round, and its helpful staff can provide visitors with brochures and information on Marblehead.

Abbot Hall is also home to "The Spirit of '76," the famous painting also known as "Yankee Doodle Dandy" and considered one of the most inspiring patriotic paintings in America.

Old Town has mansions dating from the 1600s, old church burial grounds, and a fort dating from before the Revolutionary War. There are also several streets of terrific specialty shops selling everything from nautical supplies to stained-glass windows.

For history buffs, Marblehead is a treasure trove. The very first warship of the American Navy, the *Hannah*—commissioned by George Washington in 1775—was built here.

Elbridge Gerry, one of the signers of the Declaration of Independence and later vice president of the United States under James Madison, was born in Marblehead, in a house that still stands. The second-oldest Episcopal church in the United States is in Marblehead.

Marblehead also has some of the most opulent "merchant prince" mansions in the country. These were homes of the entrepreneurial giants of Marblehead's clipper-ship days.

Down the street from Abbot Hall is a fascinating 18th-century church burial ground, behind the Unitarian Universalist Church on Mugford Street. The first headstone was laid in 1736. Many of the stones have beautiful carvings: cherubs, urns, and hands clasped together.

Death was a constant visitor to the Puritans who settled this area. Many of those buried in the yard were children. The headstone of Samuel Swasey, who died as a young adult, has an especially succinct message on it: "Death is a debt to Nature due / As I have paid it so must you."

Down the hill from Abbot Hall is the Lee Mansion at 161 Washington St., considered one of the finest examples of Georgian architecture in America. It was built in 1768 and is filled with authentic Colonial furnishings and decorations, including rare wood paneling and wallpaper made in England. The third floor contains many items of historical importance to the town. Unfortunately, the mansion is open only from May through October. But even viewed only from the outside, it is an impressive edifice.

Diagonally across the street, on Hooper Street, is the King Hooper Mansion, built in 1728. The mansion was home to Robert Hooper, a shipowner and merchant. The Georgian front rooms were added in 1745, and their ornamentation and elegance provide an interesting contrast to the older, pine-paneled rooms of the original structure. The opulent home also featured a wine cellar, slave quarters, and, on the third floor, a ballroom. (The King Hooper Mansion is open Tuesdays through Sundays from 1 to 4 p.m. There is a small entry fee.)

Other spots of interest in Old Town include the Old North Church at 41 Washington St., which was built in 1824 to replace the first religious meeting place; the Old Town House at Market Square (known as Marblehead's "Cradle of Liberty"), built in 1727, predating Boston's Faneuil Hall, and St. Michael's Church on Summer Street, built in 1714—the second-oldest Episcopal church in the nation.

St. Michael's old English bell was cracked by patriots, who broke into the church when news of the Declaration of Independence reached town and rang the bell until it cracked.

When you've filled up on history, you might want to head back to Washington Street to browse through the antiques shops and art galleries, the best of which seem to be concentrated there. For other shopping, Pleasant and State streets are home to craft shops, nautical-supplies purveyors, and boutiques.

No visit to Marblehead would be complete without a stop at Crocker Park. Perched on a hill and affording a panoramic view of the harbor, it's a terrific place to get an overview of the area and maybe—if the weather is mild—have a picnic.

From the park, you also can see the Neck, a neighborhood of many beautiful mansions and summer homes, across from Old Town. A drive through the Neck, on winding Ocean Avenue, will take you to small Chandler Hovey Park, whose lofty vantage point provides views of the ocean and the Marblehead lighthouse.

For a taste of Marblehead's maritime present, head back to State Street and the State Street Wharf, the town's public landing. Here you'll find several excellent restaurants abutting the landing.

At the end of Front Street—a walk of about 15 minutes from the landing—it's back to the past for a stop at Fort Sewall. The fort, at the mouth of the harbor, was once a rough piece of earthwork, thrown up against any attack by sea during the French and Indian Wars. It was turned over to revolutionary forces during the Revolutionary War and was improved to include first-class fortifications and barracks to house the garrison.

The history, architecture, and low-key pleasures of the off season all combine to make Marblehead a rewarding winter weekend destination.

—Pamela Margoshes

Directions from Philadelphia: To get to Marblehead, take Interstate Route 95 north and loop around to the north side of Boston. Near Danvers, take the exit for Route 114 east (Salem/ Marblehead) and follow into Marblehead. For more information, contact the Marblehead Chamber of Commerce at 62 Pleasant St., Marblehead, Mass. 01945; phone 617-631-2868.

Vermont still works

MIDDLEBURY, VT.

FOUR-YEAR-OLD JEREMY, BORN and raised in Los Angeles, knew something was different as soon as we got out of the car.

"Daddy, I smell something," he said.

I inhaled deeply. "Son," I replied, "that's clean air."

Yes, the air was still clean, and the greenness of the fields and woods was almost shocking. Just as I had hoped.

I had left this part of Vermont about 20 years before. A reunion at Middlebury College brought me back for a weekend, providing a chance to revisit old haunts, see old friends, and show my family an important piece of my past.

There was much to revisit. I spent four years of college here, and two summers as well. Much of that time was taken up exploring the surroundings—hiking, skiing, driving, biking, even a spot of canoeing here and there. Well, the news from here is: Vermont still works.

After two decades' absence, I found a place that managed to remain largely unspoiled. The Middlebury area appears to have found a way to grow and prosper—moderately—without selling its soul. And it appears, in many respects, to have its environmental act together.

Our visit lasted for a long weekend, and included a stay at a friend's farm near the village of Addison. From there, we hiked a bit, meandered around in our rented car, and loafed a lot. Our tour was far from comprehensive, but it provided some sense of what had changed, and what had not.

Take the view from the college's hilltop campus. Late in the morning of our second day, the muggy weather broke, the sun came out and the haze burned off to reveal a sparkling summer day. We could look west over miles of rolling pastures toward the Adirondack Mountains in New York State. To the east, the forest seemed to stretch unbroken all the way to Bread Loaf Mountain, 12 miles away.

My wife, Eileen, turned to me and said, "Oh, so this is what you meant."

Other things have not changed. There are still no billboards, thanks to a statewide ban enacted while I was in college. And I found no vast new housing subdivisions. In general, the place looked a bit tidier and more prosperous than I remembered. A lot of farmhouses were freshly painted.

Vermont remains untrashed and unspoiled largely because the people who live there are determined to keep it that way. But geographical luck also plays a part: Vermont is far enough from New York and Boston to be spared a lot of population pressure. From Philadelphia, it's about a seven-hour drive. And it's small: the 1990 census found just 562,758 people in the state—one-third the population of Philadelphia spread out over an area 25 percent larger than New Jersey. Burlington, the largest city, has fewer than 40,000 residents.

Not that small is any guarantee. Vermonters began to realize in the '60s that they had something worth preserving. And even though the state was then regarded as a conservative backwater, the legislature enacted some stunningly progressive environmental laws.

Vermont was among the first states to pass a bottle bill, for example. In 1967, the legislature also enacted a statewide ban on billboards, the nation's first and since followed by only a handful of states.

Anyone who considers those largely symbolic gestures can look to what followed. In the early 70s, in response to a pitched battle over a condo project at Stratton ski area near Manchester, a comprehensive land-use law called Act 250 took effect.

Essentially, Act 250 makes it difficult for developers and their pals in local government to sneak a big, ugly project through the local planning and permits process. Before a development can be built, its backers have to convince a local citizens' commission that the area can handle it—that air and water quality will not suffer, that the schools won't be swamped, that the highways can handle the traffic, and so on.

It sounds simple, but 20 years later, with only modest refinements, it still works. It scares the schlock development away.

Things are far from perfect. The water quality in Lake Champlain is a continuing embarrassment, because of sewage problems from around Burlington. But they're dealing with that as well.

Vermont is clearly much more eager now in its pursuit of the tourist dollar. Nobody had ever heard of bed-and-breakfast inns when I left in the early '70s. Now it seems as if every 10th house in the state is a B&B. There were no commercial bicycling tours back then—there were hardly any bikes. Now bike tours are a major industry.

The commercial districts of towns such as Middlebury and Bristol have been spruced up, and the commercial mix has a decidedly '90s cast. A nice-looking store in Middlebury sells Oriental carpets now. There's even a Mexican restaurant, for Pete's sake. Twenty years before, the closest taco was probably somewhere in the Bronx.

We spent most of one day on a ramble by car through the Green Mountains. We drove over Appalachian Gap and stopped for a look at my favorite old ski area, Mad River Glen. One of its lifts is a funky, inefficient single chairlift dating from the 1940s. I recalled hearing that it had been badly damaged in a fire a few years before and had to be extensively rebuilt. But lo and behold! They had rebuilt it as a funky, inefficient single chairlift. Now that's tradition.

We stopped again a few miles down the road to look at Sugarbush. This is a much larger, glossier, more commercial ski resort (we old Mad River regulars used to call it Mascara Mountain), and I wanted to see how it had fared in the development wars.

Answer: remarkably well. Yes, there were condo developments scattered back in the trees near the base station, but they did a fair job of blending into the hillside. The development struck me as far more restrained than some of the mountain-flattening stuff I have encountered at big ski resorts in the West.

After Sugarbush, we looped south for a stop at Texas Falls, deep in the woods by a side road near Middlebury Gap. The falls are a series of narrow chutes and plunges, and the biggest single drop is about 12 feet. In my reckless youth, I swam here with my friends, riding the falls from pool to pool.

We found the water cool and sparkling clear. There was but one change: The Forest Service has posted "No Swimming" signs.

The natural pleasures of Vermont are small in scale—no towering, snow-clad Alps or mighty Grand Canyons—but great in number.

In fact, while there are many things to do in Vermont on a vacation, the one thing you must do is set aside time to simply explore. There's an accessible aspect to Vermont that lets you find your own special places.

One of my special places is a simple dirt crossroads near the Lemon Fair River between Middlebury and Bridport. The foreground is a field of wildflowers. In the middle distance are a red barn and a pasture dotted with black and white Holstein cows. Behind them, a low, wooded ridge. And on the horizon, a 75-mile panorama of the Green Mountain crest, from Mount Mansfield to Killington Peak.

There's nothing really special about my places, other than that I feel a bit proprietary for having found them. Turn off the highway onto almost any side road—especially if it's not paved—and you'll find yours.

—Rob Waters

Directions from Philadelphia: Take the Garden State Parkway north to the New York Thruway (I-87). Take the Thruway north to Albany (exit 24), continue north on I-87 to Route 149. Take 149 east to Route 4 north and east, to Route 7 north.

For more information, contact the Vermont Travel Division, 802-828-3236.

The call of the sea

MYSTIC, CONN.

THIS IS WHERE I WOULD MEET the captain. He'd puff on his pipe, look me up and down, and decide whether I had the right stuff. Finally, he would say, "Sailing on the morning tide, laddie. Be aboard. Whalin' will make a man of you."

I was on my way, trudging along the railroad tracks, when my father caught up with me. The old sailing ships were all gone, he explained, and boys didn't run away to sea anymore. They stayed home and went to school. No more sailing ships! My 11-year-old heart was shattered.

The sea mysteriously calls out to small boys. Living inland is no protection, as my father learned, so you might as well bring your boy to Mystic Seaport. And if you don't have a son or grandson, come anyway. Mystic will find the small boy in you.

We drove here from Philadelphia on a weekend, crossed the road from the parking lot, and suddenly stepped into the 19th century. We were in a bustling seaport, the masts of sailing ships towering over the buildings, and exciting things were happening everywhere.

One nice thing about Mystic Seaport is that you can visit any time during the year and have a grand time. There are about 130 special activities each year: weekends for seniors in April; a lobsterfest weekend in May; a sea-music festival in June; a horse-and-carriage weekend and an antique-and-classic-boat rendezvous in July; a fish fry and family photo weekend in September; a chowderfest in October; family friendship weekends in November, and the Seaport Christmas throughout December.

You get the picture: A three-ring circus is small-time compared to Mystic.

A carriage ride from Chubb's Wharf took us around Mystic and helped us get our bearings. (A wagon takes passengers along the same route, but we'll always opt for elegance.) Our driver pointed out the 60 or so historic buildings on the 17-acre site, brought here and restored to re-create the feel of a New England seaport.

In most of the buildings, we discovered, something interesting was going on. Crafts workers were building small boats in the boat shop, making barrels in the cooperage, and carving figureheads in the ship-carver's shop. Iron workers were busy in the shipsmith, sailmakers in the sail loft, printers at the Mystic Press. Oysters were being sorted in the Thomas Oyster House; fish were being preserved in the smoke house.

We stopped by the 1874 lifesaving station, which houses a coastal rescue boat and gear, examined the vintage dry goods and hardware in Stone's Store, saw the tiny desks at the one-room schoolhouse, sat in a pew at the little 1889 Gothic chapel, admired the Block Island hand pumper in the firehouse, and inspected the bar in the sailors' tavern.

An interesting stop was the Henry B. du Pont Preservation Shipyard, which has the equipment and the craftsmen to perform any task required to restore and preserve wooden vessels. A lift dock with a 375-ton capacity can raise any of the seaport's ships out of the water. An 85-foot spar lathe can turn a new mast. In the large main shop, a gallery gives visitors a bird's-eye view of the activity. Other facilities are nearby—a lumberyard and sawmill, a metalworking shop, and a paint shop.

All this was simply a prelude to seeing the stars at Mystic, the tall ships. The most famous is the bark *Charles W. Morgan*, the only wooden whaling ship still afloat, the last surviving square-rigged American ship of the 19th century. It was restored in the shipyard here, and it's a proud beauty. If it doesn't make your heart pound, then Kansas is the place for you.

Launched in 1841, the *Morgan* sailed out of New Bedford, Mass., making 37 voyages to the South Seas in search of whales. It was laid up in 1921, after petroleum and electricity made whale oil obsolete. It had a brief theatrical fling in the 1920s as the setting for silent films.

After nearly perishing in the 1938 hurricane, the *Morgan* found a permanent home here on the eve of World War II. The *Morgan* has been designated a National Historic Landmark. To learn more about it, see the 30-minute film "Whales, Whaling and Whalemen," shown four times a day at the Meeting House. The vintage footage is exceptional.

Other tall ships here include the 111-foot, full-rigged training ship Joseph Conrad, built in Denmark in 1882 and used in the seaport's sail-training program, and the 123-foot 1921 Gloucester fishing schooner *L.A. Dunton*, a veteran of the Grand Banks fishing fleet that Kipling immortalized in *Captains Courageous*. We boarded all three ships, climbed around, went below to inspect the crew's quarters, took pictures of ourselves at the wheel, and let our imaginations soar. In my mind, I was in the bow of the whaleboat, harpoon in hand, ready for a Nantucket sleigh ride when the harpooned whale made a run for it, dragging the boat along.

"You look strange," Margo, my companion, said. "Are you all right?" Of course I was all right. What do women know about these male fantasies, anyway?

We had a quick lunch at the Gallery near the entrance, and the food was fast and good. A hearty clam chowder, followed by fried flounder, seemed appropriate for the occasion. If you don't want to take the time for a proper lunch, you can get hot dogs, ice cream, lemonade, cookies, and other snacks from costumed vendors around the grounds. We can vouch for the freshness of the popcorn from a steam-powered vintage stand.

Over lunch, we chatted about Mystic. Before the Civil War, Mystic yards built clipper ships, including the *David Crockett*, whose average performance on more than 25 runs around Cape Horn to San Francisco was never equalled. The town then was the home of prosperous merchants and fishing and whaling captains, but went into a decline when shipbuilding fell on hard times in the 1870s.

The Marine Historical Association Inc. was formed here in 1929 to establish a museum to preserve the remnants of America's maritime history. The name was changed in 1978 to Mystic Seaport Museum Inc. I objected to the word museum. Although Mystic has the artifacts and authenticity of a great museum, the word doesn't suggest the fun to be had here. I love museums, mind you, but I don't go to them for fun.

Enough! It was time to get out on the water. We boarded the 57-foot *Sabino*, a handsome 1908 coal-fired passenger steamboat, for a four-hour cruise on the river. It was a perfect way to get a closer look at some of the other jewels in the seaport's collection of 400 or so historic vessels.

Beauties that caught our eye included the two-masted *Sharpie*, the oyster sloop *Nellie*, the Noank smack *Emma C. Berry*, the Friendship sloop *Estella A.* and the exquisite 61-foot yacht-schooner *Brilliant*. More boats are on display in the small-boat exhibit and the north boat shed.

Our favorite, though, was the handsome but odd-looking *Annie*, a survivor of a long-forgotten class called Sandbaggers that once raced for big money on Long Island Sound. They were 29-footers but were allowed to carry as much sail as they could handle. The *Annie*, with a long, downward-curved wooden bowsprit and a bumpkin (pronounced boom-kin), could carry as much sail as a 60-footer. To keep it from capsizing, its crew of 14 kept busy moving sandbags around the cockpit. There are alternative ways to get out on the water. Sailors may hire a 12-foot Beetlecat at the Lighthouse Point Boat House; for landlubbers, there are classic wooden rowboats. Both are excellent craft for exploring the harbor.

If you have children in tow, tow them to the hands-on Children's Museum to see the collection of 19th-century toys and games. They can assemble small hulls, masts, and sails and launch their creations in an old claw-footed bathtub. A special area for the under-7 set has replicas of century-old children's clothing they can try on.

Everybody enjoys the planetarium. The evening show is followed by stargazing through telescopes on the lawn. A computer in the lobby gives a simple introduction to steering by the stars. Classes are offered in celestial navigation, dead reckoning, and astronomy.

Mystic is in the education business in a big way. It is the home of the Frank C. Munson Memorial Institute of American Maritime Studies, which gives graduate-level courses in American maritime history. Undergraduates come here for the semester-long Williams College-Mystic Seaport program, to study maritime history, art, literature, oceanography, and marine biology.

High school groups come on day trips, and seaport teachers visit area classrooms. Some lucky teenagers stay aboard the *Joseph Conrad* for a while, learning the fundamentals of sailing, small-boat safety, and other maritime subjects.

I found some special places at Mystic. In the Wendell Building was a superb exhibit of figureheads and ship carvings and a display of ship models, scrimshaw, and marine and ship paintings and prints.

I spent a happy hour browsing in the G.W. Blunt White Library, one of the greatest maritime libraries anywhere. Its collection includes 60,000 books and periodicals, 500,000 manuscripts, 7,000 maps and charts, and an archive of oral-history tapes.

My other find was the Mystic Seaport Stores and Gallery next to the entrance. You won't find the usual souvenirs there (they're in the Variety Store across from the village green), but for something truly special, this is the place. A bookstore offers a large selection of marine books. Sailors can shop for clothing and foul-weather gear.

The Gallery has ship models, prints, paintings, wood carvings, and sculpture that range in price from several hundred to many thousands of dollars. I lusted after a carving of an eagle and a masterful model of the USS Constitution, but they would have set me back about $12,000, and that's farther back than I care to go.

In the cool of the evening, we went to the village green to hear the Silver Cornet Band. The day had been long, and we were pleasantly tired. As we relaxed, I made the mistake of looking at the list of the day's events. We had missed more than we had seen.

Where were we when the wheel-boat demonstration was going on? Or the Dead Horse Ceremony, whatever that was? Margo would have enjoyed the 19th-century garden tour. I was of two minds about the Breeches Buoy Rescue, but I certainly would have liked the lecture "Scrimshaw: The Folk Art of the Whaleman."

"We are coming back here," I said as we were leaving. "I don't want an argument. We are coming back here."

"Yes, little boy, we'll come back."

Now what did she mean by that?

—Chuck Lawliss

Directions from Philadelphia: To drive to Mystic Seaport, take the New Jersey Turnpike to the George Washington Bridge exit, cross the bridge, and pick up the Cross Bronx Expressway to the New England Thruway (Interstate 95). Mystic Seaport is one mile south of Exit 90 on Route 27.

Mystic Seaport is open every day of the year except Christmas. Hours vary through the year. For more information, including a schedule of events, write to Mystic Seaport Museum, Box 6000, Mystic, Conn. 06355-0990, or phone 203-572-0711. Parking is free in two large lots across from the entrance. Admission at press time was $15 for adults, $7.50 for ages 6 to 15, free for children 5 and under. The seaport offers various membership plans that lower the price of admission. Admission includes all activities, except the carriage and wagon rides, boat rentals, and rides on the steamer Sabino.

Neighbor cities, worlds apart

NORWALK AND STAMFORD, CONN.

THIS IS A TALE OF TWO CITIES, one that is embracing its past and one that has dramatically moved away from it.

Norwalk and Stamford are just a few miles apart on the north coast of Long Island Sound. Both were founded about 1640. Both are about the same size today.

But while Norwalk still has that small-town Connecticut look, Stamford has converted much of its center into a skyscraper farm. Because of this, the two can make for an interesting weekend beyond Manhattan, yet still within Saturday-night striking distance of Broadway —less than an hour away by train.

You can still find the soul of old Stamford, but you have to look very hard. The city decided during the 1950s that, because of its proximity to Manhattan, its future lay in office space. Thus, the town center is glass towers and indoor parking lots; at least there are some good restaurants.

Norwalk decided its future lay in its past, and even built its grand new Maritime Center—an aquarium, museum, and IMAX theater—in the restored 19th-century Norwalk Ironworks. And its historic South Norwalk area has become a charming enclave of art galleries, restaurants, craft shops, and stores.

To begin a visit here, start with Norwalk. Get off the Connecticut Turnpike (Interstate 95) at Exit 16 and follow the signs to the tourist office to pick up maps and brochures and to plan your visit.

From here, head for the Maritime Center, where playful harbor seals splash in an indoor-outdoor pool near the entrance. Inside is a tank with sharks, stingrays, and other kinds of marine life found in Long Island Sound, and there are at least 20 other aquariums containing sea creatures both exotic and commonplace.

The center leads visitors through exhibits that start with a shallow salt marsh and progress through deeper and deeper waters.

There is a "touch tank" where children can handle sea stars and shellfish. A "sandy shore" exhibit identifies the maritime detritus you may encounter while walking along the beach.

"Dirty Water Blues" is an exhibit in which visitors follow a "river" through rural, suburban, and city areas to the estuaries and bays of Long Island Sound. Along the way, you get a fish's-eye view of sources of pollution.

A powerful and dramatic exhibit in the center's museum is "Shark!" This covers 7,000 square feet of space. The exhibition includes live sharks and rays, as well as a number of interactive devices that help to tell the story of how the 375 species of shark have survived for so long, and why they are now threatened.

A boatmaking exhibit shows various vessels in different stages of construction. And from Memorial Day through Labor Day, a 30-minute boat ride takes you from the dock near the Maritime Center to Sheffield Island and its historic lighthouse. It's a pleasant place for a picnic.

The center's restaurant and oyster bar has a large mural depicting oyster shuckers—one of the Depression-era murals created for the Works Progress Administration in the 1930s. The mural was originally in a high school, but the center restored it and moved it there. Fifteen other WPA murals adorn the walls of Norwalk City Hall.

Just a short walk down Water Street from the Marine Center is Washington Street, the heart of what's called the "SoNo district," for South Norwalk. The first thing you will see is Jeremiah Donovan's wonderful old (1892) tavern, and you should not leave town without tasting its terrific clam chowder.

Strolling up Washington Street, you can stop in a deli, buy ice cream, or eat at places named Sweptaway or Pasta Nostra.

Downtown, at Wall Street and East Avenue, the Mill Hill Historic Park is the site of several historic buildings—the Town House Museum, the School House, and the Governor Thomas Fitch law office, which dates to 1798. These building are open Sundays from 1 to 4 p.m., but you can visit the park any time to view the structures from the outside and, perhaps, peek in a window or two.

This 50-room mansion was built in 1868 for LeGrand Lockwood, a millionaire stockbroker and railroad magnate. He hired the finest craftsmen to work with the finest materials to create his mansion, which predates by 20 years the elegant residences of the New York and Newport plutocrats.

The granite exterior is imposing, but it's the interior that dazzles.

From the marble flooring at the entrance to the delicate paintings in the "Card Room" to the sweeping staircase with its 260 carved and inlaid balusters, the museum is a remarkable showcase of decoration.

The home is rich in plaster, wood, and marble carvings. It also has exceptional murals, stenciled walls, and inlay work throughout. The rooms are large and, though opulently decorated, the overall effect is not overwhelming. There is a sense of cohesion and airiness.

Several of the rooms have been restored to their original beauty, including the conservatory, the dining room, and the drawing room. Upstairs is a collection of music boxes dating to the early 19th century. The mansion is open from March to mid-December, Tuesday through Friday, 11 a.m. to 3 p.m., and Sunday, 1 to 4 p.m.

To get to Stamford from Norwalk, take the Merritt Parkway, Route 15, southeast to Exit 35. This will deposit you in the northern part of town, a short distance from the Stamford Museum & Nature Center—118 acres of museum, sculpture, lake, demonstration farm, and picnic area.

And birds. The center attracts lots of people-friendly waterfowl that will rally round any human who seems disposed to feed them. From the picnic area, you pass the otter pool and enter Heckscher Farm, with its farm animals and exhibition of tools built around the theme "The Farmer's Year." There are demonstrations of how to make cider and maple syrup.

The center's museum, called the Manor House, is the former home of Henri Bendel of fashion fame.

The museum has several galleries that display art from its own collections and from other sources in a number of exhibitions. It also houses a planetarium, an observatory, a Northern American Indian room, and a natural history room. On the first floor is an exhibition of antique bottles drawn from collections around the country, most notably from the Corning glass collection. Museum hours are 9 a.m. to 5 p.m., except on Sunday, when it's 1 to 5 p.m.

Outside there are also some nature and sculpture trails.

Also worth a visit in Stamford is the Historical Society, south of the Nature Center on High Ridge Road, which has displays relating to the history of Stamford and Connecticut and dating to the 17th century. The museum is open from noon to 4 p.m., Tuesday through Sunday.

The Historical Society also maintains the Hoyt-Barnum House, at Hoyt and Bradford streets. Stamford's oldest building (1699), it has been restored and furnished with period furniture and is open from 3 to 6 p.m. Thursday to Saturday from May to October. New York's Whitney Museum has a branch in the center of town that has exhibitions put together from its main collection.

One place you don't want to miss is called the United House Wrecking Co., a huge, barnlike building filled with everything from junk to antiques and the mundane to the bizarre. Statuary, some of it out-landish and funny, decorates the large yard and the spacious interior. There are antique typewriters and cash registers, totem poles, huge vases, old street signs, gargoyles, and much more. United Wrecking is at 535 Hope St., south of the nature center.

—John Corr and Marjorie Matthews Corr

Directions from Philadelphia: Take the New Jersey Turnpike north to the George Washington Bridge. Cross the bridge and follow I-95 across the Bronx and into Connecticut. Then follow the route out-lined above.

For information about Stamford, write to the Greater Stamford Con-vention and Visitors Bureau, One Landmark Square, Stamford, Conn. 06901, or call 203-359-4761. For information on Norwalk, contact Coastal Fairfield County Tourism, 297 West Ave., Norwalk, Conn. 06850, or call 203-854-7825.

They all came to Newport

NEWPORT, R.I.

PEOPLE HAVE BEEN DRAWN HERE for many reasons, for many centuries.

The abundance of fish and shellfish in the surrounding waters, where Narragansett Bay meets the Atlantic Ocean, brought American Indians long before the country's recorded history began.

The first white settlers, refugees from Massachusetts, came here in 1639 seeking a place where they could worship in freedom. The toler-ance they established soon drew other religious outcasts: Quakers in 1657 and Sephardic Jews in 1658.

By the early 1700s, merchants and seamen were thronging here

from Britain and the West Indies, making Newport one of the busiest
and most important Colonial ports.

In the 19th century, it was not freedom or wealth that drew the visitors, but the summer breezes. Southern planters early in the century,
and New York's elite after 1880, fixed on Newport as the place to be in
July and August. Astors and Vanderbilts led the parade of wealthy New
Yorkers who built fabulous summer mansions and called them "cottages," spent the afternoons coaching up and down Bellevue Avenue,
and made the town the yachting capital of America. The place remained a summering spot for the affluent well into this century.

By the 1960s, Newport was also bringing in the masses—well, all
right, the middle class—with events that remain inextricably linked
with that decade: the annual Folk and Jazz Festivals.

Now, in the 1990s, it can be your turn. Newport still beckons the
traveler with its water, boats, and breezes, its Gilded Age "cottages" and
blocks of Colonial-era houses, its museums and music festivals.

The trip can be done in a weekend, but a weekend is hardly enough
time to take it all in. You may want to add a day or two.

First, a bit of orientation. Downtown Newport is split roughly into
two sections, the pre-Revolutionary jumble of narrow streets along
Thames (pronounced Thaymes) Street and the western waterfront, and
the 19th-century mansion district that faces the sea to the east along
Bellevue Avenue. The waterfront jumble is best explored on foot, but
you'll want to use a car along Bellevue Avenue, where streets are wider
and there's more distance to be covered.

A good introduction to the city is the Museum of Newport History,
which opened in December 1993. It's housed in the 1770 Palladian-
style brick market building, and its exhibits of photographs, paintings,
and artifacts trace Newport from its original Indian encampments to
the present day. There are lots of voice-overs, too, with readings from
contemporary journals and descriptions of life and events.

The museum is on Thames Street at Washington Square, the heart of
the Colonial-era town. The streets that fan out from it are dense with
lovingly restored houses, most owner-occupied and not open to the
public. But a wander around gives a wonderful feel for life in a prosperous Colonial town.

For an inside look at one Colonial's life, walk or drive the short distance to Hunter House, on Washington Street, a restored Colonial merchant's home that's open to the public and outfitted with furniture by

Newport's pre-eminent Colonial cabinetmakers, Goddard and Townsend.

A walk in the Washington Square neighborhood will also take you past, or into, three houses of worship that symbolize Rhode Island's history of toleration.

On Touro Street is the Touro Synagogue, the oldest surviving synagogue in North America. Built in 1759, it is patterned after the mother synagogue of the Sephardic diaspora in Amsterdam. You can't just wander through it, but there are frequent guided tours except on the Sabbath and holy days.

Down Farewell Street is the 1699 Quaker meetinghouse, the oldest religious building in Rhode Island. It's open only by appointment, but worth walking past. The wooden structure is massive, but appropriately plain.

At Spring and Church streets is Trinity Church, whose steeple towers over the surrounding trees and is visible from the waterfront. Inside are the traditional box pews, as well as Tiffany stained-glass windows, a rare wineglass pulpit, and an organ that legend says was tested by composer George Frideric Handel in England before being shipped to the United States.

A short walk south of the museum along Thames Street brings you to the waterfront. Much of it has been tarted up with T-shirt stores, souvenir malls, bars, and outdoor restaurants that attract the singles crowd after dark. But walk out onto Bowen's Wharf during the day and you'll find Aquidneck Lobster Co., where fishing boats still unload and you can walk past tank after tank of live fish and lobsters to get a flavor of the old working waterfront.

If you're like most tourists, though, the Newport you really want to see is the Gilded Age colony—with its immense accretions of marble and vermeil, silk and brocade, sculpture and parquet and crystal—that housed turn-of-the century New York society during its summer "season."

The biggest "cottage," and the one that attracts the most visitors, is the Breakers, designed by Richard Morris Hunt for Cornelius Vanderbilt II, the grandson of the Cornelius who created the New York Central Railroad. Of its 70 rooms, 33 were used by servants. Even the children's playhouse is monumental, with three full-sized rooms and a working fireplace.

As the oldest Vanderbilt of his generation, the second Cornelius was the de facto head of New York society, and in building the Breakers he felt obliged to outdo the rest of Newport. The public rooms on the ground floor, including a music room and a morning room, are as outrageously baroque and encrusted as one might expect. The family bedrooms, however, are a bit more restrained, in a style said to be more in keeping with the tastes of Cornelius and his wife, Alice Gwynne. Restraint, however, is all relative: There are damask and brocade a-plenty, and bathrooms are supplied with salt as well as fresh water.

One of the bedrooms open to the public is that of daughter Gertrude Vanderbilt Whitney, a sculptor whose frustration at museum snubs of women artists led her to found the Whitney Museum of American Art in New York.

Women were the movers and schemers of New York social life, as many Newport mansions show. Rosecliff, for example, was the folly of Theresa Fair Oelrichs, whose husband, Hermann, was the American agent for his family's North German Lloyd shipping line. Tessie had come into a fortune in her own right: Her engineer father had made a pile mining Nevada's Comstock silver lode.

She had Stanford White model Rosecliff after the Grand Trianon, Louis XIV's outbuilding escape from the court at the Versailles palace. The house is dominated by the biggest ballroom in Newport, 40 feet wide and 80 feet long, with arched doors that open onto a garden on the west and to the lawn overlooking the ocean on the east. Crystal and ormolu chandeliers hang from a ceiling of carved and molded decorations that surround a panel painted to look like a cloud-filled sky.

Rosecliff will look familiar to anyone who saw the movie *The Great Gatsby*; some of its scenes were filmed here.

Marble House, built for Cornelius Vanderbilt's younger brother William Kissam Vanderbilt and his wife, Alva, is "a tremendous example of an architect run amok," Newport historian Eileen Warburton said in an interview, but is interesting also because its exhibits and furnishings show the metamorphosis of a social climber into a woman of purpose.

Alva Vanderbilt was "the first woman to bob her hair, the first to drive a car and the first to divorce her husband," according to Warburton. After her second husband died, she became active in the movement to give women the vote and opened Marble House for fund-raising events.

South and west of town, a peninsula jutting into the bay is ringed by Ocean Drive, which provides both famous ocean views and the entrance to Hammersmith Farm, the summer White House of John F. Kennedy. The 28-room house overlooking Narragansett Bay is open to the public.

If all this history isn't enough, Newport has plenty to offer sports and culture buffs, too.

The 19th-century Newport Casino, built as a club for high society and site of the first national tennis championship in 1881, is home to the International Tennis Hall of Fame. Enclosed within the casino's oval are grass courts that can be rented by the hour, and a restaurant in the casino serves both indoors and at tables by the court's edge.

Sailors might investigate the Museum of Yachting, whose exhibits include large-scale replicas of America's Cup contenders of the 1930s, and the fascinating Hall of Fame for Single-Handed Sailors, which honors men and women who made long ocean journeys alone.

For culture vultures, the Newport Art Museum collects and displays Newport and New England art. And there's theater, too, at Stage 3, the Rhode Island Repertory Theatre.

—Andrea Knox

Directions from Philadelphia: Newport is about a six-hour drive from Philadelphia. Take the New Jersey Turnpike north to the George Washington Bridge, cross the bridge, and follow I-95 through the Bronx until it becomes the Connecticut Turnpike and crosses into Rhode Island. Follow 95 to 138 east to Route 1 north to 138 east again to Newport.

For more information about forthcoming events and accommodations, call the local Convention and Visitors Bureau at 401-849-8098.

Paul Revere's home

BOSTON, MASS.

> Listen, my children, and you shall hear
> Of the midnight ride of Paul Revere.
> —Henry Wadsworth Longfellow

TO MOST AMERICANS, the Fourth of July marks the nation's birthday. But ask any Bostonian worth his beans and he'll tell you that the 18th of April is when U.S. history really got started. For it was on that date at 10 p.m. in 1775 that a 40-year-old gold- and silversmith (and part-time dentist) named Paul Revere left his small wood frame house on North Square to embark on the midnight mission that would become immortalized by Henry Wadsworth Longfellow.

That house, which was already 90 years old when Revere moved in with his wife, Sara, their five children, and his elderly mother, Deborah, is still standing today—the last remaining structure from 17th-century Boston. Each year, some 200,000 people walk through its rooms, soaking up the atmosphere of at least one family's lifestyle in Revolutionary Boston.

Many visitors to the city like to visit "the Reveres' place" in April, when New Englanders celebrate Patriot's Day, a period filled with parades, battle reenactments, musters, and ceremonies that commemorate the events of April 18–19 and the start of the American Revolution. Two lanterns are hung in the steeple of nearby Old North Church, guns roar as the Battle of Lexington heats up once again, and you can usually find a modern-day version of Paul, himself, riding off in a cloud of dust to warn of the British approach. (The Boston Marathon, now a regular part of the Patriot's Day activities, was added in 1897, a bit later in history.)

There is something to be said for a walk through the three-story structure any time of year. Take it all in and you'll come away not only learning a lot about the way people lived in those days, you'll also shatter a few myths.

For example, you'll discover that the midnight ride was not a total success. Revere made it to Lexington, where he succeeded in warning John Hancock and Sam Adams of the British approach. From there, he set out toward Concord, but never arrived. Riding with William Dawes, a second courier, and Samuel Prescott, a local doctor, he was intercepted by a British patrol halfway to Concord. Dawes evaded the patrol but lost his horse and never reached his destination. Revere was detained for a short time, his horse was taken from him, and he was forced to return to Lexington on foot. Only Prescott escaped successfully and completed the mission to Concord.

Revere, now a wanted man, couldn't return to Boston, so he stayed in Watertown, where he printed currency for the Provincial Congress and did other work for the cause. It was not until almost a year later that he was able to return to his family and the house at 19 North Square.

When Revere bought the place in 1770, the house had already changed hands several times since its construction in 1680 by Robert Howard, a wealthy merchant. It had also undergone several alterations. The roofline was raised, with windows added to the third story. New doors, clapboards, trim, and windows helped update the home for the Revere family.

Today, the house reflects both its original 17th-century appearance and the later Revere period, so the self-guided stroll through the four rooms available to visitors provides a pretty good impression of the way the Reveres lived. For urban women such as Sara (and Paul's second wife, Rachel, whom he married in 1773 after Sara's death), managing the household was a full-time job, with food preparation a major portion of the task.

The kitchen, with its wooden crossbeams and low, white ceiling, is typical of the period. Iron pots, kettles, and other cooking utensils hang over the brick fireplace, foodstuffs hang from the walls. Nearby, on a small wooden table, sits a bowl filled with eggs. It was probably also the job of each Mrs. Revere to raise the chickens.

Next to the kitchen on the first floor is a room called The Hall. The oak-beamed room was certainly the most versatile in the Colonial house. At various times of the day it was used as a parlor, dining room, spare bedroom, workshop, and business office. The English and American furniture in this room actually reflects the period before the Reveres moved in, probably a bit closer to what was used by Robert Howard. The pieces include a press cupboard used to store linens, a red, wool-covered daybed, a three-cornered chair, and gateleg table. Don't look for carpeting; bare floors were the norm. Any wealthy Colonial family that could afford carpeting probably used it as a table covering.

Upstairs, in the yellow and white "Best Chamber," are several pieces of furniture that actually belonged to the Revere family. They include the bow-front dresser to the left of the bed; a large upholstered chair, now re-covered in a period cream, red, and green floral print on cotton cloth; and a ladies' work table with a green sewing basket on it. The four-post bed is a period piece, but not one actually used by the Reveres. Here again, the room is multifunctional, serving as both the master bedroom and an elegant parlor. The practice of using rooms for several different purposes was especially common in middle-class homes, which often didn't have separate parlors or sitting rooms.

On the way into the children's room is a fascinating showcase containing several original Revere silver engravings as well as an ad for his dental services. (He made house calls.) It was between 1768 and 1775 that Revere supplemented his income by cleaning original teeth and wiring in false ones—a trade he had picked up from a Dr. John Baker, the local surgeon-dentist.

A look at the small upstairs children's room makes you wonder whether Revere was a magician as well as a silversmith and dentist. Between Sara and Rachel, there were 16 children, and it's hard to see where he put them all. But according to Revere House curator Edith Steblecki, the Revere offspring were born over a 30-year-period, and five died in infancy. The others moved away from the family as they married, and so it was likely that there were never more than five to seven children living in the home at one time. There are also two more rooms in the third-floor attic that aren't restored.

Like the person it was named for, the Revere House itself has quite a history, reflecting the colorful Boston North End neighborhood in which it stands. Revere sold the place in 1800. After 1820, the North End became an immigrant neighborhood, populated in turn by African Americans, Irish, Eastern European Jews, Portuguese, and then Italians, who remain in large numbers today. During the 19th century, the house served as a tenement, grocery store, bank, and even a candy and cigar factory.

In 1905, when the building was scheduled to be demolished, Revere's great-grandson, John P. Reynolds, Jr., organized support to save the house. Today, there are an estimated 1,000 living Revere descendants, including a great-great-great-grandson (named Paul Revere Jr.) who is president of the memorial association that runs the Revere House.

But don't look for too many similarities between today's Paul Revere and his legendary ancestor. "I don't ride horses!" the current version proclaims.

—Bert Shanas

Directions from Philadelphia: Take the Garden State Parkway north to the New York Thruway (I-287). Follow 287 east across the Tappan Zee Bridge to I-684. Take 684 to I-84 northeast to the Massachusetts Turnpike. Follow to Boston.

ॐ

Beyond the witches

SALEM, MASS.

WHEN I WAS ABOUT 11 YEARS OLD, an old woman pulled up in a car near the Salem Common, where I was playing, rolled down her window, and said in a Southern accent, "Do you know Hester Prynne?"

"What?" I eyed her suspiciously. Was this what they meant when they said to beware of strangers?

"Hester Prynne," she repeated, making the name two syllables Preein. "Do you know her?" There was a mischievous glint in her eye.

"Sorry, lady, I don't," I said, edging away.

"Then, young man, you should be better-read!" And off she went.

That's how tourists visiting Salem, Mass., were in those days—a literate bunch, and a little odd, too. They knew their Hawthorne, and expected Salem boys to know the heroine of Hawthorne's *The Scarlet Letter*.

I miss those days, and those kinds of tourists. Visitors still come in droves today, but most of them not for Hester Prynne's sake, nor to see the birthplace of *The Scarlet Letter's* author; they come for witches.

Oh, witches have always been big here: the high school football team is the Fighting Witches (W-I-T-C-H-E-S Rah! Rah! Rah!) and the city's official logo —a witch riding on a broomstick—adorns every police car and is embossed on my high school ring. And witches were a very big deal for the town in 1992, the 300th anniversary of the infamous Salem witch trials.

Salem is more than witches, though, as those who were asked dumb questions about Nathaniel Hawthorne know. The city claims an important literary legacy as birthplace of one of the most influential American authors of the 19th century. Salem's bloody history served as inspiration for his two most important novels: *The House of the Seven Gables* and *The Scarlet Letter*.

Despite the community's influence on Hawthorne, Salemites have a right to be skittish about honoring him—he didn't like his hometown, and made no secret of the fact. He was mortified by the witch trials and the role played by his ancestor, Col. John Hathorne, one of the trials' judges, calling the episode "a hideous epoch." And he railed against Salem's stodgy parochialism as the town settled into sleepy tranquillity in the 1820s and the 1830s, after Salem ceased to be significant as a port.

"Salem is my dwelling place," he wrote disparagingly; yet he lived 37 of his 60 years in Salem, residing there off and on from his birth in 1804 until his final departure from the town in 1849, obsessed by its past, wishing to escape its present.

The depth of the Salem-Hawthorne connection was unknown to me, a native son. Only upon this visit to my hometown did I discover that despite the author's ambivalent relations with his birthplace, Salem can claim an astounding wealth of Hawthorne memorabilia available to serious Hawthorne students or to casual visitors who may want a break from the relentless witch-hunt hoopla.

But what can the visitor see?

First there is the House of the Seven Gables itself (it actually has eight gables), the 17th-century mansion that served as the inspiration for the novel. Built in 1668, it is a marvelous example of 17th-century architecture with steeply pitched, overhanging roofs and black clapboards. Located at the foot of Turner Street right on Salem Harbor, the house is officially known as the Turner-Ingersoll House, but the locals call it the Gables.

Hawthorne's cousin, Susannah Ingersoll, lived there when he was a young man, and he was a frequent visitor to the house. During Hawthorne's time, the house had only five gables; the others had been removed during the many alterations the house had undergone as owners remodeled to fit changing styles.

Today, the exterior looks much as it did in the 18th century, with all gables intact and large framed windows replacing the original casement windows. It's a brooding, melancholy edifice with clapboards that ". . . grew black in the prevalent east-wind . . . " and had "a meditative look," as Hawthorne wrote in the novel.

Inside, though, the low ceilings and brightly painted and papered rooms and the large windows overlooking the garden and the sea beyond offer a cheery contrast to the rather gloomy exterior.

Six rooms are open to the public, and, with the exception of the 17th-century kitchen, are furnished with period pieces from the 1830s and '40s, when Hawthorne was visiting the place, so that the Hawthorne connection with the house remains paramount. Many of the furnishings are originals that belonged to Susannah Ingersoll. Of particular interest to Hawthorne enthusiasts is the serpentine-front desk located in the parlor overlooking the harbor; this desk was owned by the Hawthorne family, and was most likely used by the author himself.

Perhaps the most interesting feature in the house is the secret stairway, a twisting staircase built inside one of the house's large chimneys around the time of the witch trials. It was forgotten for more than a century and only rediscovered in the 1880s while the house was being renovated. Its original purpose a mystery, the secret stairway was removed during the remodeling; this one is a reconstruction.

The House of the Seven Gables has name recognition, but many of the 150,000 yearly visitors aren't sure what it really means. "Prior to the 1970s people came here because they had read the novel," says David Goss, director of The House of the Seven Gables (his statement made me think of the southern woman of 28 years before), "and that served this institution very well. In the 1970s and '80s we see people who have heard the name, but are only aware that it's a spooky, old house, and they seem obscure about the Hawthorne connection. Our responsibility is to fill them in on the literary and historical context."

Visitors should take the time to visit the grave of Hawthorne's great-great grandfather, Col. John Hathorne of witch-trial infamy, who is buried in Charter Street Cemetery in the heart of downtown Salem. According to legend, the judge was cursed by one of the convicted witches. This supposed curse weighed so heavily on Hawthorne that he inserted the "w" in his name to disassociate himself from his relative.

The curse affected his writing as well, for in *The House of the Seven Gables*, convicted witch Matthew Maule points from the scaffold to his judge and executioner, Colonel Pyncheon, and shouts, "God will give him blood to drink!" The connection between Hawthorne's family and his fictional Pyncheons is unmistakable. Nonetheless the cemetery, scattered with old tombstones set amid towering oak trees, offers a spot to take a break during the walking tour of Salem.

Those wishing to know more about Hawthorne's literary life should visit the James Duncan Phillips Library of the Essex Institute, located on Essex Street, which contains the world's largest Hawthorne collection. More than 10,000 pieces of Hawthorniana are housed in the institute, including virtually every edition of Hawthorne's works, and many editions in which Hawthorne's works have appeared or have been reviewed.

The collection includes correspondence between Hawthorne and his literary contemporaries, including Emerson, Thoreau, and Melville, and letters written to family members. There are also many photographs of Hawthorne and of his contemporaries, as well as Charles Osgood's 1840 oil portrait, the most famous likeness of the author. The institute even includes the manuscripts of a newspaper he published himself before he left Salem to attend Bowdoin College.

"There is no collection like it in the world," says William T. La Moy, director of the library.

That all may seem daunting to the casual tourist, and indeed most of the users of the collection are scholars. But La Moy points out that local high school students use the library as a resource when writing term papers, and tourists do come in to ask to see Hawthorne's signature or to see his famous portrait.

La Moy says, "People often see us after visiting the Gables; they come here to complete the visit." Annually, about 2,500 people use the library.

Another way to "complete" a Hawthorne visit is to see the place in Salem where he worked for three years: the Salem Custom House at 174 Derby St., operated today as part of the Salem Maritime National Historic Site (the oldest National Historic Site in the country). From 1846 to 1849, Hawthorne was Surveyor of the Port of Salem, a political job he got through his connections with President Franklin Pierce, a Democrat and classmate at Bowdoin. Hawthorne needed the job to support his growing family; he was 42 years old and had had only minor literary success to that point.

The Custom House, built in 1819, is an imposing, two-story, red-brick Federalist structure. To enter the front door, visitors must climb a flight of granite steps, at the top of which stands a double row of white pillars supporting an elegantly carved balustrade. On the roof of the building a carved golden eagle with outstretched wings keeps watch over the long-ago deserted harbor.

The sparsely furnished room where Hawthorne labored is on the first floor and offers a sweeping view of Derby Wharf and Salem Harbor. Visitors can see such Hawthorne artifacts as his pen and his weighing scales (to weigh cargos). The remaining rooms open to the public are decorated in the opulent style of the 1870s and 1880s, long after Hawthorne was dead, and are the original furnishings provided by Custom House officials from that period.

Hawthorne lost his job at the Custom House when administrations changed in Washington, and he was forced to look for other work. Ironically, this commenced the most productive period of his literary life; shortly after his dismissal, he published *The Scarlet Letter*, in 1850.

His unhappiness over his firing is borne out in the preface of *The Scarlet Letter*, when he used the eagle over the Custom House as a metaphor for the U.S. government: ". . . she has no great tenderness, even in her best moods, and, sooner or later . . . is apt to fling off her nestlings, with a scratch of her claw, a dab of her beak . . ." Political sour grapes!

All of the Salem houses in which Hawthorne lived still stand. The Hawthorne birthplace, where he was born on July 4, 1804, is located on the grounds of the House of the Seven Gables and is a noticeable example of a mid-18th-century frame house. A 2½-story structure with gambrel roof dominated by a large central chimney, it was a typical residence for Salem's working families of Hawthorne's time and shows the humble beginnings of the author, whose family fortunes had declined after the death of Col. John Hathorne.

It stands in vivid contrast to the grandeur of the Gables. Unlike the gaily papered Gables, the birthplace's walls are whitewash with reddish-brown and blue paneling, reflecting the somber Puritan influence of Salem's working classes.

Originally, the Hawthorne birthplace was located on Union Street, a narrow lane that runs between Salem Common and Derby Street. One of my earliest memories is from 1958, when the house was moved, propped up on huge timbers on a flatbed trailer. Ever so slowly, the old house crept down the street toward the harbor and its "final" resting place on the grounds of the Gables.

Other Hawthorne residences are private homes scattered throughout the city and are not open to the public. These include the house at 10½ Herbert St., one street over from Union. It was the home of his mother's family, the Mannings, where the author lived for the better part of 30 years, and where he wrote his first novel, *Fanshawe*, and early short stories published as *Twice Told Tales*.

I used to live in the former Hawthorne residence at 14 Mall St., near Salem Common, Hawthorne's home during most of his Custom House years, and where he wrote The Scarlet Letter. We lived on the second floor, where Hawthorne's mother and sisters lived. The author and his wife and children lived on the first floor; his study was on the third floor. Sharing the fate of many of Salem's large 18th- and 19th-century houses, it has been converted into condominiums.

Hawthorne lived briefly on Chestnut Street, the most elegant street in Salem, lined with exquisite Federalist mansions. The house, number 18, where he lived in 1847, just after his appointment as surveyor, is a three-story, wood-frame structure, reputed to be the oldest residence on Chestnut Street, built before 1800. Despite its elegant location, the house proved too small for Hawthorne's growing family, so he moved to Mall Street.

After losing his surveyor's job, Hawthorne left Salem for good. Although he never returned after 1849, and lies buried elsewhere, his mark on the city is indelible. Any visitor to Salem, even one with only the most passing interest in the author, will find a fascinating trove of Hawthorne lore in the "Witch City."

And a certain southern woman would be glad to know that I have made my acquaintance with Hester Prynne.

—James F. Lee

Directions from Philadelphia: The drive is about seven hours. Take the New Jersey Turnpike north to the Garden State Parkway and follow the parkway north and into New York State to Interstate 287. Take I-287 east and across the Tappan Zee Bridge to Interstate 684. Take I-684 north to Interstate 84. Follow I-84 east, through Hartford, Conn., and into Massachusetts where it meets Interstate 90, the Massachusetts Turnpike. Take the turnpike east to Route 128 north. From Route 128 exit to Route 114 east and follow it into Salem. Salem has a new set of tourist signs and markings that are quite easy to follow.

Of the Hawthorne residences, only the birthplace is open to the public. Other Hawthorne-related sites include:

The House of the Seven Gables (includes the Hawthorne birth-place and two other historic houses), 54 Turner St., Salem, Mass. 01970; phone 508-744-0991. Open every day except Thanksgiving, Christmas, New Year's Day, and the last two weeks in January.

James Duncan Phillips Library of the Essex Institute, 132 Essex St., Salem, Mass. 01970; phone 508-744-3390. The library is open Tuesdays through Fridays (Mondays, also, during the summer). Call for hours.

Salem Maritime National Historic Site, Custom House, 174 Derby St., Salem, Mass. 01970; phone 508-745-1470. Open year-round. The National Historic Site also maintains Derby Wharf and several nearby buildings, including a visitors' center; the Derby House, home of America's first millionaire; and a West India Goods Store.

A tour of country towns

SALISBURY, CONN.

WITH ITS TIDY, WHITEWASHED SHOPS and rebuilt 18th-century town hall, Salisbury could be a movie set for the ideal New England village.

Situated in the far northwestern corner of Connecticut, this is an elegant country town. One would be surprised to see a real farmer walk down Main Street; a BMW fits this place better than a John Deere.

Just a four-hour drive from Philadelphia, Salisbury is a good place to begin a weekend in the Southern Berkshires.

One could easily spend two days in this picturesque village or use it as a starting point, as we did twice, for a tour of other country towns.

Salisbury and three communities across the border in Massachusetts —Sheffield, Great Barrington, and Stockbridge—offer an eclectic mix of cultural attractions and natural beauty.

Salisbury covers 60 square miles of luxuriant meadows, roaring streams, pretty ponds, and impeccably restored farmhouses, many of them the country homes of affluent retirees.

Strolling through Salisbury's small business district, one can stop for crumpets at the Chaiwalla Tea House or pick up something to read at the tiny and tastefully cluttered Lion's Head Books.

To be invited into one of Salisbury's elegant homes is probably the best way to enjoy the place. But less fortunate out-of-towners will have to find a place to stay. And there are some to be found.

An ideal place to continue a weekend of relaxation is Sheffield, a short drive north from Salisbury on Route 41 and then right on Berkshire School Road to Route 7. There is not a great deal to Sheffield other than antiques shops, bed-and-breakfasts, beautiful scenery, and historic homes. But that's enough.

We stayed at the Orchard Shade (413-229-8463), an excellent bed-and-breakfast on Maple Avenue just off Route 7, we walked on Sheffield's beautiful country roads, also ideal for biking, and, on a clear weekend in September, gazed at the stars from the porch of the inn.

A little farther north on Route 7 is Great Barrington, a bustling commercial center in a scenic setting. If Ralph Lauren seems the fitting style for Salisbury, hiking boots and jeans seem more appropriate here. Although it is not as quaint as the two other towns, the center of Great Barrington has handsome red-brick commercial buildings, built at the turn of the century after a fire destroyed much of the business district. Now, there are interesting shops and restaurants that attract the young and the hip.

It is worth going to a movie at the Mahaiwe Theater on Castle Street no matter what is playing. Built in 1905, the Mahaiwe is a relic from a bygone era of moviegoing. There are actual opera boxes alongside the stage, which is framed in intricately worked stone. A vintage projector and old movie bills are on display in the lobby. The movie house also hosts performances by the Berkshire Ballet and the regional orchestra.

Not surprisingly, given the setting, the Great Barrington area has plenty to offer in the way of outdoor activity. There is downhill skiing at Butternut Basin Ski Resort's 21 trails in Great Barrington, and at Catamount, in nearby South Egremont.

We visited Beartown State Forest, a good place to camp, hike, cross-country ski, fish, and view the Berkshires from on high. We recommend taking a circuitous route to the park, traveling east on Route 23, making a left on Monument Valley Road and a right on Stony Brook

Road. The drive to the park affords spectacular panoramas of brilliant fall foliage.

Once you are at Beartown, it is worth taking a detour to the village of Tyringham, which holds little of interest other than one of the most unusual houses ever built. It's the Tyringham Gallery, once the studio of sculptor Henry Hudson Kitson. Half grotesque and half cute, the building looks like a witch's cottage in a ghoulish fairy tale. It has odd-size stained-glass windows and roof tiles that appear to be melting. In the summer, works of local artists are displayed there.

Traveling farther north, one comes to Stockbridge, a town that clearly caters to the tourist trade. It has the sort of small-town charm one would expect from a village that claims Norman Rockwell as a native son. The famous illustrator is memorialized in a museum, appropriately situated at the intersection of Main and Elm streets. It is open all year and houses the largest collection of Rockwell originals anywhere.

From May to October, there are tours of several historic houses in town, including one built in 1739 by a missionary to local Indians; Naumkeag, an elegant summer house built for a former ambassador to Britain; and Chesterwood, the former country home of Daniel Chester French, sculptor of several American public monuments, including the Abraham Lincoln at the Lincoln Memorial in Washington.

One can also take a stroll through the Berkshire Garden Center, a 15-acre botanical garden with a terraced herb garden and a woodland walk.

From June to October, Berkshire Walking Tours (413-738-5224) offers one-hour guided walks through Stockbridge. There are noteworthy shops in Stockbridge, and it's the site of the Berkshire Theater Festival, one of the oldest summer theaters in the country; Tanglewood, the summer home of the Boston Symphony Orchestra, is in Lenox, about 15 minutes away. There are numerous lodging options in Stockbridge, including the Federal House, a small inn with a highly recommended restaurant, and the Red Lion Inn, a huge complex that dominates the center of town. Both inns are on Route 102, the main street through Stockbridge.

New Yorkers and Bostonians are becoming increasingly attached to Stockbridge and the other towns of the Southern Berkshires and, given the relatively short distance, there's no reason why Philadelphians shouldn't join in.

Opting for a scenic route home, we took Route 102 to Interstate 90 West, making an exit at 22 South. In Millerton, we picked up Route 44 and then 199, which leads to the Taconic Parkway and eventually to the Tappan Zee Bridge. Along the way, we traveled through some of New York State's most scenic farmland.

For more information, contact the Salisbury Chamber of Commerce, Lakeville, Conn. 06039, phone 203-435-0740; the Southern Berkshire Chamber of Commerce, 413-528-1510; or Berkshire and Greater Springfield Bed & Breakfast Homes, Box 211, Williamsburg, Mass. 01096, 413-268-7244.

—Laura Quinn and Anthony R. Wood

Directions from Philadelphia: Take the Garden State Parkway north and pick up the New York Thruway (I-287) east across the Tappan Zee Bridge. Follow 287 to I-684 north, then to 22 and 44 north to Salisbury. The drive is about 4¹/₂ hours.

Folk-art paradise

SHELBURNE, VT.

THE PLACE LOOKS as if a giant child had neglected to put away the toys.

Here is a depot, there a steam locomotive. Over there, a lighthouse. Plus a covered bridge. Among the buildings scattered about are a one-room schoolhouse and a jail. And in the middle of it all, high and dry, sits a paddle-wheel steamboat.

The hodgepodge is all part of the Shelburne Museum, which is on 45 acres of beautifully landscaped land on Lake Champlain, 10 miles south of Burlington. The setting is exquisite. To the west, across the broad lake, you can see the Adirondacks; to the east are the Green Mountains.

We're here to see one of the great collections of Americana—one that attracts folk-art lovers the way Gettysburg attracts Civil War buffs. And we came on a Friday night, to make sure we had two full days to see everything.

The Shelburne—just outside the tiny village of the same name—is not a conventional museum; it's what you might call a collection of collections. One happens to be old buildings and other structures; they, in turn, house other collections.

Nor is Shelburne a restored village such as Old Sturbridge in Massachusetts or Mystic Seaport in Connecticut. All the buildings of a typical New England village are here—most of them moved from other sites—but they are not arranged in any sort of village setting. The remarkable woman who created this museum felt that restored villages were dishonest.

The woman was Electra Havermeyer Webb. She was born in 1889, the daughter of Henry Havermeyer, an immensely wealthy sugar baron. The Havermeyers, guided by their artist friend, Mary Cassatt, assembled a collection of old master and French impressionist paintings, some of which now hang in the Metropolitan Museum of Art in New York.

The Havermeyers were nonplussed when their daughter became a collector, not of impressionists, but of folk art. She bought her first cigar-store Indian in 1907, before the terms folk art and Americana were known. She also started buying such items as weather vanes, merchant trade signs, carved eagles, ships' figureheads, quilts, samplers, toys, hatboxes—almost anything old and beautiful and American that struck her fancy.

In 1910, Electra Havermeyer married J. Watson Webb, whose family owned a large summer estate here. They had five children, but this did not impede her collecting. Displaying her acquisitions soon became a problem, though, so her husband, a great-grandson of Commodore Cornelius Vanderbilt, began buying buildings to house them. Finally, they decided to turn it all into a museum, which they did in 1947 and opened to the public in 1952.

A word to the wise: You really can't see it all in one day, no matter how hard you try. (That's why all tickets are good for two days.) There are almost 40 museum buildings, 25 of them historic gems, and practically all of them are chock-full of fascinating things.

When you buy your ticket, see the eight-minute introductory slide show, and pick up the free brochure, "Shelburne Museum Map and Guide"; it will save you many steps. To save time, consider skipping the craft demonstrations at the blacksmith shop, the weaving shed, and the print shop.

Your first stop should be the *Ticonderoga*, a steel-hulled 220-foot side-wheel steamboat built in 1906 and said to be the only vessel of its kind still in existence. It's the largest and most unusual item at the museum. Now a National Historic Landmark, the *Ti*, as it is called in these parts, was an excursion boat on Lake Champlain until 1953.

Nearby is an old friend of the *Ti*'s, the Colchester Reef Lighthouse. The small white-frame lighthouse, which was built in 1871 and decommissioned in 1933, was moved here in 1952. Inside is a collection of maritime and whaling paintings and prints, figureheads and scrimshaw, and early maps and charts.

For something entirely different, walk up the gentle rise to the small white Greek Revival building that the Webb children built as an unusual memorial to their mother. It contains six of the 17 rooms from their apartment on Park Avenue in New York, faithfully re-created in every detail and containing the Webbs' furnishings, including art inherited from Electra Webb's parents. As you wander about the rooms, you'll see works by Degas, Monet, Cassatt, Goya, and Rembrandt.

One of my favorite stops at the museum is the Shelburne Railroad Depot, built in 1890 by W. Seward Webb, J. Watson Webb's father, to service the estate. Seward Webb was president of the Rutland Railroad and held many other posts. The depot is full of railroad memorabilia. On the tracks outside are a 1915 Baldwin steam locomotive and the Grand Isle, a luxurious private car that Seward Webb gave in the 1890s to the governor of Vermont.

If you have children with you, head directly for the horseshoe-shaped Circus Building, custom-built to house a 518-foot hand-carved miniature circus parade created by the contemporary artist Roy Arnold. It has bandwagons with musicians, cage wagons with animals, and riders and clowns and everything else that makes a circus a circus. It is a delight. Also on display are 40 hand-carved, full-size carousel animals and a wonderful collection of circus posters.

A real old-fashioned carousel is outside. Give the children a ride or two; it's free. And if they get out of hand, mention that there are stocks and a pillory outside the Castleton Jail.

Children also love the Toy Shop, with its handmade wooden toys, trains, banks, music boxes, and many other playthings. Electra Webb's personal collection of 1,500 dolls from all over the world is also on display in the oddly named Variety Unit, a two-story red-brick house built in 1835.

Before you call it a day, you must see the collections of quilts and samplers. Both are in the building called the Hat and Fragrance Unit, and both are exceptional.

We were spending the night at what once was Shelburne House, the Webbs' 45-room mansion, on a rise with a panoramic view of the lake. It now is the Inn at Shelburne Farms, with 24 guest rooms; an excellent restaurant serving dinner and breakfast, and a range of recreational facilities, including tennis, canoeing, croquet, hiking, lake fishing and swimming, and a game room for rainy days.

The facilities were wasted on us. After an early breakfast the next day, we toured Shelburne Farms before returning to the museum. Shelburne Farms is a 1,000-acre national historic site devoted to "preserving, maintaining and adapting its historic buildings and landscape for teaching and demonstrating the stewardship of natural and agriculture resources."

When all this land was the Webbs' private estate, it consisted of 3,800 acres, which were landscaped by Frederick Law Olmsted (who also designed Central Park in New York and a small part of Fairmount Park in Philadelphia) and forested by Gifford Pinchot.

Our tour included the 1890 Farm Barn, which was the headquarters for the estate—a five-story monster that housed offices, telephone and telegraph stations, stables, fire equipment, wagons and sleighs, blacksmith and carpenter shops, and hay, among other things.

Arriving at the museum, we began our second day in another barn, the Horseshoe Barn, which contains about 200 carriages, sleighs, farm wagons, Conestoga wagons, trade wagons, and stagecoaches. Horse-drawn farm machinery and other implements are in the adjacent Red Shed. In the 1834 Shaker Shed, a $2^1/2$-story building brought here from the Shaker Village at Canterbury, N.H., is a collection of antique woodworking tools, the centerpiece of a large collection of tools and household implements.

We visited the historic buildings next, including an 1830 schoolhouse that now houses early maps and calligraphic drawings. We toured the 1783 Stagecoach Inn, which came from Charlotte, just south of here, and exhibits carved eagles, cigar-store Indians, trade signs, and weather vanes.

We were beginning to fade, but we pushed on to the period houses, all of which have been restored and filled with vintage furniture. Among them is the Prentice House, a 1733 saltbox that is the oldest house in Shelburne.

We lingered next in the Webb Gallery, home of three centuries of American artwork, including a number of primitive paintings and early portraits. And of course, we stopped in at the museum store in the Diamond Barn.

And we still didn't see everything. For example, we missed the American Indian artifacts and North American big-game trophies in the Beach Lodge. And we also missed the old doctor's and dentist's offices upstairs at the General Store. And at least a few other exhibits.

But if we had seen everything, we might not come back.

And that would be a shame.

—Chuck Lawliss

Directions from Philadelphia: Take the New Jersey Turnpike and the Garden State Parkway to Interstate 87-287 (the New York Thruway). Follow I-87 north to Albany and continue north on I-87 (now the Adirondack Northway) to the Lake George exit. Take Route 97 north to Crown Point, cross the bridge into Vermont, and follow Route 22A and Vermont 7 to Shelburne.

The Shelburne Museum (802-985-3346) is open daily, 10 a.m. to 5 p.m., May 21 to October 23. At press time, tickets were $15 for adults, $6 for children. At other times, the museum is open only for a guided tour at 1 p.m. daily; admission was $6 for adults; $2.50 for children.

For more information about the Burlington area, including accommodations, contact the Burlington Convention and Visitors Bureau, 802-863-3489.

A well-kept travel secret

SPRINGfiELD, MASS.

FEW NEW ENGLAND TRAVELERS place Springfield on their must-see lists. But maybe they should.

It has most of the basic categories of New England travel—museums, town green, 19th-century buildings, natural beauty. It lacks a famous college, but is within an hour's drive of Smith, Mount Holyoke, Amherst, and the University of Massachusetts.

And although the word Springfield never produces the frisson in the basketball fan that Cooperstown does in a baseball enthusiast, it has the basketball hall of fame—officially called the James Naismith Memorial Hall of Fame, after the YMCA instructor who developed the game to keep his older students from going stir-crazy in the winter of 1891–1892.

Founded by Puritans in 1636, Springfield, a town of about 150,000 just north of the Connecticut border in western Massachusetts, is without doubt one of New England's best-kept travel secrets.

Springfield was the gateway to what is called Pioneer Valley, the valley of the Connecticut River, along which early settlers made their first homes. Springfield was home to an armory—whence came the Springfield rifle. That is now a weapons museum containing one of the largest collections of military small arms in the world—part of the Springfield Armory National Historic Site (413-734-8551).

After that, Springfield became primarily a small industrial town, which it is to this day.

The place to begin to see Springfield is Court Square, the town green and a simple square of grass crossed by brick paths and studded with huge trees, a tall pillar topped by a Civil War memorial, and several statues, as well as a great antebellum-looking lion fountain and a little Victorian cast-iron cupola. Along the paths are inviting red benches of wood and cast iron.

Around the square are a host of noteworthy buildings. First, facing the square, is Old First Church, the obligatory simple, white, clapboard church, with a tall spire topped by a rooster weathervane. Built in 1819, the church stands on ground first used for religious purposes in 1636, when the city was founded.

Across Court Street from the church is a distinguished group of civic buildings: the low, gray, columned, classical twins of City Hall and Symphony Hall, and, between them, the 300-foot stone campanile that is Springfield's signature building. Modeled after a Venetian bell tower, the slender, stark white campanile features a clock and a carillon of bells.

Among the other structures is the lovely Court Square building, a five-story, yellow brick confection with arched windows, iron pillars, and a little green tower. It's on the corner of Main and Elm streets and houses the Springfield Convention and Visitors Bureau (413-787-1548).

And, take a look at one more: the stone Hampden County Courthouse, a gray, crenelated castle with a tower that sort of hides behind the Old First Church. The courthouse was designed by H.H. Richardson, and it's worth examining to see what Richardson's buildings looked like when things didn't go just right.

For a look at what happened when they did go right, head east of Court Square to 18 Salem St., where stands one of his best—a brownstone church that features outstanding examples of the arches, towers, and turrets that can make Richardson's buildings so delightful.

The church forms a little island between Salem and Mattoon Streets. A walk down Mattoon will reveal an almost entirely restored row of upper-middle-class Victorian houses—a glimpse of Springfield as it must have looked around the turn of the century.

From Mattoon Street, if you head south on Chestnut Street, you won't walk very far before you find the Quadrangle, a grouping of four museums and the Springfield City Library around a central green that gives Springfield a campus setting of its own. And what's more, the museums are free.

The Museum of Fine Arts (413-732-6092), on the west side of the little tree-lined square, is a simple beaux-arts building, lit by an atrium, that houses 19 galleries, with concentrations in impressionist and contemporary art. Across the square is the Springfield Science Museum (413-733-1194), easily the equal of many similar science museums in New England and including a "please touch" section that will delight children. On the north side of the Quadrangle is the Connecticut Valley Historical Museum (413-732-3080), specializing in local history and including a few excellent period rooms.

But the two best stops are across the quad: the George Walter Vincent Smith Art Museum (413-733-4214), a buff-colored Italianate terra-cotta masterpiece built in 1896 by the importer and philanthropist whose name it bears, and the City Library (413-739-3871), on the Quadrangle's south side.

The art museum, with a little cloister along the side and a tower, has beamed ceilings and carved wooden walls almost rococo in their design. The collection—a lot of armor, masks, and swords from Asia, as well as, oddly, realist paintings—is highly eclectic, and even includes a sarcophagus and a life-size smiling Buddha.

The Italian Renaissance–style library is a quite spectacular finish to the Quadrangle.

A two-story, coffered blue dome supported by white Corinthian columns stands above the central court, and lintels of plaster and wood top the doorways leading to side rooms. Just the lightest touch of gilt here and there lends a regal air to this public building.

Beyond the Quadrangle, Springfield doesn't just roll up its sidewalks. There's the Springfield Symphony Orchestra (413-733-2291), a regional orchestra that plays a full season of classical music in Stanley Park in nearby Westfield. There's a fine regional theater, Stage West (1 Columbus Center, 413-781-2340), that augments its season with a month each summer in the Berkshires. There's Zone Art Center (395 Dwight St., 413-732-1995), a lovely and unusual gallery focusing on new and alternative art by artists from the area.

There's Riverfront Park, along West Columbus Avenue, a beautiful stretch of lawns, benches and pleasant places to watch boats on the Connecticut River or listen to a band concert in the summer. And there's the Civic Center (on Main Street across from Court Square, 413-787-6600) for conventions and large events.

Finally, there's the Hall of Fame at 1150 W. Columbus Ave. (413-781-6500). The museum houses the expected relics and holy sepulchres of basketball, including some floorboards from the gym in which Naismith, in December 1891, invented the game. Every development in the game is documented, and if there's any historical question you have, you can get it answered here. In one area are television screens, where visitors can choose scenes from the greatest games played.

But what makes this hall of fame different from others is that it doesn't concentrate purely on the pros. There is, for example, a wall of pictures of children playing basketball around housing projects. And there are participatory exhibits, including a shoot-out at the end of the visitors' tour.

You stand on a moving conveyor and get a chance to shoot at any of a bunch of hoops, close and far, as you move slowly by them.

Let me tell you: You may not have seen it on the evening news, but I sank a lovely, arcing 30-foot rainbow to close out my day. Fump! Nothing but net.

And did I go home happy.

—Scott Huler

Directions from Philadelphia: Take the Garden State Parkway north to the New York Thruway (I-287) east across the Tappan Zee Bridge. Follow 287 to I-684 north, then I-84 north to Hartford. Take I-91 north into Massachusetts and to Springfield.

∾

The caloric side of Vermont

WATERBURY, VT.

WE PLANNED OUR TRIP with all good intentions—an early-summer weekend in Vermont where we would visit a little-known museum that specializes in Americana, walk the funky streets of Burlington, and maybe take a dip in Lake Champlain if it wasn't too cold.

Instead, we went on a two-day eating frenzy.

And what a binge it was. Banana-and-nut ice cream fresh off the assembly line at Ben & Jerry's main factory. Rich and intense chocolate truffles from a confectionery shop run by a former White House pastry chef. Fresh-made apple cider from a hugely popular cider mill. Dense and creamy Vermont Cheddar cheese from a farm that makes it on the premises. Portuguese sweet bread from a gourmet store that bakes 10 different kinds of loaves. And a fabulous meal of Greek-style seafood and Indian tandoori chicken at a terrific Burlington restaurant.

Face it, given a choice between museum-hopping and pigging out on world-class food, wouldn't you, too, give in to your palate?

As I mentioned, it wasn't really planned this way. I tend to think of Paris or New York, Rome or Barcelona, when it comes to gastronomical glory. But as we quickly came to learn, the stretch of northern Vermont around Waterbury and Burlington offers a number of epicurean delights that rank up there with the very best.

We arrived in Waterbury on a Friday night, checking into a quite acceptable Holiday Inn. Our plans were to head west the next day toward Burlington and spend at least a full day—and maybe two—at the Shelburne Museum, which has a massive and justly famous (among aficionados) collection of American folk art. How was I to know that Ben & Jerry's factory, which gives tours and, more importantly, free samples, was only a mile or so down the road?

First thing on Saturday morning, I was in line at the tour desk, where for $1 one can purchase a ticket and learn how two quirky, left-wing guys from Long Island make a fortune selling ice cream with funny-named flavors. It's told in slick, slide-show fashion and is amusing, but clearly all of us on the tour were a lot more interested in sampling the product than hearing propaganda—even if it's commendable propaganda such as the company's concern for the disappearing Brazilian rain forest.

Our tour guide didn't let us down. She brought us up to a windowed room that overlooked the ice cream assembly line, lowered a bucket down, and pulled up a half-dozen or so pints of "Chunky Monkey" banana ice cream so fresh, it hadn't even gone into the factory freezer yet. As an ice cream fanatic who rarely ventures beyond chocolate, I can report that it was nothing short of incredible.

To wash it down, my next stop was Cold Hollow Cider Mill, a few miles down the road in Waterbury Center. The business claims to be one of Vermont's most visited attractions, and it certainly seemed to be, judging from the crowd that morning.

My wife (who foolishly skipped Ben & Jerry's) and I watched a brief demonstration of how cider is pressed and then headed into the main store. The cider here, made year-round, is top-notch, as is the apple juice, but there's a host of other delicious foodstuffs to sample and buy—including cider doughnuts, jams, apple butter, and fancy mustards. Don't ask me why, but this part of Vermont is heavy into gourmet mustard.

By this time, though, I knew I would have to save some room for dessert, for we had learned the location of Green Mountain Chocolate Co., about 10 miles south on Route 100.

I had read about this place before, and how it is owned by Albert Kumin, who served as pastry chef during Jimmy Carter's administration. The articles claimed that the place sold the best chocolate truffles outside of France.

I no longer doubt it. Green Mountain Chocolate is more than just a candy store; it is a chocoholic's paradise. In addition to mounds of different varieties of truffles and other chocolate treats, there are cakes, fudge, chocolate-dipped strawberries—all reasonably priced—and a remarkable display of chocolate handicraft, including thin-walled chocolate boxes and ears of corn completely formed from chocolate, down to the individual kernels and even the silk.

(I later made the criminal mistake of leaving a small box of truffles in a hot car. There was, of course, only one remedy: a return visit on Sunday. The second time around, I bought more truffles, along with a small chocolate cake filled with white chocolate frosting and topped with raspberry purée. Considering its ingredients, it was remarkably light—and superb.)

But I digress. To work off the estimated five million calories already consumed that morning, we took a short hike through Little River State Park, a pretty forest dotted with the remains of 19th-century farms. Then we finally headed to Burlington.

Alas, it was time for lunch.

We decided to stop at Leunig's Old World Café, at 115 Church St. in downtown Burlington. Leunig's is French in style, with outdoor tables along the sidewalk, and an eclectic menu that includes French, Spanish, Greek, and Mexican dishes, among others. The highlight of the meal was the $5.25 Neptune Salad, a Caesar salad topped with a sizable portion—considering the price—of real lobster meat.

We left the restaurant and, to our astonishment, discovered that less than a block away the city was celebrating its sixth annual Green Mountain Chew-Chew Vermont Food Fest, held every June. That's right, an entire city square of food booths set up by dozens of local restaurants. (There are also music and entertainment.)

At other times, I would have simply dived in, sampling from the diverse selection of edibles, ranging from spring rolls and crab fritters to sushi and blackened swordfish, with many portions costing just $1. But it was barely midafternoon, and I had already eaten at least five times. With remarkable restraint, I resisted.

Of course, the day was not over. That afternoon, we walked around

Burlington, an artsy college town that is kind of an East Coast Berkeley. In our wanderings, we made a fine discovery—the Gourmet Food Exchange at 88 Church St. It was near closing time, so the bakery personnel downstairs offered a free sample of Portuguese sweet bread, one of the several kinds of breads offered each day. The sweet bread and French-style rolls were excellent.

Dinner time found us at The Daily Planet—no, not a newspaper office, but a terrific fern bar and restaurant on a downtown side street. It is extremely popular and its food is extremely good, comparable, in fact, to many of the top restaurants in Philadelphia or Boston.

I ate the Greek Seafood Pasta—featuring a sauce of scallops, shrimp, goat feta cheese, spinach, and tomatoes. My wife, a fan of Indian food, enjoyed skewered tandoori chicken with tomato chutney. It seems somewhat out of place to discover great Greek and Indian cooking in a Vermont college town, but it is all here.

Satiated at last, we retired for the evening at the Sheraton in South Burlington.

On Sunday, we finally did make it to our original destination—the Shelburne Museum, a sprawling and wonderful display of Americana, (including quilts, cigar store Indians, circus memorabilia, and a full-size steamer ship) just outside Burlington. No doubt we could have spent the full two days there—instead of just a few hours—had we not been sidetracked by our stomachs.

Speaking of which, the food at the museum isn't anything special. But they do make and sell superb Cheddar cheese at nearby Shelburne Farms. Like much of the food we found in this scenic area of Vermont, I highly recommend it.

—Steve Stecklow

Directions from Philadelphia: Take the Garden State Parkway north to the New York Thruway (I-87). Take the Thruway north to Albany (exit 24), continue north on I-87 to Route 149. Take 149 east to Route 4 north and east, to Route 100 north. Follow 100 for almost 60 miles to Waterbury.

Ben & Jerry's gives daily tours from its factory in Waterbury. Cold Hollow Cider Mill can be found at Route 100 in Waterbury Center. Green Mountain Chocolate Co. has two locations—along Route 100 in Waterbury, about three miles south of the town, and in Stowe Village at Park and Main Streets. In Burlington, Leunig's Old World Cafe is at 115 Church St. The Daily Planet is at 15 Center St. The Shelburne Museum is on Route 7 in Shelburne, seven miles south of Burlington. Shelburne Farms is a couple of miles away on Bay and Harbor Roads, just off Route 7.

♋

A kinder, gentler Woodstock

WOODSTOCK, VT.

I REALIZED, as soon as I drove into town, that it was going to be hard to get lost here.

Central Street runs straight through the center of town. River Street follows the river. Mountain Avenue curves along the base of the mountain. Church Street starts right at the stone church. And almost everything is within walking distance of the town green.

Even those who have never been to Woodstock may know something of its reputation. It has been a favorite New England tourist destination for more than half a century, ever since establishing what it still claims was the nation's first rope tow for skiing in the mid-1930s.

This Woodstock is not to be confused with the one on the edge of the Catskills in New York State, where the famous 1969 rock concert was held. This is a kinder, gentler Woodstock—one of Vermont's most cosmopolitan towns and one of its prettiest. Woodstock today draws people for its expensive boutiques, art galleries, restaurants, and historic buildings, all clustered around or near its postcard-perfect town center.

The town's greatest claim to fame, though, is that several dozen millionaires call it home, including its most famous residents, Laurance Rockefeller and his wife, Mary Billings Rockefeller, whose family has ties to the area that go back four generations. Nearly a dozen inns and bed-and-breakfasts, including the Rockefeller-owned Woodstock Inn and Resort, lie within a short distance of the town green.

I had been to Woodstock before—been swept into its shops and along its sidewalks with crowds of brightly dressed tourists, and admired its historic graciousness and old-New England lines. But this time I came in search of something else. I wanted to do more than appreciate the facade; I wanted to get to know the place, the character of the town itself, a town that was founded in 1761. To do that, I came in spring—just past mud season, with no snow to ski on, no foliage to peep at, no perfect summer weather to bask in. And that was the point: Almost no tourists. This is the time, locals say, to get a feel for the real town, the one they know and love—certainly not the Woodstock of high summer season, which tends to make the town the New Hope (Pa.) of the Green Mountains.

Frank Teagle came to Woodstock in 1946, after the war "back before it was discovered," he says, "back before you had to make a date to cross the street."

He's lived here ever since, doing more things for the town than he'll ever let on. Everyone in town knows him; his nickname, in fact, is Mr. Woodstock. And everyone knows his most famous contribution—the town blackboard.

This huge piece of slate, better known as the Town Crier, once hung in a local one-room schoolhouse. I discovered the blackboard one evening at dusk, as I rounded the corner at Central and Elm streets. The overhead light was on and a young couple stood before the board, settling a dispute about what time the movie started down at the old opera house.

The answer was written right there, in neat white chalk lettering: The first showing was 7:30. I also noted when the Billings Farm & Museum opened the next day, the hours of the Raptor Center up the road, and the starting time for the spaghetti supper at the Unitarian church.

Every few days, rain or shine, for 40 years, Frank Teagle has been erasing old information and adding new announcements to the Town Crier. People send him messages on postcards, which he likes the best, or they call him on the phone—usually during dinner, he jokes. Or, they stop him on the street and ask him to be sure to include their event.

The best way to see Woodstock is to walk the town, and one of the best ways to do that is with Don Wheeler, who meets visitors several times a week at the information booth on the green for guided tours. (Call the Chamber of Commerce at 802-457-3555 for exact days and times.)

Wheeler is a rarity—he was actually born in town some 60 years ago. Over the years, he's become an expert on Woodstock, and when he doesn't have an answer ready, he simply refers to his stack of yellowed index cards, which are filled with names and dates.

As we walked the town, he pointed to an innocent-looking home that began life as the town jail, then became a tavern. He didn't want us to miss the little round window on the house that used to be the schoolhouse; the kids could look through there and see the town clock to tell when lunchtime was near.

Donald Wheeler knows his history. But he also remembers such places as the old inn with its long front porch and its row of Lincoln rockers, filled with maiden ladies from Boston and New York City. He remembers when the little brick house on the green used to be down where the supermarket now stands. He recalls the two widows who lived at No. 4 Mountain Avenue and were famous for their crazy clothes and their unusual driving habits: When they went out for a spin, one would steer and the other would shift.

Later that evening, I walked alone through the silent streets, past gardens of tulips and lilies, daffodils and impatiens, their colors still bright in the night shadows. I peered through arched windows with billowing lace curtains. At one home, the porch light was on, and a mother robin sat on her nest tucked high in a corner above the front door.

Then I headed down to the covered bridge over the Ottauquechee River. One of the newest structures in town, the bridge was built not in 1869, but in 1969—as a tourist attraction. How could such a cute town get along without a covered bridge?

The bridge fools a lot of people, nevertheless. It's got wide boards that creak underfoot, and when I stood on the walkway and leaned over the edge, the Ottauquechee River rushing below, the breeze lilac-sweet against my face, it could have easily been 100 years old.

And if you really want old covered bridges, there are two originals nearby over the Ottauquechee—one three miles west, built in 1877, and the other four miles east, at Taftsville, built in 1836.

Back in the center of town the next day, not far from Frank Teagle's blackboard, I found F.H. Gillingham & Sons, a place that really is old. At Gillingham's you can buy organic pickles, sun-dried tomatoes, anchovy paste, and all sorts of groceries, including, if you're so inclined, 45 different kinds of mustard. Without leaving the store, you can also stock up on sandpaper, vegetable seeds, wooden spoons, or dog biscuits.

Today, F.H. Gillingham's great-grandsons, Jireh and Frank Billings, carry on the tradition their mother's grandfather began. Somehow the spirit of the place has lasted through the years, including the fact that they still make deliveries.

Best of all is the smell inside the store—an aroma of fresh-ground coffee beans, spices, cheeses, chocolate, and well-oiled floors. If someone ever wanted to bottle a scent and call it "General Store," this is where they'd come get it.

That afternoon, I checked out Sugarbush Farm, run by Larry and Betsy Luce. It's one of the last large working farms in the area and a place that welcomes visitors. Sugarbush is five miles outside town; take U.S. Route 4 east to Taftsville and turn left over the covered bridge, at the sign for the farm.

Betsy Luce remembers growing up on this 540-acre farm and carting milk to the end of the long dirt road. She recalls the year the barn burned down, and, especially, the time her father hired a farmer named Luce to do the haying and his son, Larry, came along to help. Thirty years and five children later, Betsy and Larry are still milking cows, smoking cheese, and sugaring, as well as a host of other daily chores.

The farm is a few miles outside town and off Route 4, at the very end of a twisty, bumpy dirt road. The giant barn leans and tilts against the sky, its weathered sides patterned with lighter boards where old ones have been replaced.

The smokehouse (you'll smell it before you see it) is next to the little dirt parking area, across from the white clapboard house. There's no fancy gold-painted sign here that says you can buy cheese (which you can), just a metal screen door that slams shut as you enter the back wing of the house where a half-dozen people are cutting, waxing, wrapping, and labeling cheese.

When I walked in, I found cheese-tasting heaven: mellow, sharp, smoked, with sage, name it. There was syrup, too, from the lighter, sugary-sweet kind to the darker, stronger stuff that tasted a little like molasses.

In the sugar house, behind the giant cooler that holds the cheese, I learned that it takes 40 gallons of sap to make one gallon of maple syrup, and saw a sap hydrometer that measures sweetness.

The Luces don't charge visitors. They hope that folks will walk away having bought some of that cheese (they sell samplers of four half-pound bars) or a quart of syrup, or jams, mustards, or a few other items.

Yes, this may still be country, but it's not bumpkin. (They had gone so far as to install a toll-free number for customers who want to call in orders: 800-281-1757).

There was one more spot to visit. Even though it's only five minutes from the center of town, in the far corner of Faulkner Park, the trail up Mount Tom remains one of Woodstock's little-known secrets.

The mountain, like much of Woodstock, is largely owned by the Rockefellers, who deeded their home and 500 acres of land, including Mount Tom, to the National Park Service. (They have life tenancy on the property, but eventually it will become Vermont's first national historic park.)

Meanwhile, the hiking trails are always open. My walk was a nature lover's dream: Heart-shaped columbine, yellow trout lily, jack-in-the-pulpit, and purple trillium (also known by its less flattering name, Stinking Benjamin).

Halfway up, in a cool, dark stand of hemlock, I could hear the chimes tolling the hour from the town below. After a final steep scramble to the top, I sat down to enjoy the view.

The town of Woodstock stretched out below, a jumble of brick and white clapboard, bell towers, and church steeples, and narrow, winding streets.

It looked, I thought, like the New England town of every imagination.

But Woodstock is for real, of course. And from here, it looked just about perfect.

—Suki Casanave

Directions from Philadelphia: Woodstock is about a seven-hour drive from Philadelphia. Take the Garden State Parkway to the New York State Thruway. Take the Thruway north to Albany, Exit 24, and continue north on I-87 (the Adirondack Northway) to Exit 21, Route 149, just above Glens Falls. Take Route 149 east to U.S. Route 4 and follow Route 4 north and east into Vermont, through Rutland and past Killington to Woodstock.

For more information on Woodstock, write or call the Chamber of Commerce, Woodstock, Vt. 05091; 802-457-3555.

Some attractions:

Billings Farm & Museum, a picture-perfect, educational farm with Jersey cows, Morgan horses, a Victorian creamery, other exhibits. Route 12. 802-457-2355.

Kedron Valley Riding Stables, guided riding tours along miles of beautiful trails. Box 368, South Woodstock, Vt. 05071. 800-225-6301 or 802-457-2734 or 802-457-1480.

Vermont Institute of Natural Science and Raptor Center, a "living museum" full of rescued hawks, owls, eagles, and other birds of prey. Church Hill Road. 802-457-2779.

Walk on the Wild Side, a five-mile walk up 500-foot Mount Tom leaves twice weekly from the Woodstock Inn, starting in June (call for times). 802-457-1100.

Woodstock Historical Society, at the 1807 Dana House Museum, which displays period furnishings. 26 Elm St. in Woodstock. 802-457-1822.

4

Washington, Maryland, and Virginia

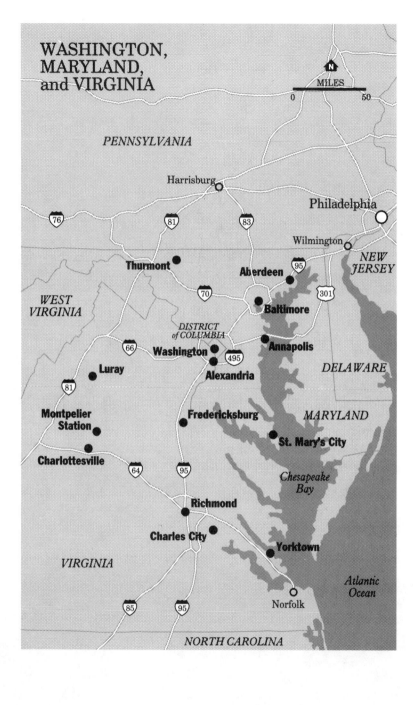

WASHINGTON, MARYLAND, and VIRGINIA

MILES
0   50

N

PENNSYLVANIA

Harrisburg

Philadelphia

76   81   83

Wilmington

NEW
JERSEY

Thurmont   Aberdeen   95

WEST
VIRGINIA   70   301

Baltimore

DISTRICT
of COLUMBIA

66   Washington   Annapolis

Luray   495   DELAWARE
Alexandria

81

Montpelier
Station   Fredericksburg   MARYLAND

St. Mary's City

Charlottesville

64   95   Chesapeake
Bay

Richmond

Charles City   Yorktown

VIRGINIA   Atlantic
Ocean

85   95   Norfolk

NORTH CAROLINA

The Ordnance Museum

ABERDEEN, MD.

IF YOU'VE DRIVEN to Baltimore or Washington, I'll bet you've seen the signs. They're dirt-brown, and they stand along the bustling flat stretch of Interstate 95 that passes over the Susquehanna River near where it empties into Chesapeake Bay.

Ordnance Museum, Exit 85.

Most drivers, of course, zoom right by, some having no clue what an ordnance museum might be, and others knowing but not caring.

Maybe the signs should say "Tanks for the memories." For here sit rows and rows of old military tanks, lined up to fight the battles of World War II and Korea and other conflagrations of the past.

American Sherman tanks and German Tiger tanks. British Honey tanks and a mammoth Soviet Stalin tank. Italian tanks and French tanks. Czech tanks and Japanese tanks.

So many tanks—and you're welcome. Free. Every day, including Sunday.

"We have the world's largest collection of armored fighting vehicles here," said W.F. Atwater, the museum director.

Situated about halfway between Philadelphia and Washington, the U.S. Army Ordnance Museum makes a fascinating stop on a weekend journey through the I-95 corridor. Those who want to weekend right in the neighborhood—instead, perhaps, of Baltimore or Washington—might consider overnighting in the historic nearby waterfront town of Havre de Grace, just a few miles up the road.

The ordnance museum sits at the northern edge of the 72,500-acre Aberdeen Proving Ground, an Army facility just down the road from Havre de Grace, which is at the head of the bay. You can get off I-95 and be at the museum in five minutes.

Each year, despite the rather uninspiring signs, 200,000 people find their way to the museum, which consists of a two-story building containing exhibits on ordnance, plus the 25-acre "tank and artillery park." The park contains 225 tanks and artillery pieces, including Nike and Hercules missiles from the early Cold War.

Many who come to visit are active members of the Army assigned to the Proving Ground, where the weapons of the future are being tested.

Many others are soldiers of the past, particularly World War II, who come to look again at the weapons once used by—and against—them. Not a veteran myself, I discovered the museum one day when the ride home to Philadelphia was getting too long, and I needed a break. Later, I returned with my family on a Saturday. I confess that our two daughters, ages 14 and 10, wouldn't get out of the car; they sat and read. But my wife, Gail, to her surprise, was as strangely captivated as I was by this museum devoted to the history and development of ordnance, from the Civil War to Vietnam and beyond.

My *Webster's* defines ordnance thusly: "All military weapons, together with ammunition, combat vehicles, etc., and the equipment and supplies used in servicing them."

I guess that must include the staff car that Gen. John J. "Black Jack" Pershing used to cruise around France in World War I—because it's here. We also saw an "earthquake-producing" bomb from the 1950s and a Gatling gun from the 19th century.

Inside the museum building, Gail spent a long time looking at a glass case showing the development of shrapnel, which the exhibit says was invented in 1784 by Lt. Henry Shrapnel to "fill the need for an effective projectile for use against troops in the open." In other words, to blow apart a lot of young men all at once.

"I couldn't help thinking," Gail said, "about how all that intelligence and creativity was poured into weapons of destruction."

Indeed.

Outside, we heard a blast of artillery in the distance. Then we heard a whole barrage. When I later asked Atwater what was up, he said, "They're testing projectiles; they're testing propellants. No big secret about that."

The Ordnance Corps, which is headquartered at Aberdeen, is also working on the development of lightweight armor plate made from a nylonlike material for the tanks of the future.

The Army's main battle tank at the moment weighs 60 tons, Atwater said. The biggest plane the United States has can carry only two of them. That's why it took five months to complete the buildup for Operation Desert Storm; the tanks had to be shipped by sea.

"The next war may be 'Come as you are,'" Atwater said. And so the Army wants a lighter tank it can airlift. Somewhere in secret, on the sandy plain of Aberdeen, such tanks may be scooting around right now.

Most of the Aberdeen Proving Ground is restricted to visitors. But you can drive right onto the property and follow signs to the museum without being stopped. The entrance road, in fact, is the first exhibit. Along it you will see a mile of tanks—retired American tanks, some of them prototypes that were never put into production.

Clearly, tanks are the main attraction around here.

Anyone who has ever seen a World War II movie will recognize the German Panther tanks parked at the museum. Maybe also the famous Soviet tank of World War II, the T-34. The Panthers and T-34s clashed in some of the legendary tank battles of history. In one battle on the Eastern Front, at a place called Kursk, 6,000 tanks faced off in combat.

"If you were going to pick the best tank of World War II, I think the buffs would get into an argument as to which was the best one, the Panther or T-34," Atwater said.

Both were superior to the best American tank of that era—the Sherman, which Atwater said had a better suspension than the others but had puny armor and was badly outgunned.

Now these old enemies sit side by side on the grass, their long barrels all pointed in the same direction. The array includes tanks from a half-dozen countries and times. They look ready for some battle in "The Twilight Zone."

A sardine-can tank from World War I. A diminutive Japanese tank left on the battlefield at Okinawa. A Soviet-made tank captured in the Korean War. A Soviet T-55 captured by Israel in the 1967 Middle East war.

The museum even has a Soviet T-72 taken from the Iraqis in the Persian Gulf War, Atwater said, though it isn't yet on display.

Most of the foreign tanks—at least enemy ones—were shipped across the sea and up the Chesapeake for what Atwater called "technical intelligence purposes." If the Army could see how they were put together, it figured, it might learn how to defeat them in battle. And if they were any good, it might copy them.

Of even greater interest was the V-2 rocket—the first ballistic missile. Some 4,300 of these terror weapons were launched by the Germans, most against London and Antwerp, before the Allies finally got their hands on one intact.

Found in May 1945 when the Nazis abandoned the concentration camp at Nordhausen, that first captured V-2 now rests here. It sits, rusting and peeling, under a metal canopy outdoors.

And I've got to tell you, it still looks sinister.

So does a 230-ton German railroad cannon nicknamed Anzio Annie by the Allies. Too big to be moved except by train, the gun fired 550-pound shells from a 70-foot barrel. Now it, too, rests forever at the museum, still sitting on rails.

A plaque says: "This giant railway gun was used by the German army against Allied troops attempting to break out of the Anzio beachhead in 1944," taking "a very heavy toll in life and equipment."

Looking up the long, fat barrel, we could hardly imagine that such a weapon was used against human beings.

But no matter how big a weapon gets, no matter how fearsome, somebody will always try to top it.

Thus, very close to Anzio Annie, we saw Atomic Annie. Made by the United States in the 1950s, Atomic Annie was as big as its predecessor—and it could fire a nuclear shell.

"It's like, 'Let's see who can make the most destructive weapon,'" Gail said.

Right again.

—Tom Infield

Directions from Philadelphia: To get to the Army Ordnance Museum by car from Philadelphia, take Interstate 95 south to Exit 85. Turn left onto state Route 22 (Aberdeen Thruway), and drive three miles to the Aberdeen Proving Ground gate. The drive from Philadelphia takes about 1 1/2 hours.

The museum is open seven days a week, noon to 4:45 p.m., Tuesday through Friday; 10 a.m. to 4:45 p.m. Saturday and Sunday. Admission and parking are free. Tours are self-guided, and most outdoor exhibits carry explanatory plaques.

A host of weekend destinations—Baltimore, Annapolis, Maryland's Eastern Shore, Washington—are within an easy drive of the museum.

Adams-Morgan

WASHINGTON, D.C.

THERE IS A PLAQUE on the house at 1831 Wyoming Ave. here marking the last residence of North Pole explorer Adm. Robert Peary, who bought the home in 1914 and lived there until his death in 1920.

And it may be the only historical marker in all of Adams-Morgan, an eclectic neighborhood in the city's northwest section.

There is nothing, for instance, to tell you that the Wyoming, a turn-of-the-century luxury apartment building, was where Dwight and Mamie Eisenhower lived for nearly nine years.

No guidebook points out the house that Al Jolson bought for his parents.

There is no marker at the apartment Lyndon and Lady Bird Johnson rented for $42.50 a month in 1935, or the shop where Charles Lazarus began Toys R Us. Or the place where reporter Carl Bernstein was living on the night of the Watergate break-in.

But these are just a few of the hidden places sprinkled throughout the 240 acres of this colorful, offbeat, multicultural area. Adams-Morgan has gone through a half-dozen reincarnations in the last 100 years and became something of a tourist destination primarily because of its proliferation of restaurants in the late 1980s and early '90s.

Fortunately, there's a man who knows the neighborhood well, is constantly discovering more, and is willing to share his knowledge with just about anyone. Each Sunday, Anthony Pitch leads a two-hour walking tour of Adams-Morgan, regaling his audience with tales of the presidents and radicals and authors and artists who have passed through this neighborhood. The tour starts in front of the Wyoming, which is at 2022 Columbia Rd., at 11 a.m. (Phone 301-294-9514.)

The tour is fascinating—and it's free. Pitch won't accept money, not even a tip. His reward, he says, will come when he finishes his book on self-guided walking tours of Washington. What he's doing now, he says, is getting in practice.

Adams-Morgan, says Pitch, is something of a yuppie paradise. It is close to downtown, relatively safe, and very picturesque.

While not nearly as famous as the Georgetown section, its neighbor to the west, Adams-Morgan already rivals Georgetown for real estate prices. Large brick and stone townhouses that could be bought for $30,000 in the 1970s go on the market for $400,000 or more today.

Perhaps you only know Adams-Morgan from its restaurants. The neighborhood is home to some of the most diverse and eclectic eating establishments in the city, most of them on a stretch of 18th Street that's just a few blocks long.

And even if you've never heard of Adams-Morgan, it's likely you've caught glimpses of it at the movies. Remember the opening frames of *In the Line of Fire,* in which Clint Eastwood waits to be picked up by his partner? That was filmed on 18th Street in the heart of Adams-Morgan.

How about the walk taken by Tom Cruise and Kevin Pollack—Pollack's wheeling a baby stroller—in *A Few Good Men*? That's 20th Street near the Airy View apartments. *Dave* and *The Pelican Brief* also feature scenes of Adams-Morgan. Hollywood has discovered it because it's in a good location, it's quiet, and it generally doesn't have a problem with traffic congestion.

That doesn't mean, though, that's it's off the beaten track. Adams-Morgan sits right behind the gigantic Washington Hilton and Towers, just north of Dupont Circle and south of the National Zoo.

Once, though, it was considered the boondocks. That all changed when the 18th Street trolley began running in 1892, followed five years later by a streetcar extension on Columbia Road. Developers saw the potential; in 25 years, 26 apartment buildings went up, many of them still standing and retaining traces of the luxury for which they were noted shortly after the turn of the century.

Three on Columbia Road, the main thoroughfare in Adams-Morgan, are the Wyoming (No. 2022), Woodley (No. 1851) and Norwood (No. 1868). Built in 1905, the Wyoming, which has two large wings, has housed many members of Congress, but its most famous residents were the Eisenhower family. Dwight, Mamie, and the children lived there—during the times that Ike was not working overseas—from 1927 to 1936. It is considered one of the finest examples of a turn-of-the-century luxury apartment house.

On one of the top floors of the circa 1917 Norwood, a building covered with decorative plasterwork, lived Congressman William Bankhead. He eventually became Speaker of the House, but his daughter's fame has long outlasted his. Her name was Tallulah.

The Woodley, completed in 1903 as the first apartment building on

Columbia Road, is noted primarily as a onetime investment property of Woodward & Lothrop's Sam Woodward, whose partner, Alvin Lothrop, built a mansion at the southern tip of Adams-Morgan where Columbia Road, Connecticut Avenue, and California Street intersect. The building, assessed at $5 million, is now used by Russia as a trade mission.

Slightly less luxurious was the Woburn at 1910 Kalorama Rd. LBJ moved there in 1936, a year after his marriage. A frequent guest was Speaker of the House Sam Rayburn.

Mintwood Place, a street that curves between Columbia Road and 19th Street, was known as Admiral's Row because so many Navy people lived there. The pastel colors of the well-maintained townhouses are reminiscent of Rainbow Row in Charleston, S.C. At 1863 Mintwood Place, a bright yellow building that sticks out, lived Sen. Thomas Gore, the grandfather of author Gore Vidal and the first blind senator to serve in Congress, from 1907 to 1921. (Perhaps, says Pitch, he was a distant relative of Vice President Al Gore.)

A block away, Biltmore Street was General's Row, where the Pentagon's generals once lived. The building at the corner of Biltmore and 19th Streets is where *Washington Post* reporter Carl Bernstein lived when he and Bob Woodward broke the Watergate story. He later married writer-director Nora Ephron and the couple moved to the Ontario (on Ontario Road), one of the finest apartment addresses in Adams-Morgan and Washington. The first wing of the Ontario was begun in 1903; General Douglas MacArthur lived there at one time.

The strait-laced MacArthur undoubtedly would not have been pleased with the residents who inhabited Lanier Place, around the corner from the Ontario. The street in the 1960s became the home for inhabitants of the radical movement, including members of the Catonsville Nine and Chicago Seven. This was not exactly unknown to the Federal Bureau of Investigation.

A generation earlier it had also been well known to Al Jolson, whose father, Rabbi Moses Yoelson, and stepmother moved to 1787 Lanier after Jolson made it big in the first talkie, *The Jazz Singer*. His father, the leader of a congregation in southwest Washington for 30 years, died there in 1946.

It was around that time—right after World War II—that Adams-Morgan's fortunes began to slip. Many of the stately homes were broken into single rooms and efficiencies, and a transient population moved in. The area became run down, property became cheap.

In 1955, a year after the Supreme Court decision in *Brown* vs. *Board of Education* declared segregated schools unconstitutional, the principals of the white John Quincy Adams school and the black Thomas Morgan school agreed to merge and the area took its name from the new school.

In the next decade, hippies and American leftists began arriving, drawn by the low rents. At the same time, there was an influx of anti-Castro Cubans. The Cubans paved the way for other Spanish-speaking peoples, and the two populations—American liberals and foreign nationals—lived peacefully side by side.

Restaurants and cafés began opening along 18th Street, and soon that is what the street, and the neighborhood, became best-known for—its eclectic food. Today there are about 75 restaurants that seem to represent almost as many countries—from Senegalese to Vietnamese, from Italian to West Indian, Ethiopian to Spanish and Mexican, and so on, plus gourmet, vegetarian, pizza, and deli places.

By the late 1970s, the yuppies had discovered Adams-Morgan and they've been moving in ever since.

Today, Adams-Morgan is, in the words of author Barbara Raskin, "a truly tan community. Residents who stuck out several racially tense eras eventually found themselves living in a politically, culturally, and artistically integrated area. On alternately quiet and raucous streets, haves and have-nots live next door to each other, constantly surprised by their coexistence."

That quote is taken from her bestseller *Current Affairs*, set largely in Adams-Morgan.

Raskin should know what she's talking about.

She lives on Wyoming Avenue—right across the street from Admiral Peary's old home.

—Ralph Vigoda

Directions from Philadelphia: From Philadelphia, take Interstate 95 south to Interstate 495 west (the Washington Beltway). Take the beltway west to Exit 33, Connecticut Avenue South. On Connecticut Avenue, about a half-hour of city driving will take you to the National Zoo. A few blocks past the zoo is the intersection of Connecticut Avenue and Calvert Street. Turn left on Calvert and go about a half-mile to 18th Street. A right on 18th puts you in the heart of Adams-Morgan.

The boundaries of Adams-Morgan are U Street on the south, Rock Creek Parkway on the north, Connecticut Avenue on the west, and 16th Street on the east.

For more information, including information about accommodations, contact the Washington, D.C., Convention and Visitors Association, 1212 New York Ave., N.W., Suite 600, Washington, D.C. 20005. Phone 202-789-7000.

ɔ

A lot of George Washington

ALEXANDRIA, VA.

GEORGE WASHINGTON SLEPT HERE.

He ate here. He worshiped here. He bartered at the farmers market here. He hung around and mooched off a bunch of Colonial muckymucks here.

"And," said the woman in the visitors center, "when you go up the steps to Gadsby's Tavern and put your hand on the railing, remember that George Washington went up those same steps and put his hand on that same railing."

Whew! George knew Alexandria.

In fact, if Ol' George is your bag and if you get a kick out of what America looked like before it was America, this is the place to be. His presence hangs everywhere over this delightful city, where he spent much of his time when he wasn't down on the farm a few miles away at Mount Vernon. And there is such a wealth of historical offerings—the real thing, too, not the rebuilt-for-tourists kind in Williamsburg—so many good restaurants, such charm that, as we found out, a weekend is barely enough to see it all.

The original intention of our party of four was to spend a leisurely afternoon in Old Town Alexandria and the rest of the weekend strolling the mall in Washington, 15 minutes away by the George Washington—who else?—Parkway.

As it turned out, we couldn't get enough of Old Town, squeezing Washington into a couple of twilight hours on Sunday.

And if your taste runs more toward, say, the 19th century than the 18th, there's plenty of that here, too. After all, this is where another famous military man spent his growing-up years. Robert E. Lee lived in a house on Oronoco Street, before heading off at age 18 to West Point.

Lee's boyhood home is just three blocks from Christ Church, where George and Martha bought pew No. 60 for 36 pounds, 10 shillings after the building was completed in 1773.

The church is three blocks from the Stabler-Leadbeater Apothecary Shop—owned and operated by the same family for 141 years—which looks pretty much as it did in 1792.

The apothecary is a couple of blocks from the imposing Atheneum, built as a bank in 1850 and used today by the Northern Virginia Fine Arts Association. And the Atheneum is two blocks from the Torpedo Factory, opened just after World War I. Home to more than 150 artists and their studios and galleries, it is Alexandria's most visited spot.

The point is, the town is a walker's dream. If you have to bring the car, park it at a meter—the city provides a certificate allowing tourists 72 hours of free parking—and forget about it.

Old-time architecture? Federal, Georgian, Greek revival, and the oddly named, tall and narrow Flounder style—it's all here. Shopping? Boutiques and galleries—from old bookstores to mini-malls to popular clothing shops such as the Gap and Banana Republic—line the streets. Black history? You can find everything from the site of an early slave market to the home of George Seaton, a prominent free master carpenter. Like the waterside? The town sits right on the Potomac, and there are lots of places to skip stones.

Still, in many ways this place is a well-kept secret, overshadowed by Washington. We visited over a President's Day weekend—the largest Washington's birthday parade in the country takes place here then—and felt nearly alone. In some of the historic residences, we had the tour guide to ourselves. At three restaurants, at the peak dinner hour, we were seated immediately. Things, of course, pick up considerably in the summer.

The city has its roots in the 1670s, when John Alexander bought 6,000 acres next to the river. It wasn't until the 1730s, though, that the establishment of a tobacco warehouse by a number of Scottish merchants spurred heavier settlement. Alexandria was incorporated by the Virginia Assembly in 1749; in 1791, Congress made it part of Washington and, at the same time, ensured that it remained residential by prohibiting construction of public buildings.

A building boom began in 1846 and lasted until the Civil War when the area became part of Virginia again, but the town remained somewhat sleepy until the 20th-century growth of Washington.

Much of the effort to preserve the heritage began in earnest during World War II. The result is that the entire Old Town district is on the National Register of Historic Places.

The oldest building, the Ramsay House at 221 King St., is the official visitors center. Built in 1724 and moved to the King Street site 25 years later, it's the logical starting point. Here you can pick up the free parking pass, grab a couple of brochures, including a self-guided walking-tour pamphlet, and chat with the enthusiastic workers.

The question is, where do you go from there?

The suggested walking tour takes about an hour if you want only to glance at the more famous landmarks. But if you follow just the tour, you might miss Captain's Row, the 100 block of Prince Street, still cobblestoned and once the street of many ship captains. Or you might not get to the Odd Fellows Hall on South Columbus Street, the early site of the first school for females in Virginia—thanks to money from Martha Washington—and a major gathering place for black societies and organizations after the Civil War.

That's not to say you should ignore the suggestions. But you can modify them.

We began with two hours at the Torpedo Factory, where thousands of men and women once made torpedo shell cases. After World War II, the place was used to house everything from Nazi war records used in the Nuremburg Trials to dinosaur bones for the Smithsonian Institution. It opened in 1974 as an art center, and today, artists must pass a jury review before applying for studio space.

The site also houses a small laboratory and museum about Alexandria archaeology. It's a good introduction to what you'll see around the town—such as the home of John Carlyle, built in 1752-53 by the wealthy Scottish merchant, and the place where Colonial governors met with Gen. Edward Braddock in 1755 to plan strategy for the French and Indian War. It's interesting to note that the estate was a waterfront property when it was built, but is now two long blocks from the Potomac.

Although called the grandest of Alexandria homes, we found it less interesting than some of the other historic homes. This was partly the fault of our ill-informed and nervous guide. The tour—we were the only ones in the house at the time—consisted of her reading small index cards as we moved from room to room. In one room she got halfway through before she realized the card was the wrong one.

On the other hand, the guide at Lee's boyhood home knew so much about the house, the Lee family (his father was Revolutionary War hero "Light Horse Harry" Lee), and the area that the information was almost too much to process. We found a happy medium at the large clapboard Lee-Fendall house across the street, which was decked out for a Victorian funeral, complete with a casket in the living room. We learned much about the sexist funeral practices of the 1800s—and heard the story of the ghost of a former nanny that reputedly inhabited the house.

The home, built in 1785 by Philip Fendall, was frequently visited by Washington and, later, the Lees; Fendall, in fact, married a trio of Lee women. It was also for 32 years the 20th-century residence of labor leader John L. Lewis.

For a sobering thrill, go to Christ Church. Washington's pew is preserved in its original rectangular shape. When he worshipped here, the church was unheated and the family would huddle together around red-hot stones placed on the floor. The Lee family pew is across the aisle.

The small graveyard on the grounds is also worth some time. You'll find tales of woe from two centuries ago on the few headstones that are still readable. On one, a widower laments his wife's death, which left him with two children. On another a man is praised for his fortitude in bearing up to an illness that lasted more than three years.

Perhaps that unfortunate gentleman fought his illness with medicines obtained at the Stabler-Leadbeater Apothecary on South Fairfax Street. Certainly, the records show, the Washingtons and Lees were customers, and people such as Daniel Webster, Henry Clay, and John Calhoun were known to stop by. No longer does the apothecary stock Rice's worm-destroying drops or Wright's Indian vegetable pills. But it does have antique drugstore furnishings and a fascinating collection of early medicine bottles.

A few other things are popular on tourist lists: the Old Presbyterian Meeting House, where Washington's funeral sermons were preached;

the Lloyd House, with its collection of rare books and records of Alexandria history; and the George Washington Masonic National Memorial, a 333-foot tower that houses such Washington memorabilia as the family Bible, and a clock that was stopped at the time of his death.

A little farther out is old Fort Ward, a 45-acre park that was the site of one of the 68 forts built to protect the city of Washington during the Civil War.

There are also Gadsby's Tavern Museum and adjacent restaurant. Washington was a frequent guest at the tavern, which also hosted John Adams, Thomas Jefferson, and Lafayette. Although the restaurant had "tourist trap" written all over it—complete with waiter and waitresses in Colonial garb—we couldn't help ourselves and walked in for dinner. We were pleasantly surprised. The prices weren't outrageous, the portions were huge—my 10-year-old had a children's plate that had enough food for two adults—and the food was quite good.

All that, and a chance to walk down the steps where Washington once stood.

For more information, contact the Alexandria Convention and Visitors Bureau, 221 King St., Alexandria, Va. 22314, phone 703-838-4200; the Alexandria Black History Resource Center, 638 N. Alfred St., Alexandria, Va. 22314, phone 703-838-4356; and the Washington, D.C., Convention and Visitors Association, 1212 New York Ave., N.W., Washington, D.C. 20005, phone 202-789-7000.

—Ralph Vigoda

Directions from Philadelphia: Follow I-95 south, past Washington, to Alexandria.

~

Beyond Chesapeake Bay

ANNAPOLIS, MD.

WE HAD BEEN HERE BEFORE—once to a wedding at the Naval Academy chapel, another time for a sailing weekend on a 42-footer out of the yacht club. But both times the city itself was no more than a pleasant blur. Throwing rice and hauling lines and seeing old friends left little time to explore its treasures or experience its delights.

So, driving down from Philadelphia on a crisp, sunny Saturday, we congratulated ourselves on our cleverness. It was out of season—winter, in fact—and we would have the place to ourselves. We would poke around, see the sights, relax over a good dinner, get lots of sleep, do the Sunday crossword puzzle. Oh, how wrong we were!

Nearly as many visitors come here in the winter as in the summer. Unlike Cape Cod, say, which goes comatose after September, Annapolis goes merrily along, almost impervious to the changing seasons. When you think about it, why not?

Chesapeake Bay is hardly its only asset. The winter is mild—more enjoyable, for us, anyway, than the wilting heat and humidity of summer. And for millions like us who need a change from the annoyances of the city, it is an easy drive and a welcome change.

The mention of Annapolis usually conjures up the Naval Academy, sailboats, and historic buildings. True, but you can add good times to the list. There's a dance in the old girl yet.

Annapolis is a lot older than Baltimore, its much bigger sister, and it has been the political capital of Maryland since Colonial times. For a while, it was the nation's capital. The Continental Congress met here from late 1783 until the summer of 1784. The first settlers, we learned to our surprise, were Puritans fleeing religious harassment in Virginia. They called it Anne Arundel Town for the wife of the second Lord Baltimore, proprietor of the crown colony of Maryland. In 1695, it was renamed Annapolis for Princess Anne of England.

This city of 35,000 has more than its share of historic buildings. Our guidebook listed more than a dozen worth visiting. In 1766, Thomas Jefferson was so impressed with the stately Georgian mansions here that he wrote to a friend: "The houses [in Annapolis] are in general better than those in Williamsburg."

The Naval Academy has been here since its founding in 1845, and its 4,500 midshipmen are much in evidence on weekends. The academy overshadows tiny but prestigious St. John's College, whose 400 students pursue a unique curriculum based on the great books of Western civilization. In 1784, St. John's succeeded King William's School, which first welcomed students in 1696. Alumni include Francis Scott Key and two nephews of George Washington. (A popular spring event is the croquet match between the "mids" and the "Johnnies" accompanied by baroque music and champagne.)

Once, fishing boats filled the harbor, but the skipjacks and bugeyes have given way to a fleet of pleasure craft. Chesapeake Bay is one of the great sailing areas in the country, as crowded on summer weekends as the Schuylkill Expressway at rush hour.

After lunch, we visited the mansion of William Paca, who built this magnificent structure overlooking the old city and the harbor before he became governor of Maryland in 1782. It is the pride of Historic Annapolis, the local historic preservation group, and rightly so, for Historic Annapolis saved it.

For 58 years, most of the Paca house was hidden under the plaster and paint of a 200-room hotel, Carvel Hall. When the hotel was marked for demolition, Historic Annapolis rescued it after a battle with developers. The mansion was not only meticulously restored, decorated, and furnished with period pieces, but a parking lot was dug up to re-create Paca's garden, complete with a brick canal and Chinese Chippendale bridge.

I would not like to get into a fight with the Historic Annapolis people. They even beat up on the Navy. In 1962, the Navy wanted to appropriate three residential blocks to expand the academy. Historic Annapolis made up booklets showing why the neighborhood was architecturally and historically important and sent them to every preservation group in the country that had a congressman on the Joint Armed Services Committee. They also were asked to write to President John F. Kennedy, and reportedly his desk was piled with letters saying, "Don't destroy Annapolis!" The Navy solved its problem with landfill, extending the academy into the Severn River.

No detail is too small to escape Historic Annapolis' watchful eye. At the Middletown Tavern, a historic restaurant and watering hole at the harbor, the wife of the owner told us, "We were painting the front when they descended on us. We were using the wrong shade of brown. We had to stop, get the right shade mixed up, and start all over again. But I remember when the old part of town was really junky and not many visitors came here. I guess it's a small price to pay."

One treasure that didn't need restoring was the splendid State House, whose steeple-topped dome is the highest thing in the city. Some state capitols have grandeur, this one has elegance. Begun in 1772, it is said to be the oldest state capitol still in use. A superb portrait of George Washington by Charles Willson Peale hangs in the Old Senate Chamber.

We also visited the "New Annex," added in 1905 (in Annapolis, that's practically yesterday), which contains the new Senate and House of Representatives. The Maryland Legislature has one habit we wish our people in Harrisburg would adopt: one 90-day session that starts in January, at which they do their business, balance the budget, go home, and stay there.

That was just enough sightseeing for an afternoon. But strolling down the hill to our inn, Gibson's Lodgings, shop after shop called out to us. In the Ship and Soldier Shop, I found dime-store doughboy models from World War I, some of them now costing up to several thousand dimes. A few doors away at John Willoughby Antiques, it was love at first sight when I spotted a large model of the tug *Philadelphia*. And The Smoke Shop at the corner had a display of Zippo lighters and meerschaum pipes in the window. My companion was busily buying napkins and some knickknacks at the Annapolis Country Store, and an embroidered pillow at the Peake House. And there would be a lot more shopping before we would make it to our room.

We had earned a quiet evening, but happily it was not to be. We had booked a table at what is considered the best of the 20 or so restaurants in Annapolis, the Treaty of Paris in the Maryland Inn, an establishment that has been ministering to weary travelers since the Revolution. For openers, I had a few beauties from the oyster bar; my companion had the crab bisque. We both chose house specialties: grilled rock fish in a dill sauce and a perfectly cooked Maryland duck with cherry sauce, accompanied by a Caesar salad that was mixed at the table.

For dessert we moved to the inn's King of France bar to savor the sweet sounds of Charlie Byrd, a master of the amplified guitar who lives in the area and plays here frequently. Backed by a bassist and drummer, also fine musicians, they played to a properly reverent audience. For reasons that escape me now, a pub crawl seemed the sensible thing to do. In this city of 35,000, everything is in walking distance from everything else.

The next day, my companion and I walked through the Naval Academy. We followed some midshipmen into Dahlgren Hall and found ourselves watching Navy give Georgetown a hockey lesson. From the ceiling at one end of the vast arena hung a Yellow Peril, an open cockpit seaplane once used here as a trainer. Navy was leading, 10–1, in the second period, so we pushed on to the chapel.

"Chapel" is the wrong word; it is as big and impressive as a cathedral. In a room below the chapel, the remains of John Paul Jones, brought here from his original burial place in France, are in a crypt similar to that of Napoleon's in Paris. Near the chapel is the academy museum, the repository of Navy history. We gazed at beautifully carved figureheads, paintings of famous battles, incredibly detailed ship models, scrimshaw, and the memorabilia of the great heroes: Decatur, Farragut, Dewey, Peary, Nimitz.

We had one more stop before heading home, and I couldn't find it. An obliging midshipman came to the rescue. "Tecumseh is right over there behind the cedar trees, sir," he said.

And sure enough he was, looking as grim as ever. I explained to my companion that the statue was the academy's good luck symbol. Midshipmen tossed coins at it before exams, and it was decorated and painted before every home football game.

The coast was clear now, and I bounced a quarter off Tecumseh's forehead. I'm not a midshipman, but you never know.

—Chuck Lawliss

Directions from Philadelphia: Annapolis is a 125-mile drive from Philadelphia. Take Interstate 95 south to the exit for the Francis Scott Key Bridge near Baltimore, then follow Maryland Route 2 into Annapolis.

Pick up a free copy of The Insiders' Guide to Annapolis and Chesapeake Bay, which includes a calendar of events, at the Visitor Information Booth on the harbor, City Dock Street, 410-280-0445. The booklet also is available at the city's Office of Public Information and Tourism, 160 Duke of Gloucester St., phone 410-280-0445.

For a 48-page events calendar write: Office of Public Information and Tourism, 160 Duke of Gloucester St., Annapolis, Md. 21401, or call 410-269-0223.

The Visitor Information Center at the Naval Academy (410-263-6933 or 410-267-3363), is in Rickets Hall at Gate No. 1, near the intersection of King George and East streets. Tours are daily from March to Thanksgiving. The Naval Academy Museum is just inside Gate No. 3; open to visitors daily, except Thanksgiving, Christmas and New Year's Day. The museum and other buildings are open from noon.

The historic William Paca House (410-263-5553), 186 Prince George St., is open daily except Monday and holidays. There are three tours a day at the State House (410-974-3400), on State Circle. Open daily except Thanksgiving, Christmas, and New Year's Day.

ॐ

April in Virginia

RICHMOND, VA.

ONCE IN A WHILE, come spring, I long for my childhood home, Virginia.

In memory, anyway, springtime there is long and lush and dependable. A whole lot of sunny, sweater-only days. Soft, warm breezes. Soaking rains that turn winter's dreary brown to vibrant green almost overnight.

And the gardens. Peach, cerise, and lavender azaleas in profusion. Dogwoods flowering pink and white on lawn after lawn. Sturdy old magnolias ladling sweet perfume from their delicate white blossoms.

I am enchanted and lulled by these mental images, even though I realize they are embellished by 20 years of living elsewhere. So I was readily attracted to the notion of visiting Virginia for an April during the state's annual Historic Garden Week.

But first, a confession: What I know about growing flowers and plants wouldn't fill a trowel. Spider and asparagus plants and a bamboo palm or two have been part of my household decor for years. But for most of my adult life, I had no inclination—indeed, no place—to grow anything outdoors. My interest in gardening was budding at best.

I wasn't sure I'd enjoy Garden Week, then, if it amounted to dull recitations about soil acidity and sawdust mulches, accompanied by casual references to plants by their Latin names. A daisy may be a *dimorphotheca aurantiaca*, but I didn't need to know.

A close friend who is a skilled gardener—her arrangements of blossoms from her own garden rival any done professionally—would be a fine companion for the trip, I decided. Certainly she could help me understand what I was seeing, and maybe I could educate her a little, too. Having grown up in Minnesota and Connecticut, she had never before traveled to Dixie and knew none of its charms.

(As it turns out, open houses are as much an attraction as open gardens on many of the Garden Week tours. The Historic Garden Week guidebook describes the unusual architectural and decorating touches in the houses, along with any special horticulture. But the garden theme is ever present in the colorful and sometimes exotic arrangements created by local garden clubs to grace rooms in the houses.)

We set out driving south on Interstate 95 after work on Friday. We had to be back in the office on Monday morning and did not want to spoil our relaxation by trying to cram in too many distant gardens so that we'd have to do a lot of driving on Saturday. The four-hour trip to my sister's house in Richmond, where we could stay both nights for free, was plenty of road time, along with the Sunday drive back.

Luckily, one of the counties very close to Richmond—Hanover—was among the six locales offering house-and-garden tours that Saturday. And, luckily again for us, one of the two places in the state with tours scheduled that Sunday was Fauquier and Loudoun counties, in northern Virginia. We would be able to stop there on Sunday without a huge detour as we made our way back to Philadelphia.

It was late Friday when we reached Richmond. But before we went to sleep, my brother-in-law, a history teacher, briefed my friend on the high spots of historic Richmond that he would show her on a short car tour the next evening, after the day's garden viewing. She hooted when, after mentioning the statue of Stonewall Jackson on Monument Avenue, he asked, "You know who that was, don't you?"

"Of course, I know!" she shrieked indignantly. "A Civil War general." Maybe the weekend's education would be one-sided after all, I thought.

Our choices of what-to-do-when were limited by the Historic Garden Week schedule, as set forth in a detailed book published by the Garden Club of Virginia and made available about six weeks before Garden Week. The gardens selected for the tour are changed each year.

Saturday dawned drizzly, but my expert-gardener companion, my sister, and I set out enthusiastically, driving about 15 miles north of Richmond on Route 1 to the first stop we wanted to make on the Hanover County tour, the Greenfield Garden. Its 20 acres of well-planned, lovingly tended plants turned out to be the most elaborate garden we would see all weekend.

The 18th-century country house at Greenfield, once an abandoned dairy farm, was not open. At other stops on our tour, the open houses—their rooms graced by elaborate arrangements done by members of local garden clubs—were as much an attraction as the grounds around them.

But the varied Greenfield Garden was a real education for me and even impressed my experienced friend.

OK, here's where I admit that until that time I had never stopped to think that a garden was anything more than a spot where plants were tended and grown. I had never even thought of a gardener trying for an emotional effect beyond, say, simple beauty.

But as our clump of about a dozen folks under umbrellas trod the pebble paths at Greenfield, my mind was opened to different possibilities.

"A garden is to appreciate the use of many senses," said our guide, Wayne Ambler, a horticulture teacher at a local high school. He took us through a "no-talking zone," in which we were invited to listen to the sounds of the rain and a meandering brook. These, too, he said, were to be savored as part of the garden.

Certainly there was plenty to savor at Greenfield.

Ambler led us through a "desert" portion, full of cactuses I would never have expected to see growing in Virginia soil. It was even sprinkled with a few shards of bone, for desert effect. We tourists could imagine the kick the gardener, who Ambler said was "obsessed" with his gardening hobby, got out of placing the bones.

The Greenfield Garden seemed to have it all: a Japanese garden, complete with stones, a lantern, and a dwarf Japanese maple; an allhosta garden; a grass garden; a rare-rock garden; a lake for irrigation; a rock wall; assorted wild flowers; three gazebos; a pine forest; a boxwood border. And a wisteria that refuses to bloom. (I admit, I was glad to hear it. Mine won't either.)

As we left the Greenfield Garden, we encountered Jerry Huntsinger, who designed and cultivated it. "A garden is supposed to be an escape from reality," he told us, explicating the philosophy that guided his work. "A garden is not real life."

Huntsinger told us he didn't mind the day's wet weather because "the rain makes the colors in the garden more vibrant. Bright sun tends to blur the colors." Here was a man who was clearly able to find pleasure, even joy, in his gardening obsession.

After a homey chicken-salad lunch provided at a local school by the Doswell Ruritan Club, we headed to the two other homes on the Hanover tour. Approaching Pebble Hill, a Williamsburg-style house built in the early 1970s, we drove up a long, winding driveway bordered by white pine trees. Inside we found floors, beams and cabinets made from pine that had been salvaged from a well-known old Richmond drugstore. A stunning arrangement of yellow and orange tulips and white dogwood brightened the sunroom of the house.

Across the street at Pinehurst, a 50-year-old Colonial-style brick home with recent additions, we were again impressed by the Ashland Garden Club's floral arrangements. I especially liked the corkscrew willows, hyacinths, tulips, azaleas, and coral honeysuckle gracing the piano downstairs. Upstairs, I was most taken with the 14-by-20-foot bath area, featuring skylights and an oversize tub with a view of the landscaped rear grounds.

The Greenfield Garden, Pebble Hill, and Pinehurst were enough for us for one day. We spent the evening after dinner on a quickie drive-by tour of some of Richmond's historic sites, including Monument Avenue and the Jackson statue.

Some of our Sunday garden touring was informal and self-directed. We drove north on I-95 but abandoned the highway at Fredericksburg for the picturesque back roads. It was a lovely sunny day, and our drive toward Loudoun and Fauquier Counties, along Route 17, thrust us into breathtaking panoramas of rolling Virginia countryside. I cajoled my friend to concede that, indeed, my native state was truly God's country.

We had made reservations for brunch at the 1763 Inn, a few miles west of Upperville on Route 50. The inn had advertised in the Garden Week guidebook, and it was conveniently close to the houses we would visit that afternoon along Route 709. Most of the entrees on the inn's German-American menu were heavier than we wanted at midday, but we ordered omelets and enjoyed the cheerful atmosphere—print curtains, old photographs on the wall, plank floors—and a view of the pond out back.

It was a short drive from the inn to the three houses we would visit on the Loudoun-Fauquier tour.

That afternoon, in the heart of Virginia horse country, we were reminded a couple of times that the nation's capital, with all its power and wealth, was nearby. At our first stop, Ardarra—a 58-year-old restored home whose Gaelic name means "Grand Old Trees"—we encountered the lady of the household in the cutting garden.

She was lamenting the fact that her gardener had forgotten which weekend the tour was, so she and the household staff had been forced to hustle to get ready for visitors. "I had to go out, and I spent a great deal of time pulling weeds and wild onions," said Lila Ash, whose husband, Roy, a co-founder of Litton Industries Inc., was director of the Office of Management and Budget under Presidents Richard Nixon and Gerald Ford.

After a stop at Waterford Farm, which featured a master-bedroom suite overlooking rolling fields and an eight-acre pond, we moved on to Friendship Farm, an 1816 farmhouse with walls full of photographs and memorabilia from the Civil War to the present. There, we found this disarming note in a typewriter:

We beg your pardon
If our garden
Isn't really at the ready.
The reason is
The season is
A little bit unsteady.
JWS, April 20, 1990

The house is a country retreat for former Representative James W. Symington (D-Mo.).

As we were leaving Friendship Farm to begin our drive back to Philadelphia, I overheard a man in a light-blue hat remark with satisfaction to his female companion, "Well, we saw them all, and it's only 20 after 4."

We felt satisfied, too, although our approach had not been so comprehensive. We had set out to enjoy an unhurried spring-weekend trip and still manage to see some spectacular houses and gardens, and we'd done it. Plus, I had learned something about gardens.

As for my friend, on the way home, she acknowledged that she had also learned something. She had indeed known who Stonewall Jackson was, she said.

"But I have to admit, I thought he was a Yankee."

—Carol Horner

Directions from Philadelphia: Follow I-95 south to Richmond.

Every spring, the Garden Club of Virginia sponsors Historic Garden Week in the last full week of April, to raise money to restore the gardens and grounds of historic landmarks. The homes and gardens selected for Historic Garden Week tours change each year. To learn which have been selected for current year's tours (as well as days and hours of opening and admission prices), contact: Historic Garden Week in Virginia, 12 East Franklin St., Richmond, Va. 23219; phone 804-644-7776 or 804-643-7141.

On the waterfront

BALTIMORE, MD.

MEDIA HYPE CAN BE a dangerous thing, but Oriole Park at Camden Yards can handle it.

Built on the edge of Baltimore's downtown just three blocks west of the ever-popular Inner Harbor, the Orioles' new $105 million brick-and-steel playground is a Shibe Park–like throwback to the intimate ballyards of yesteryear. Any baseball fan who considers Philadelphia's stadium complex a wasteland will find it hard to believe that the same Interstate 95 that leads to Veterans Stadium can, two hours to the south, deliver you to such an alive and downright fun baseball destination.

Of course, with its waterfront renaissance, Baltimore had been a prime weekend family getaway long before the Orioles moved downtown to Camden Yards.

Over the course of two days earlier this summer my parents, wife, children, and I, in addition to taking in a game at Camden Yards, visited Babe Ruth's birthplace; toured the National Aquarium in Baltimore, and enjoyed it as much as ever (though the dolphin show in the new Marine Mammal Pavilion was disappointingly brief); browsed through the shops and food courts of Harborplace; feasted on the world's best steamed hardshell crabs, and took an enjoyable water-taxi ride through the harbor to Fell's Point, an intriguing old waterfront community with shops, taverns, and restaurants that's a combination of South Street and Society Hill-in-the-making about a mile east of the Inner Harbor.

But baseball was our primary order of business, and we were not disappointed. After parking our car at the Sheraton Inner Harbor, one of many good hotels ringing the tourist area, a short walk up the hill brought us within view of one of the stadium's singular features: the restored Baltimore & Ohio Railroad Warehouse, at 1,016 feet one of the longest buildings on the East Coast.

Making our way around the historic eight-story building, whose west side forms the rightfield backdrop, we joined the crowd pouring through the Eutaw Street gates, giddy with good fortune: Their team was battling for first place; they were cheating the modern-day nature of things by seeing a day game on real grass in a jewel of a baseball-only stadium, and they had one of the toughest tickets in town.

I had purchased our upper reserved seats six weeks in advance—good thing, too, because the 47,000-seat stadium was sold out, the 29th such sellout in the first 42 home games.

Beyond the gate, we were each rewarded with an Oriole beach towel—a giveaway we hadn't expected. The street, now a pedestrian mall between the warehouse and the outfield, offers a number of eating possibilities, as does the warehouse, which also features Babe's Pub and a parental nightmare: the well-stocked Oriole store.

But Baltimore knows how to eat, so we got in the longest line, which was quickly forming behind a tent redolent with hickory charcoal smoke: Boog Powell's Barbecue Tent. While we waited, we stole a peek at the field, an emerald checkerboard of real grass. The Orioles and the Milwaukee Brewers were loosening up 16 feet below us in centerfield. They were running atop the site where, during construction, archaeologists unearthed the remains of Ruth's Cafe, one of the saloons Babe Ruth's family owned and lived above while Ruth was at St. Mary's Industrial School in West Baltimore.

But the 10-cent soup the Babe's mother served for lunch couldn't have matched Powell's sliced-pork sandwich. A power-hitting star of the Orioles' great '70s teams, Powell usually greets customers and signs autographs. He wasn't present this day, but the pork I slathered in thick barbecue sauce, the baked beans alive with cayenne pepper, and the good coleslaw more than made up for his absence.

We ate our sandwiches at one of the picnic tables scattered about the street, sharing the table with a retired season-ticket holder whose cap was festooned with Oriole pins. "I like it, it's like a picnic atmosphere here," he said of the bustling scene. Good description—happy people, bottles of imported beer iced down in tubs, and plump sausages grilling in the open air.

The climb to our seats just beyond third base brought another pleasant surprise: a cheerful, courteous attendant who spritzed and wiped down our good but nonetheless nosebleed seats.

"This is quite a facility," agreed the man next to me, retired Navy Captain Jim Brunson, who had come up from Ponte Vedra Beach, Fla., to visit his son and his family. As the Orioles took batting practice, we had a hard time deciding where to look. Down on the field, where batted balls were dying in the grass and caroming oddly off the asymmetrical outfield wall? Or up higher to a grand view of a city comfortable in its embrace of both the past and the present? To right field, 460 feet from home plate, the imposing warehouse that has prompted Oriole scouts to conclude that some rare prospects have "warehouse power"? To the scoreboard topped with Oriole weather vanes and a gold-leaf clock whose numerals have been replaced with the 12 letters: BALTIMORESUN? To the 1911 Italianate Bromo Seltzer tower peeking above the light standards in left-center? Or to dead center, beyond the terraced bullpens and shady picnic area to the modern skyscrapers of downtown Baltimore?

I was eventually jolted from this reverie by the singing of the national anthem. Sports customs, like food, define a culture, and Oriole fans put a distinct stamp on the song penned less than three miles from here by screaming out the second "O" ("O say does tha-at star-spangled . . . ") in fealty to their only major-league team.

The O's responded with an interesting, well-played game. They had bashed three home runs and were up 7–2 in the seventh inning before the Brewers' Franklin Stubbs parked a Ben McDonald pitch in the bleachers in right-center. And the crowd booed loudly—not at McDonald, as it turned out, but at the miscreant who held onto the ball for a while before following Oriole-fan tradition and heaving it back onto the field.

Then came the top of the ninth, the crowd up on its feet raucously dancing and playing air guitar to the "Wild Thing" song as relief closer Gregg Olsen made his way to the pitcher's mound. Dark clouds boiled out of the northwest, and the crowd nervously roared with every lightning bolt that ripped into the area.

Soon it was raining in windswept sheets, and the giveaway towels were doubling as damp raincoats. On the field, Olsen was just one out away from finishing the game when he fell off the slippery mound while throwing a pitch and the umpire suspended play.

When the rain tapered off, we scampered down to some of the excellent (and now vacant) lower reserved seats behind home plate, but after the ground crew again covered the infield with a tarp, we called it a day and headed back to our hotel.

My wife and kids went swimming. My father and I were headed for Babe Ruth's birthplace and a glass of draft English ale at one of the taverns that rim the stadium area. We met what was left of the crowd spilling out of the park.

"Did the Orioles hold on?" I asked.

"Yeah," one young man said. "One pitch and a fly ball to [Mike] Devereaux in center and it was over."

He laughed at the absurdity of sitting through a 64-minute rain delay for just one pitch. We laughed at our good fortune in not having missed anything.

As Rex Barney, the Orioles longtime public-address announcer would say, "Thank youuuuuuu," Baltimore.

—Bruce E. Beans

Directions from Philadelphia: Drive south on Interstate 95 to Baltimore. Orioles tickets are tough at any time, but especially on weekends.

The Orioles information number is 410-685-9800. Call, too, for information about tours of Oriole Park, including the dugout, press box, club level, and party suites. The Babe Ruth Birthplace Museum and Baseball Center houses displays devoted to Babe Ruth, the Orioles, and Maryland baseball. The rowhouse is at 216 Emory St., just off the 600 block of Pratt Street, and a couple of blocks from the stadium. Phone: 410-727-1539. Hours: 10 a.m. to 5 p.m (7 p.m. if the Orioles are playing at home).

The Inner Harbor, with its famed center for shopping and noshing and with the National Aquarium, can easily fill the time when the O's aren't playing. For information on harbor activities and events, contact the Baltimore Area Visitors Center at 1-800-282-6632. It will supply information on hotel packages and the Orioles schedule, too.

ᏫᏫ

The homes of the rich

CHARLES CITY, VA.

THE VERY RICH FASCINATE ME. I like to see how they live, poke around their mansions, hear the gossip, learn how they got their money and, sometimes, learn how they lost it, too.

If you share this minor quirk, hurry to the banks of the James River in Tidewater Virginia. Here you can visit some of the most opulent and historic mansions in the country and pick up enough juicy stories for a dozen dinner parties.

Plantations are a nice change from the big city and as much fun to visit as any of the places Robin Leach goes.

The great plantations of the James share a common origin. To attract colonists, the Virginia Company of London, the group of financiers that had the rights to settle America, gave large tracts of land to men who had the funds to transport people to Virginia. Their plantations prospered, becoming by the mid-1700s large-scale agricultural and commercial operations.

The wealth and power of the plantation owners was built on tobacco, which they exported to England, and the gangs of enslaved Africans who grew it for them. Their mansions were centers of hospitality and social life and they made entertaining almost an art form.

But years of growing tobacco depleted the soil. Plantations began to decline, and the Civil War just about finished them off. During Reconstruction, most of the great houses stood empty, and many were vandalized or destroyed. Decades later, some were restored, by the descendants of the original owners in some cases, and by new money as well. And a relative handful remain accessible and open to the public today.

Our first stop on our weekend was Carter's Grove, originally owned by Robert "King" Carter, the wealthiest and most powerful of the Tidewater planters. His grandson, Carter Burwell, inherited the property and in 1750 began to build an elegant brick mansion with a remarkable series of carved, paneled rooms and detached, flanking dependencies. He also expanded the property by buying five neighboring plantations.

Carter's Grove was the Burwell family seat until they moved west in 1792. For more than a century, it passed through the hands of various owners, declining with the times. In 1928, Archibald McCrea, the son of a president of the Pennsylvania Railroad, and his wife, a tobacco heiress, purchased Carter's Grove and transformed it into a symbol of their wealth and social standing. The Colonial Williamsburg Foundation acquired it in 1964 and now administers it.

At the reception center, an audiovisual presentation, "A Thing Called Time," compresses 400 years of history into 14 minutes. On the way to the mansion, we stopped at the reconstructed slave quarter where a black interpreter told how the slaves lived. Beneath their shacks were pits where they stored their few possessions. Nearby were small garden plots, a corn crib, and enclosures for chickens. The ramshackle slave quarter would haunt us as we toured the mansion.

The great house has been changed since it was completed in the 1750s. The roof was raised, a third floor added, the dependencies enlarged, and linked to the main building by complementary structures, called "hyphens" by the architect. The furnishings are vintage antiques and tasteful reproductions. The elegant woodwork, however, is original.

Many interesting stories are associated with Carter's Grove. Two brief ones: Both George Washington and Thomas Jefferson were turned down in marriage in what is called the "Refusal Room." And during the Revolution, a British cavalry officer slashed the railing when he rode his horse up the great staircase. It must be true; we saw the slash marks.

The formal garden on the river side has been restored and planted with 18th-century ornamentals. A short walk from the garden is the partly restored Wolstenholme Towne, the original settlement that was destroyed in the Indian uprising of 1622.

Carter's Grove was my companion's favorite; mine was Berkeley, our next stop. This Georgian mansion, built in 1726, is said to be the oldest three-story brick building in Virginia. Benjamin Harrison, son of the builder and its second owner, was a signer of the Declaration of Independence.

William Henry Harrison, Benjamin's third son, was the Indian fighter known as "Tippecanoe" who became the ninth president in 1841, but died of pneumonia a month after his inauguration. His grandson, Benjamin Harrison, was the 23rd president.

Here at Berkeley, English settlers came ashore on December 4, 1619, and observed what many say was the first official Thanksgiving in America. (A framed letter from the Kennedy White House apologizes for crediting the Pilgrims with that honor.) George Washington, and later the nine succeeding presidents, dined here. Thomas Jefferson directed the installation of the handsome woodwork and the double arches of the great rooms.

From July 2 to August 16, 1862, General George McClellan made his headquarters at Berkeley, and President Lincoln visited twice to confer with him. One of his generals, Dan Butterfield, helped his bugler compose a new tune for "lights out." When the melancholy notes of Taps rang out, the buglers of other divisions repeated the call, and Confederate soldiers across the James could hear the haunting melody.

When the Seven Days' Battle drove McClellan back from Richmond, the deserted mansion was used as a field hospital, and much of the remaining furniture was burned in the fireplace for heat. Union soldiers were the last people to occupy Berkeley until it was purchased in 1905 by John Jamieson, who as a drummer boy had once been there with Union troops.

After Jamieson's death, his son, Malcolm, restored the mansion and made Berkeley a working plantation again. Today the Jamiesons use the two upper floors as their living quarters, while visitors tour the entrance hall, the great room, the dining room, and the master's study on the first floor. Malcolm's wife, Grace, did her research, chose interior colors close to the original, and furnished the rooms with exceptional 18th-century antiques.

After the tour, we walked down the five restored landscaped terraces to the river and through the formal boxwood garden, rose garden, and ladies' winter garden.

After a restful night at Edgewood, a plantation near Berkeley, we drove to Westover, one of the finest examples of a Georgian domestic complex in the country. Built by William Byrd II in 1730, Westover has come to symbolize the high level of architecture achieved in the Colonial era. The outbuildings and the original gardens complement the mansion.

One of the Westover legends concerns Byrd's daughter, Evelyn, whose marriage to the rakish grandson of the Earl of Peterborough was forbidden by her father. She died in her late 20s, of a broken heart, the story goes, and yes, her ghost is said to walk still at Westover.

A small church on the grounds originally served the families of Westover, Shirley, Berkeley, and other nearby plantations, and the parishioners would drop by Westover after services. Mrs. Byrd tired of entertaining them, we are told, and had the church moved four miles away. We also enjoyed learning that the small brick building called "the necessary," which housed the toilet, had a fireplace to warm it in the winter.

We also visited neighboring Evelynton, which originally was owned, like Westover, by Byrd. He sold it, and the plantation's ownership changed hands several times before it was purchased by Edmund Ruffin, a secessionist who later became famous for firing the first shot at Fort Sumter. Ruffin also was a well-known agriculturist who developed methods to restore the productivity of the exhausted land along the James.

The war all but destroyed Evelynton. As for Ruffin, after some thought he convinced himself that suicide was the most honorable choice, and his final diary entry ended, "I hereby repeat my unmitigated hatred to the perfidious, malignant, and vile Yankee race."

Although the Ruffin family managed to keep the plantation, it was not restored until the 1930s. John Augustine Ruffin, Jr., a great-great-grandson of Edmund, built a Georgian Revival house on the original foundation, borrowing the best elements from historic plantation houses in the area, and furnishing it with period antiques.

Before heading back to Philadelphia, we visited Shirley, a plantation founded in 1613 and deeded to Edward Hill in 1660. The mansion was begun in 1723 by the third Edward Hill for his daughter Elizabeth, who married John Carter, son of King Carter. Finished in 1738, and still largely in its original state, it is an architectural treasure filled with family portraits, original furniture, crested silver, and memorabilia.

Ann Hill Carter was born here and married "Light Horse" Harry Lee in the mansion. Their son, Robert E. Lee, received part of his schooling in the converted laundry house.

And the rest, like the James River plantations, is history.

—Chuck Lawliss

Directions from Philadelphia: Follow I-95 south almost to Richmond. Pick up I-295 south and east to Route 5, about 20 miles. Follow Route 5 south and east for another 20 miles to Charles City.

A very perfect place

CHARLOTTESVILLE, VA.

SOMETHING ABOUT OUR WEEKEND was troubling us, but we couldn't decide what. We enjoyed our day, the weather was beautiful, our dinner was lovely. Then, over coffee, my companion suddenly said, "Our problem is that Charlottesville is too perfect. It intimidates us."

She was right. The town nestles near the Blue Ridge Mountains, where the vistas are long, the sun warm, the breeze cool. Everywhere you look, there's a scene that belongs on a calendar: horses in rolling pastures, elegant farms, vineyards, the historic buildings in the charming town, the elegant University of Virginia campus.

There's always something to do. Opera in the garden of Ash Lawn-Highland mansion and the concerts of the Charlottesville and University Symphony Orchestra. Plays at the university's Culbreth Theater, band concerts at the Downtown Mall. The county fair in late August. Wine festivals. Art and craft festivals. Steeplechase racing. Polo. A festive holiday season.

To top it off, Charlottesville is Thomas Jefferson's hometown. After retiring from the presidency, he came back to Monticello, his "little mountain home," which he had designed and built while still in his 20s. He proceeded to found and design the University of Virginia, his "academical village," and, in his spare time, he invented all sorts of neat gadgets.

The perfect man in the perfect place. It is intimidating, isn't it? But perfection isn't the worst problem to have on a weekend, and we decided to relax and enjoy it.

While the dew was still on the lawn, we explored the university, with its famous serpentine walls and its handsome red-brick buildings trimmed with white. The centerpiece of the campus is the Rotunda, inspired by the Roman Pantheon. No wonder the American Institute of Architects has chosen Jefferson's design for the university as the most outstanding achievement in American architecture.

Flanking the lawn in front of the Rotunda are the east and west ranges, which contain the original student rooms. We peeked in at Edgar Allan Poe's old room (No. 13, on the west range). Poe didn't graduate, but Woodrow Wilson did. William Faulkner was writer-in-residence here for several years, and Georgia O'Keeffe once taught art in the summer school.

When I was in college, Virginia was considered a drinking school, the home of the "gentleman's C," the place where you could major in plantation management. (I once told my mother that I thought I would like to go to Virginia. She icily replied, "I bet you would." The subject never came up again.) That era is long gone, and its 16,000 students now diligently pursue learning at an institution renowned for its academic excellence.

In Charlottesville's historic district, we explored the Albemarle County Court House, which has an interesting history. In the 1820s, its north wing was a "common temple," used on different Sundays by Episcopalians, Presbyterians, Methodists, and Baptists. Jefferson, James Monroe, and James Madison worshipped here.

Near the courthouse is a statue of Stonewall Jackson astride his horse, Little Sorrel, and a few blocks away is a statue of Robert E. Lee. Two other statues, though, proved more interesting. One commemorated the Lewis and Clark Expedition, the other Clark's brother, known as the Conqueror of the Northwest.

During the Revolution, George Rogers Clark brilliantly led the fight against the British in the Old Northwest, the area around the Great Lakes. Returning home a general, he received a letter from Jefferson asking if he would lead an expedition "to research the country" between the Mississippi and the Pacific. He said the idea was "extremely agreeable" but that he had too many financial worries to consider it. He later moved into a house on the Ohio River and slipped into obscurity.

In the spring of 1803, Clark by chance saw himself being surpassed by his younger brother, William, who was sailing by in a boat with Meriwether Lewis. They were beginning their journey to the Pacific and immortality.

The town's shops invite browsing, and we stopped in a few. Palais Royal has French linen for bath, bed, and table. Pewter Corner has one of the widest selections of pewter anywhere. Crafters' Gallery displays the work of a number of talented contemporary artisans. Signet Gallery specializes in Native American jewelry and crafts, and the Sun Bow Trading Co. has some interesting Oriental rugs and tribal textiles.

We had a late lunch at the splendid Historic Michie (pronounced Mickey) Tavern, one of the oldest homesteads in the state. It was dismantled and moved here in 1927 from its original location on a stagecoach route some 17 miles to the northwest. John Michie, a Scot, purchased the original land from Patrick Henry's father and opened the tavern in 1787. His descendants owned and operated it until 1910.

Meals are served at the tavern in the 200-year-old converted slave house called the Ordinary. We feasted on fried chicken, black-eyed peas, green-bean salad, cornbread, and a tasty apple cobbler, then walked it off on a guided tour of the tavern, which contains a fine collection of pre-Revolutionary furniture and artifacts.

Downstairs, we saw the Keeping Hall, the Tap Bar in the Gentlemen's Parlor, and the wine cellar that supplied it. Upstairs were the ballroom and private quarters for affluent guests. The restored outbuildings include the kitchen, a smokehouse, a springhouse, and a gristmill, its two-story waterwheel still being turned by a millrace.

On the first floor of the gristmill is a general store, complete with post office and barber shop, a brass cash register, a cigar-store Indian, and a set-up checkerboard perched on a cracker barrel. We bought a few gifts—jars of homemade preserves, a Raggedy Ann doll, and several pairs of dice, replicas of those used by soldiers in the Revolution. On the second floor is the Virginia Wine Museum, where exhibits trace oenology in the state from the days of the Jamestown settlement to today.

The wine museum was a perfect segue to the Oakencroft Vineyard and Winery, a short drive away. Another perfect touch: a red barn that houses the winery. In front of it is a small lake, home to Canada geese and ducks. Behind it are 17 acres of grapevines, and to the side, a field with purebred Herefords. All of it is framed by mountains.

The next morning, we went to Monticello, Jefferson's justly famous home on a hilltop that commands a view of the rolling countryside and the town. He retired here, having served as governor of Virginia, minister to the court of Louis XVI, secretary of state, vice president, and, ultimately, the third president of the United States.

Architecture was his avocation, and the house was rebuilt and remodeled several times over a period of 40 years, reflecting the pleasure Jefferson found in "putting up and taking down." The entrance hall functioned as Jefferson's little museum, containing fossil bones, a buffalo head, elk antlers, and a seven-day clock of his design that indicated the day as well as the time. He equipped the house with more of his gadgets, the single-acting double doors in the parlor, and the dumbwaiters and revolving serving door in the dining room.

Jefferson also was interested in gardening and agriculture. "No occupation is so delightful to me as the culture of the earth," he wrote, "and no culture comparable to that of the garden. . . . But though an old man, I am but a young gardener."

In his original plans were ornamental and vegetable gardens, two orchards, a vineyard, and an 18-acre "grove" or ornamental forest. He experimented with more than 250 varieties of vegetables and herbs, including some 20 varieties of English pea, his favorite vegetable. The gardens here have been re-created from Jefferson's detailed records.

He brought his bride, Martha Wayles Skelton, here in 1772, and died here on July 4, 1826. The Jeffersons are buried in a small family cemetery near the foot of the lawn. Over Jefferson's grave is an obelisk, inscribed with an epitaph he wrote, curiously making no mention of the high offices he had held. His self-assessment read simply:

Here was buried Thomas Jefferson
Author of the Declaration of American Independence
Of the Statute of Virginia for Religious Freedom
And Father of the University of Virginia.

Before heading home, we just had time to see Ash Lawn-Highland, the home of James Monroe and his family—a 550-acre working farm next door to Monticello. Jefferson chose the house site and planted the orchards for his friend. The house is attractive and filled with Monroe possessions and memorabilia. The slave quarters are first-rate by the standards of the period, a reflection of Monroe's ambivalence about slavery. There is a boxwood garden, and a peacock patrols the lawn.

Everything looks comfortable, lived in. It is old-shoe, while Monticello is dancing-slipper. We wondered what Jefferson really thought about Monroe's home, and vice versa. We left convinced that this place was our favorite. Beautiful, but with just enough flaws to be lovable.

—Chuck Lawliss

Directions from Philadelphia: Go west on the Pennsylvania Turnpike to Interstate Route 81. Take I-81 south to Staunton, Va., then go east on Interstate 64 to Charlottesville. If the day is particularly clear, consider taking the much slower but beautiful Skyline Drive, which runs along the crest of the Blue Ridge Mountains, picking it up at Front Royal on the way down, or at Waynesboro on the way home. The exits from I-81 and I-64 are marked. Either way, it's about 290 miles from Philadelphia.

Charlottesville has a full complement of chain hotels and motels, both in town and on the outskirts. There are also a number of inns and bed-and-breakfast accommodations in the area. Consult the Guesthouses Bed and Breakfast Inc. reservation service (Box 5737, Charlottesville, Va. 22905; phone 804-979-7264, noon to 5 p.m., daily).

For a calendar of area events, contact the Charlottesville/Albemarle Visitors Bureau, Box 161, Dept. CE, Charlottesville, Va. 22902; phone 804-977-1783.

For exploring Charlottesville itself, begin at Virginia's Thomas Jefferson Visitor Center (just off Interstate 64 at Route 20 South; phone 804-293-6789 or 804-977-1783). Information is available on auto and walking tours in the area. A combination ticket on sale at the center admits visitors to Monticello, Ash Lawn-Highland, and Historic Michie Tavern at a substantial savings.

Directions from Philadelphia: Take I-95 south to Interstate 495—the Washington Beltway—heading west. Pick up 66 west to 15 south. Follow 15 to 29 and take 29 southwest to Charlottesville.

∾

The Civil War: A bicyclist's view

FREDERICKSBURG, VA.

IT WAS THE CLOSING WEEKEND of the Tour Du Pont. Four of us who couldn't qualify piled our bikes into a rented Chevrolet van and set off for something more bucolic than Kelly Drive. And here we found it: black velvet road winding through miles of leafy territory. We were on the battlefields.

The idea began with a touch of the national fever brought on by the PBS television series "The Civil War." Why not see some of these mournful and monumental sites up close? Like from a bicycle?

Eastern Virginia is mild through and through, forgiving in its climate (even the rain, which did come, was gentle) and low-slung in landscape and architecture. Lazy two-lanes could keep a biker going for weeks. And in the battlefields, thanks to the National Park Service, the roads are blacktopped to perfection.

We picked Fredericksburg for its proximity to four battlefields strung together as the Fredericksburg and Spotsylvania National Military Park. These were guaranteed to be undisturbed terrain. They were also guaranteed to be close to comforts for the urban marshmallow.

This was not a trip for cycling maniacs. We didn't want any rock-hopping or breathtaking hills. We didn't want to compete for anything. We wanted cushy bed-and-breakfast accommodations, a good array of restaurants, antiquing in the event of rain, and a bike-repair shop in the event of worse.

We found all of these. Here, it's only natural to depend on civilization.

Fredericksburg draws far more amateur historians than outdoor types and the town is stocked with amenities for them. Civil War nuts and genealogy buffs fill old inns, exchanging fresh historical leads over breakfast and dining well after a day of maps and museums. The airing of "The Civil War" in 1990 "sure didn't hurt" business, said Jerry Selby, who owns a small B&B in the historic district.

"Half the people in this country didn't know there was a war going on 129 years ago," he said. "Now they want to get caught up, figure out what happened."

Fredericksburg would have been historic without the Civil War.
George Washington was born just across the Rappahannock River, and
two of the main tourist attractions in town are the house he bought for
his mother, Mary, and the mansion called Kenmore where his sister,
Betty, lived in elegant Georgian fashion.

James Monroe practiced law in Fredericksburg. Patriots met there
to plot revolution. All the while, the wharves took on huge shipments
of tobacco bound for Europe.

In 1862, Fredericksburg, halfway between Washington and Richmond, was caught in the crossfire, invaded, shelled, burned, and
fought over block by block. The town of 5,000 was torn apart, but
many antebellum buildings survive, unmarked and unpretentious.

Most are in the 40-block National Historic District. The downtown
is a precious but agreeable shopping strip in certifiably Colonial housing, offering enough antique and home "shoppes" to redecorate the entire East Coast to Martha Stewart specifications.

Fredericksburg—with a population of 20,000 the biggest town
around for miles—is struggling to fend off the greater Washington-
Northern Virginia suburban spread (bumper sticker: "Don't Fairfax
Fredericksburg"). Ominously, the city's fringes appear to be giving way
to fresh subdivisions. But at places like Dinty Moore's in town, where
breakfast comes with ashtrays and grits, exurbanization doesn't seem
much of a threat to the spirit.

For the moment, Fredericksburg is safely southern: Colonial clapboard, Victorian front porches, actual accents, and courtesy everywhere.

On a warm evening, the streets are lush and hushed, except when a
pickup truck (these account for about half the vehicles in Fredericksburg) varooms past. Windows fronting on the sidewalk afford glimpses
of people watching television, fighting, and in the case of one man on
Caroline Street, performing a slow, balletic dance across the living
room. It's a nice small town.

This we discovered on Friday night, after the four-hour drive down
Interstate 95 from Philadelphia. We were nicely received at the Fredericksburg Colonial Inn, a big 1928 building just this side of the strip-
zoned, shopping-centered road from the expressway.

We strolled deeper into town for dinner, settling on a place called
Sammy T's that has a tin ceiling and a big, beautiful beer list.

Next morning, in blazing sunshine, we rode to the Fredericksburg
Battlefield, less than a mile from downtown and past the iron gates of

the Confederate Cemetery. (Union soldiers were buried in the cemetery next to the Visitor Center.)

As a national park, the battlefield is a perpetual good deal. For absolutely nothing, cheerful, knowledgeable people at the Visitor Center answer lists of questions.

With its exhibits and slide shows, the Visitor Center launches tours not only of the Fredericksburg Battlefield, but also of those at Spotsylvania, Chancellorsville, and the Wilderness, all within 15 miles.

Just outside the center is the Sunken Road, cut into a hill where Confederate artillery perched while infantrymen behind a stone wall mowed down soldiers hurled pointlessly across the plain by General Ambrose Burnside. More than 12,000 Union men were killed. Fredericksburg was to be Lee's most one-sided victory.

In the battlefields, there's an eerie quiet. Here, as if to keep the facts of carnage at a distance, the government's hand has posted signs forbidding firearms and politely asking visitors to not disturb the trenches.

Lee Drive, which winds through the Fredericksburg Battlefield, is canopied by dense woods. Our bikes pretty much commanded the road, with its luscious curves and intermediate-level hills. Even on a sunny Saturday, car traffic in the woods was sparse and pokey.

This was a good thing, because Lee Drive is where my friend Trevor's derailleur slipped a sprocket.

We knew what to do. We limped back to town on a country road, put the injured bike in the van, and drove to the Bicycle Exchange in a nearby shopping center.

Maybe it wasn't southern; maybe it was just nice. But the young woman at the shop, after fixing the derailleur with a few flicks of the wrist, said there wouldn't be any charge. "Just give me a smile," she said.

This left time for more biking around town, down by the river and on the paved path along the canal. Only on bikes would we have run across the many people fishing (bass, perch, catfish) the Rappahannock, one of the cleanest rivers in the East, or Denise and Bill Micks of Rappahannock Outdoors, who schmoozed with us on the porch of the woodsy lodge outside town where they outfit canoe and kayak trips.

Back in town, we checked into the spectacularly genteel Richard Johnston Inn, a 1799 townhouse in the heart of the shopping district.

Libby Gowin, the innkeeper, was preparing for the wedding of a couple who she said "just had to get married at the Richard Johnston Inn." We repaired to our rooms upstairs, finding armoires and quilts, a fireplace, dormer windows, and bathrooms worthy of Central Park South.

But back to biking: Having covered only 12 miles at the Fredericksburg Battlefield, we were ready for more riding territory. There is more at the Spotsylvania Battlefield, about seven miles to the southwest. This can be reached by bike and would have been if it hadn't been drizzling Sunday morning.

Again, we piled the bikes into the van. Deeper into the country, Spotsylvania was all but deserted—so much the better for biking. The roads traverse the site of some of the war's most savage fighting, and we traced Lee's 14-day holding action against Grant's 1864 drive to Richmond.

Spotsylvania is largely open field, the trenches marked along about 10 miles of road. The battlefield seemed more sad and raw than Fredericksburg, perhaps because of the terrain, perhaps because of the cold mist, perhaps because even the Park Service's painstakingly evenhanded wayside narrative evokes the horrors of hand-to-hand combat in the waning days of the Army of Northern Virginia.

We had to go back to I-95 and home, but there is more to see at the Chancellorsville and Wilderness battlefields, about 10 and 15 miles due west of Fredericksburg. These, too, can be reached by bike in an hour or two. A day should be enough to do both. If your derailleur holds together, almost anything is possible.

—Laura Mansnerus

Directions from Philadelphia: Follow I-95 south to about midway between Washington and Richmond. Pick up Route 17 east for a few miles to Fredericksburg.

A wealth of information about the area is available from the Fredericksburg Visitor Center, 706 Caroline St., Fredericksburg, Va. 22401, phone 800-678-4748; Spotsylvania County Visitors Center, 4707 Southpoint Parkway, Fredericksburg, Va. 22401, phone 703-891-8687; Fredericksburg Battlefield Visitor Center, Sunken Road, Fredericksburg, Va. 22401, phone 703-373-6122.

The footsteps of Georgetown

WASHINGTON, D.C.

GEORGETOWN IS A DELIGHTFUL BIT of Washington that looms large here despite being little more than a square mile in size.

It seems unlikely that any other piece of land in the world of comparable size has been home to—or host for—so many world players, from presidents to ambassadors to movie stars to foreign dignitaries to media moguls to writers and artists.

One of the greatest joys in spending time in Georgetown is to walk in their footsteps. To stand, for instance, on the brick sidewalk in front of 3307 N St., John F. Kennedy's last Georgetown home, where, as president-elect, he held impromptu news conferences before moving to the White House.

To wander through Dumbarton Oaks (1703 32nd St.), where the conference was held that led to the United Nations Charter.

To pause near the site of Suter's Tavern (1000 block of Wisconsin Avenue), where George Washington and others met to plan the building of the capital.

Or to hop down the 75 stairs where the devil met his match: The steep steps on the Georgetown University campus are known as the "Exorcist Steps" because that's where actor Jason Miller, the priest in the movie *The Exorcist*, fell and died, taking the devil with him.

Georgetown, with its chic restaurants and pubs and trendy boutiques, has few rivals as a place for strolling. Even on a hot summer day, the streets are comfortable, shaded by trees at nearly every step.

For the lover of history, Georgetown—a thriving tobacco port long before the District of Columbia was founded—is an obvious draw. Students of architecture can marvel at the Federal, Georgian, Gothic Revival, and Victorian buildings.

And hikers and joggers can do their thing on the towpath of the C&O Canal, the 184-mile waterway that ends (or begins) in Georgetown.

For those with more modern needs—such as a Gap, for instance—Wisconsin Avenue is a shopper's haven. Music mavens will find every taste answered along M Street. And for those tourists who feel incomplete without some fancy-schmancy waterfront shopping, like Baltimore's Harborplace or New York's South Street Seaport, Georgetown has that, too. It's called Washington Harbour, it's next to the Potomac River, and it has all the usual high-priced ethnic restaurants.

Georgetown has fabulous nooks and crannies. There are—if you don't watch carefully—as many things to miss as there are to see.

Such as the Francis Scott Key bookshop (28th and O streets), with a shelf of interesting volumes for $1. Or the 19th-century testaments to love written on the headstones and monuments in the Oak Hill Cemetery (30th and R streets). Or Briggs Hall (1514 26th St.), a ramshackle building whose history is carved into a stone in the front wall; the stone, though, is so eroded that all that can be made out is the date 1864, leaving Briggs Hall a bit of a mystery.

Or, of course, Herman Hollerith's old workshop. Herman who?

Hollerith is one name few Americans might recognize, despite its importance. A century ago, Hollerith perfected a punch and tabulating machine in his workshop on 31st Street, a few steps from the C&O Canal, that was the forerunner of today's computer. He later sold his business to a company that evolved into IBM.

Hollerith's workshop was just another delightful bit of Georgetown history not found in the standard guidebooks. But it's all there, waiting to be discovered.

On one visit, for instance, I ran across Daw's Fence. Stretching about a half block along P Street, between 28th and 29th, the fence was erected by a locksmith named Reuben Daw in the 1860s and is made of musket barrels from the Mexican-American War of 1848. Daw, the legend goes, bought from a pawn shop all the guns he needed. Nothing marks the site, however, and it was only because I had thumbed through a book called *The Washington Historical Atlas* that I knew what I was looking at.

What you'll bump into first in Georgetown depends on where you start. And where you start depends on where you park. Despite a not-undeserved reputation for clogged traffic—especially at Georgetown's main intersection of M Street and Wisconsin Avenue—free street parking is often available.

Just remember that nonresidents—those without parking stickers—are supposed to stay in one spot no more than two hours.

But that's plenty of time to get a good feel for the area. And after two hours you can get some fresh bread and cheese at a grocery, walk to

Rock Creek Park, and have a picnic. The park, on R Street, is close to a quartet of Georgetown's most famous mansions—two open to the public, two private.

The Beall-Washington House (2920 R St.), built in 1784, and its surrounding grounds cover nearly a block. The house is still owned privately, as is Evermay (1623 28th St.), erected 1792-94 by Samuel Davidson, a Scotsman who financed the construction by selling other Washington land he owned, including the site of the White House.

Open to the public are Dumbarton Oaks, erected in 1801, and famous for its art, its gardens, and its historical conclaves, and Tudor Place, intended as a shrine to the memory of the George Washington family. Tudor Place was built for Martha Custis Peter, granddaughter of Martha Washington by her previous husband, and her husband, Thomas Peter, around 1800 and remained in the Peter family until 1983.

Other homes of note are those formerly occupied by Robert Kennedy (3214 S St.), Robert Todd Lincoln, Abraham's son (3014 N St.), and the parents of Alexander Graham Bell (1525 35th St.). Bell used the carriage house on the property to set up a laboratory. All remain privately owned.

The Old Stone House at 3051 M St., dating from 1765, has no permanent living residents but is said to be haunted by ghosts who have been roaming the house since shortly after it was built. A few rooms are open to the public.

—Ralph Vigoda

Directions from Philadelphia: From Philadelphia, one of the most direct routes into Georgetown is to take Interstate 95 south to Interstate 495—the Washington Beltway—and then take the beltway west to Exit 34, which is Route 355/Wisconsin Avenue. Going south on Wisconsin Avenue from there will take you into the middle of Georgetown. There are other routes—Exit 33, Connecticut Avenue south, for example—but negotiating the streets and traffic circles may not be worth the trouble.

Georgetown, tucked into the westernmost part of Washington, is bordered roughly by 27th Street to the east and 38th Street to the west, the Potomac River to the south and the city's Uptown neighborhood to the north.

Hotels often have special weekend rates. For more information, including information about accommodations, contact the Washington, D.C., Convention and Visitors Association, 1212 New York Ave. N.W., Suite 600, Washington, D.C. 20005. Phone 202-789-7000.

∾

The Holocaust Museum

WASHINGTON, D.C.

I THOUGHT I'D CRY SOONER.

But it wasn't until my fourth hour in the United States Holocaust Memorial Museum here that the tears came.

I was probably too absorbed to cry earlier.

So was everyone else. The crowd walked through the exhibition quietly. Hushed. No tears, no sniffling. Some grim faces and shaking heads in apparent disbelief, but the enormity of the material seemed to swallow emotion.

This is not a pleasant place to visit on a weekend, or any other day. Good time is not an apt description. Powerful or unforgettable is better.

My wife, Libby, and I were there four hours, and we could have easily spent more time.

I am a sucker for information. The museum has been lauded—and rightly so—for its design and architecture, but it was its information that I will not soon forget. The horror of the Holocaust is told through its tiniest details: the date that all Jewish lawyers in Germany were disbarred; the systematic killing of physically and mentally disabled Germans; the hair of Holocaust victims—thousands of pounds of it—collected and baled.

My suggestions and complaints number but a few:

Parking is so hard to find that I suggest you take the train to Washington and then use cabs or public transportation.

Interest in the museum is so high it is almost impossible to get a spur-of-the-moment ticket. More than 2,000 free tickets are given out daily, but they're gone quickly each morning. The best move is to make reservations four to six weeks in advance. Once there, be ready for four to five hours without a break. It's not easy to stop and start the self-guided tour. Eat lunch beforehand, or have a big breakfast. There is a restaurant in the annex behind the museum. It's called the U.S. Holocaust Museum, but this museum is focused on what happened to six million Jews. Several million non-Jews died during the period as well. Although the exhibition acknowledges the deaths of many thousands of Slavs, Gypsies, Poles, Jehovah's Witnesses, communists, trade unionists, homosexuals, and others at the hands of the Nazis, there's not much more than that.

"It's a hard task balancing the centrality of the Jewish experience while never forgetting that the Nazis used the occasion to murder others," says Naomi Paiss, museum communications director.

"Without the Jews, there would have been no Holocaust. The gas chambers were not built specifically for Poles or Gypsies. We've received scattered complaints that the museum was too Jewish and scattered complaints that it was not Jewish enough."

We drove and easily found the museum—it opened in April 1993— on 14th Street past Independence Avenue. But there was nowhere to park, and, before we knew it, we were on the 14th Street bridge over the Potomac River and in Virginia.

Avoid our mistake. Look for parking as soon as you enter the Mall area, if not before. The two-hour parking meters on the street are not much help, since the museum is more than a four-hour visit. On Sundays, the meters do not have two-hour restrictions, but it's still difficult to find a space.

We paid $10 and parked in a lot at 13th and G streets, about eight blocks away. We arrived at the museum about noon. The tickets are timed, and ours said 10 a.m. The ticket-taker smiled on noting our tardiness.

The museum recommends the exhibition for children 11 and older, but younger children were there as well. We entered a waiting area. Industrial-looking elevators with gray doors took us to the exhibition. Elevators shouldn't be frightening, but these were. Ominous. No Muzak here. The pall begins.

The exhibition begins on the fourth floor and winds downward. Titled "Nazi Assault, 1933–1939," the floor is devoted to life before the Holocaust and the rise of Nazism.

But the first sounds and pictures are of American soldiers liberating a concentration camp. Soldiers shocked by what they see. Gen. Dwight D. Eisenhower, shocked. Outside witnesses. It really happened. Then to the past, to Jews playing soccer, dancing, marrying, in Latvia and Greece and Romania. The information is delivered in four, and sometimes five, ways—text, artifacts, photographs, film, and voices.

In 1933, political prisoners are sent to Dachau, dissidents and communists first. Boycotts against Jews. Book burnings. You know it will get worse.

From 1933 to 1939, 400 laws are passed to "define, segregate, and impoverish German Jews." In 1938, for example, lawyers were disbarred, nurses fired, and pupils expelled from public schools. Park benches contained signs: "For Jews Only."

The Evian Conference in 1938, a little-remembered gathering of nations in France to discuss whether to accept Jews fleeing Germany, is remembered here. No nation wanted more Jews, except the Dominican Republic, which offered to accept 100,000.

In November 1938, Kristallnacht, the attack on synagogues and Jewish businesses, further isolates the Jews. Poland is attacked in 1939. The killing of 70,000 mentally and physically disabled Germans in hospitals and asylums. The museum is crowded and the crowd keeps moving you along.

Finally, open space, a glass wall that permits a view of the first floor: steel beams, people streaming in. But etched in the glass are the names of towns that lost all or part of their Jewish population: Rawicz, Vjazd, Mielec, Jesberg. Libby calls out. She has found the Polish town where her mother's family came from—Radoszkowicze.

There is no Radoszkowicze anymore.

Not many people would be stopped by the name of a Polish town, but the pictures of the Lithuanian shtetl of Eishishok stop everyone. The little town near Vilna had a 900-year history and a population of 3,500 Jews. In two days, the Nazis killed everyone.

These are not just pictures on a wall but a tower of images three-stories high, dizzying, stretching above and below you, of skiers and lovers and swimmers and workmen and mothers with children and someone dressed as Mickey Mouse with a bouquet for an embarrassed woman, images of life, images of life, images of life.

All those people; I shuddered.

The third floor is titled "The Final Solution, 1940–1944."
Pictures and words show the decision to annihilate the Jews—mechanized murder that begins in 1941 as the first Jews are gassed in Poland. Jews are marked now—yellow stars for Parisian Jews, a yellow star for a Jewish bridegroom in Antwerp, Polish trolleys with yellow stars —for Jews only.

Jews are segregated in ghettos, too. Now the floor underfoot is cobblestones, and you are there as well. Artifacts of the Warsaw ghetto, papers and public notices hidden in milk cans, buried and found.

More from the ghetto. Film of bodies being buried in Warsaw. No narration—none needed. Money in the ghetto. I never thought about money in Warsaw or Lodz. Residents had paper bills with pictures of local Jewish leaders. Bizarre, almost comical.

Germans invade Soviet territory, accompanied by death squads, mobile killers who murder Jews and communists and Gypsies. September 1941, Babi Yar, the Ukraine. Soviet saboteurs had blown up several German buildings. Germans thought that the residents of Babi Yar had assisted the Soviets. They hadn't.

More than 33,000 Jews of Babi Yar were told to be at the Jewish cemetery with their money and belongings at 8 a.m. to be resettled. If they failed to come, they would be shot.

They came, and were shot.

The Germans used their railroads to move not just troops but also those headed for the death camps. Despite the burden of war and the Final Solution, "no scheduled train failed to move."

Trains with Jews on their way to Treblinka may have carried as many as 100 in a freight car. A freight car is there, in the exhibit.

It is so small.

There are pictures of Jews arriving at Auschwitz-Birkenau in May 1944. They do not know what will happen to them. It is a slave labor and extermination center, but the pre-teen girl making a face doesn't know that, nor do the two boys, 8 or 9 years old. A German officer is motioning people into two lines, one for life, one for death. What line will the girl enter? The boys?

"Arbeit Macht Frei" says the sign above Auschwitz: "Work Will Make You Free."

Some of the possessions of the ones who were gassed are here. Their stuff. Canes, combs, scissors, kitchen utensils, toothbrushes, razors, prayer shawls, mirrors.

There are benches for sitting and thinking. In this Auschwitz section, an area is set aside to sit and listen through loudspeakers to the voices of Auschwitz survivors. The stories put lumps in your throat.

"I used to dream about my mother, but I forced myself not to."

"One never knew if you were in the good line or the bad line."

"Nobody menstruated anymore. It was a blessing. No underwear, nothing. What would we have done?"

"There was one person who rubbed the little piece of dirty alcohol on your arm and the other one who had the needle. . . . He would do the numbering. So my number is 65316. That means that there were 65,315 people numbered before me."

"And we were given wooden shoes. The wooden shoes were killers, absolute killers. In the mud of Auschwitz, no socks, in the cold."

It is like dripping water, this accumulation of horror, this inhumanity. This isn't information—it's insanity's debris. This must be the end, I thought.

No.

A scale model of Auschwitz-Birkenau.

Nearby, the canisters that held the pellets that dropped through vents and released deadly gas.

Three television screens enclosed by a five-foot-high wall showing gruesome Nazi medical experiments on prisoners. Discretion is advised for children. It is not pleasant to watch. Discretion should be advised for adults as well.

Why wasn't Auschwitz bombed by American planes? "It could be executed only by the diversion of air forces now engaged in decisive operations elsewhere," explained John J. McCloy, U.S. assistant secretary of war.

The exhibition never comes out and says that McCloy lied, but it does tell visitors that in August 1944, American planes bombed a German factory five miles from Auschwitz.

Then there are the shoes, 4,000 of them, from Majdanek in Poland: sandals, boots, suede shoes, baby shoes, gold lamé, leather shoes, a room full of shoes. "We are the shoes, we are the last witnesses, we are shoes from grandchildren and grandfathers. From Prague and Paris and Amsterdam. And because we are only made of fabric leather, and not of blood and flesh, each one of us avoided the hellfire." So wrote Yiddish poet Moses Schulstein, who died in 1981.

The second floor is titled "Aftermath, 1945 to Present."

I could not imagine seeing anything more powerful than what I had just witnessed. I was wrong again.

There is the story of how Denmark stood by its Jews and resisted Nazi pressure. Only 51 Danish Jews died during the Holocaust. And the story of the Protestant village of Le Chambon in France, and how its villagers helped several thousand Jews escape.

A list of rescuers, 10,000 of them, lines the walls. The story of White Rose, the German group whose members openly protested the Nazi genocide, is told, as is the story of Jewish revolts in the Treblinka and Sobibor death camps and the Ukrainian ghettos of Tatansk and Mir.

There is the film of the U.S. Army's making Germans tour the death camps, and of the tears on the faces of the German people. There are the Nuremberg trials and the Eichmann trial in Israel and the artwork of the Jewish children in the camps.

And, finally, the film of the survivors, interviews with the men and women talking about living through hell.

"My mother actually made me believe she was not hungry. That's why I am here."

My tears begin. I am not alone.

An elderly man on screen tells how he asked a fellow prisoner why he was praying. "I am thanking God for the fact that he didn't make me like the murderers around us."

A woman says she learned a "terribly important lesson. One should never, ever, ever give up."

—Murray Dubin

Directions from Philadelphia: Take Interstate 95 south to Route 50, or New York Avenue. Follow Route 50/New York Avenue east to 14th street, go left, and before very long, look for a place to park.

The United States Holocaust Memorial Museum is at 100 Raoul Wallenberg Place (formerly 15th Street), about 400 yards from the Washington Monument, but also has an entrance on 14th Street. The phone is 202-488-0400. The museum opens at 10 a.m. and closes at 5:30 p.m. daily. It is closed for major Jewish holidays.

Each day, the museum hands out 2,300 free timed tickets. The line forms at 8 a.m. on weekends, 8:30 a.m. weekdays, and usually everyone gets a ticket, but not necessarily at the time they want.

Reserved tickets, carrying a $3.50 service charge, are available from Ticketmaster at 800-551-7328.

There is a permanent exhibit especially for young children called "Remembering the Children: Daniel's Story." The walk-through exhibit tells the story of a fictional 11-year-old boy's life through the Holocaust, beginning in a re-creation of his middle-class home and proceeding to a Polish ghetto and, finally, a concentration camp setting.

The best of two worlds

LURAY, VA.

COMING HOME WAS HARDEST for the dog. Not that we wouldn't miss the mountains, the endless farmland, the views, the silence.

But the dog—she missed the freedom. No leashes. No fences. No boundaries. No neighbors.

Every year, my wife and I promise to take a vacation with the kids (and, this time, with the dog), but far removed from parents, siblings or cronies—and big splashy resorts and nightclubs. And I am a native Virginian, always yearning to return.

This time, we chose Luray, a town best known for its famous caverns. And we loved it, but more for the above-ground attractions than the hidden ones.

We loved the incomparable Shenandoah Valley, the sublimity of the Blue Ridge Mountains, the remarkably unspoiled and undeveloped environs of Luray, and the peace of being by ourselves, all alone, swinging the kids on a tire swing, climbing the bales of hay in the barn, playing darts, and falling asleep by a fire.

For us, Luray offered the best of two worlds—an old, depressed Southern town, with a traditional main street, right down to the great five-and-dime, as well as the nearby Blue Ridge Mountains and Shenandoah Valley. The town is less than two hours from Washington, but the oozing opulence of that area has yet to reach Page County. People here still drive old pickups, and a recession is not something you just watch on the evening news.

We stayed in an old house along the Shenandoah owned partly by an old college friend—and, alas, not for rent. But Luray, smack in the heart of the valley, an easy 4½ hours from Philadelphia, is filled with inexpensive cabins, hotels, and bed and breakfasts.

The drive alone was worth the trip. The last stretch takes you on Route 211 west from Warrenton, through the rolling Rappahannock County, up over the Skyline Drive, and down into Page County, Luray, and the valley—far, far, far, far from the Schuylkill Expressway or Ellisburg Circle.

My friend's old farmhouse was hardly a premier rental property. The bathroom's only virtue was that it had running water. The shower was a Rube Goldberg contraption that only a boot-camp soldier might love. And then there were the mice in the kitchen.

But, hey, to me this was all part of the charm. There was no telephone ringing. No mailman bringing bills. No television . . . and consequently no whining by our children, ages 6 and 4, about watching it.

Our first day in Luray, we drove back up to the Skyline Drive, only about 15 minutes away. This, of course, is the curvy, idyllic drive along the crest of the Blue Ridge, part of Shenandoah National Park.

We drove down the Skyline, stopping at several scenic overlooks, for about 10 miles, until we arrived at the trailhead for Stony Man, the second highest peak in the Blue Ridge, at 4,010 feet. This is not exactly the Himalayas. The walk was an easy, painless mile to the summit—perfect for our kids.

It's a well-marked, compact dirt trail, and it crosses the Appalachian Trail. Several times the trail curves and offers some beautiful views of the valley. When we were there, there were very few other hikers, adding to the feeling that this mountain, these woods, were our own.

I frequently did this trip as a boy myself, but it had been a long time. At the top, the wind howled, so much that my wife carried Sally, 4, and Timmy, 6, clung tightly to me. The view is still humbling, and so rewarding. Virginia and the Shenandoah Valley stretch out before you. As a child, I always felt that reaching the summit of these mountains was as close as we could get to the top of the world, and the country we were surveying—the barns and silos and neatly carved farmland below, as well as the Massanutten mountain range to the west—was about as beautiful as this world has to offer.

I'm not sure my kids came away with the same feeling, but they were still young and the wind was howling so we couldn't linger too long. But to borrow from the Terminator, we'll be back.

We had packed a lunch, but found it too cold up top to eat it. Skyland, the charming, century-old lodge and restaurant, was just another mile or two down the drive. So we hiked back and ate our lunch there, ordering up some delicious hot chocolate.

(Skyland boasts 186 rooms, from quaint cabins to spacious new suites. The lodge even offers guided horseback trips and pony rides for kids. For the dates it's open, rates, and reservations: 800-999-4714. We could see the lights of Skyland from our little house in the valley at night.)

I wished I had brought a bike, because there are endless rolling country roads through the valley. One morning, we drove a few miles to Arrowhead Lake, a public park just outside Luray. This is an artificial lake, with a sandy beach, surrounded by mountains, perfect for a swim, a picnic, a hike, or a game of horseshoes. It was too cold to swim when we visited, but we hiked around the lake, chatted with the fishermen, fed the ducks, napped in the sun.

Back at the lodge, our friends had a very tippy, one-man canoe, and I felt it would be unforgivable not to try it on the river. A couple of years before, I had tubed down the Shenandoah River on a lazy summer day, and remember the river in a torpor. But in April, in the spring, the river rushes. And the water is cold.

My wife held the tie line while I settled in. I am not the most flexible man on Earth, and this canoe required one to squat very low and remain very still. She had yet to let go of the line when the canoe capsized. The kids roared. I swam after the paddle, fears of hypothermia racing through my mind. My wife wished she had brought the video camera to record the event, and perhaps earn some prize money from "America's Funniest Home Videos."

For those who are more comfortable in a regular canoe, or wish to try the river at a tamer time of year, canoes and inner tubes can be rented from Shenandoah River Outfitters in Luray (703-743-4159). Tube floats are four miles long and take four to five hours. A canoe rental includes all necessary equipment.

One morning, we took the kids to the world-famous Luray Caverns. I was worried that it would be too commercialized and crowded, and fearful that it would spoil my get-away-from-it-all state of mind.

But it wasn't too bad. I think, actually, our kids were a little young for it. The caverns themselves are dramatic—a powerful reminder of what nature and time can accomplish, and how it can be exploited for commercial purposes.

Visitors walk about a mile in the caverns, and there is one spot bathed in floodlights where you can take great photographs. Some engineer even built an electronic organ that plays the stalactites 160 feet below the surface, officially called the Great Stalacpipe Organ. We were treated only to a tape recording, but if you want to hear the real thing, I suggest you get married there. More than 200 weddings have been held in the underground "cathedral." (Phone: 703-743-6551.)

One drizzly day, we also toured all the old stores and antiques shops on Main Street, and there are scads of them. Don't expect fancy boutiques and an extension of tony Washington. Sure, there are some pricey antiques, but this is, essentially, a poor county. We also found a great five-and-dime store, and a toy store we loved, loaded with more Playmobil sets than anyplace we've ever seen. It's called Zib's Country Connection, and he does a booming mail-order business. (Phone: 703-743-7394.)

There's also a museum of antique cars, as well as horse-drawn carriages and coaches dating back to 1625, at the caverns, and a reptile center, with Virginia's largest reptile collection, another mile up the road.

—Michael Vitez

Directions from Philadelphia: Take I-95 south to Washington. At the Beltway (I-495), go west to Route 66. Take 66 west for almost 60 miles, then take 522 south to Front Royal. Pick up Route 340 south about 25 miles to Luray.

For more information on Luray, Va., and vicinity, contact the Page County Chamber of Commerce, 46 E. Main St., Luray, Va. 22835. Phone: 703-743-3915. It can send a brochure of all the motels, bed and breakfasts, cottages, cabins, restaurants, and stores in the area.

The fourth president's home

MONTPELIER STATION, VA.

THE LAWN WAS DOTTED with makeshift picnic tables where Virginia's high society sat, politely fingering their barbecued chicken and discussing their distant relatives' roles in framing the Constitution or fighting the Civil War.

We were in the back gardens of Montpelier, the magnificent, 2,700-acre estate of James and Dolley Madison—later owned by the du Ponts—to celebrate Dolley's 226th birthday.

We had stumbled onto the birthday party on a weekend visit to Montpelier, and we were warmly welcomed in by the Friends of Montpelier, despite introducing ourselves as Yankees from Philadelphia. So we dove right into the barbecue, then headed down the hill to the stone horse stables, where tubs of vanilla ice cream were being scooped out, in honor of Dolley, who introduced ice cream to the White House.

Beyond the gardens of Montpelier, we gazed out on the verdant hills that form the foothills of the Blue Ridge Mountains.

In one direction, we could spot the brick mansion bed-and-breakfast where we were staying, a short coach ride away (or so I began to think of it), where Robert E. Lee had once spent the night. Some distance farther loomed Thomas Jefferson's Monticello. All the country in between created a breathtaking scene little changed since the days when Madison and Jefferson compared grape varieties and forged a new nation.

Again and again during our stay in exclusive, rural Orange County, we lost our moorings to the present. I found myself slipping back to an era when country gentlemen farmed hundreds of acres while the women planned elaborate social agendas from their grand Georgian mansions. And while those roles might be somewhat stifling full time, it was fun to pretend, at least for a weekend.

Although we were just 20 miles from Monticello, we chose to focus our getaway on the home of the nation's fourth president, rather than its third, and the countryside that surrounds the magnificent Montpelier.

As Madison's contributions in shaping the Constitution are sometimes unfairly underrated compared with Jefferson's, so, too, is Montpelier lost in the shadow of Monticello. But if our experience is a guide, it won't be for long.

Montpelier reflects the same commitment as Monticello to thoughtful architecture, inventive farming, and beauty. In fact, parts of Montpelier's design were heavily influenced by Jefferson, a good friend of the Madisons.

But while Monticello has long been a popular travel destination, Montpelier is considered a newcomer to the historic tour circuit, since it was opened to the public only in 1987, three years after it was deeded to the National Trust for Historic Preservation.

Touring Montpelier was especially interesting because it is a research project in progress, and is presented as such. (And unlike Monticello, there are no long waits to get into Montpelier, which gets only about 200 visitors a day in high tourist season. On a perfect Saturday in May, we were able to get on the next scheduled tour.)

Upon entering Montpelier, we were surprised by how raw it was. It lacked the furniture (often reproductions) that is the focus of most historic homes, and visitors were asked instead to examine the walls, floors, and ceilings, looking for "ghosts" that indicated where and how work was done on the 230-year-old mansion while three generations of Madisons and two generations of du Ponts lived here.

We learned how James and Dolley lived here with his parents (by dividing the house in half and keeping two wings completely separate), and how Dolley arranged guests in smaller social groups according to political considerations. But mostly we learned how the house was constructed.

So focused is the tour on the changes in floor patterns or plaster marks that our guide was taken by surprise when my husband asked where James Madison had died.

"Oh, uh, just outside this dining room, here," she said, sweeping her arm past a sign hanging on the wall that said, "Change in plaster will be explained later."

It isn't until you get into the second phase of the tour—the du Pont era—that you get a sense of how the house functioned as a home.

After Dolley Madison sold Montpelier in 1844 to retire her son's gambling debts, the house changed hands six times and fell into disrepair. Then, in 1900, the property began its second life, when it was purchased by William and Anna Rogers du Pont.

Under the du Ponts' stewardship, and particularly in the hands of their daughter, Marion du Pont Scott, Montpelier became the quintessential baronial estate. The du Ponts doubled the mansion's size to 64,000 square feet, added a steeplechase course, racetrack, bowling alley, and train station to the grounds, and imposed a decidedly 20th-century look inside.

Before entering the last room on the tour, our guide felt she had to warn us about "Marion's desire to reflect her own taste" here. The first people through the door let out a gasp upon viewing the art deco-style room, with its black-and-white checked flooring, stainless-steel curved bookshelves, and red leather banquettes.

"What a shame," said one tourist.

After the house tour, visitors are free to spend as much time as they wish wandering the estate, which is surprisingly unrestricted. The formal gardens, which had been restored by the Garden Club of Virginia, provided plenty of fun for our 4-year-old, Grace, who loved the "beootiful" peonies and played hide-and-seek in the seven-foot-high boxwood hedges.

I followed the "Tree Walk," which is mapped out with a key to about 40 different species. Deep in the walnut grove, I could almost see Madison and Jefferson strolling along, discussing such weighty issues as freedom of religion or the individual conscience.

We later learned that there have been extensive archaeological surveys of 80 sites on the property, where everything from prehistoric artifacts to massive quantities of slag from the Madisons' ironworks has been uncovered.

While I was sorry to leave Montpelier, I knew we had an equally inviting mansion to return to for our overnight stay. The weekend we visited Orange County was graduation weekend at the University of Virginia in nearby Charlottesville, so we thought we'd end up staying in some roadside motel. But as luck would have it, we found what we thought was probably the nicest inn in the entire area.

Turning off the scenic country Route 231, we passed through two massive pink stone columns with granite plates announcing we had arrived at Rocklands. After driving another mile through cow pastures, deep forest overgrowth, and fields of wildflowers, we saw the white-pillared three-story brick mansion.

Innkeeper Maggie Neale showed us to our "room"—the whole top floor of a brick Colonial house behind the main 19th-century farmhouse.

A registered Historic Landmark, Rocklands was the site of a Civil War engagement on Christmas Eve, 1864, and was a resting stop for

Gen. Robert E. Lee. The present mansion was built in 1905 in the Classical Revival style by Neale's in-laws, gentlemen farmers who brought Black Angus cattle here from Scotland. The 1,800 acres of land are still farmed.

Rocklands had been open as a bed-and-breakfast for only a couple of years; after Grandma Neale died in the early 1990s at the age of 97 (her gravestone is next to the fish pond), the younger Neales turned the home first into an executive retreat and then a B&B. Considering the formality of the place, we were delighted at how welcoming the innkeepers were to our children, Grace and 8-month-old Julia.

At breakfast—an elaborate spread of eggs, bacon, French toast, fruit, scones, and biscuits—we again felt suspended in time, surrounded by beautiful antiques and a hushed atmosphere that was soon broken by Julia, eating eggs for the first time and having a lot of fun with them.

After breakfast, we headed toward the town of Orange, the county seat, where we hoped to soak up a little more 19th-century history, but found the modern-day scene more inviting. After a quick visit to the historical society, which was more like a library reading room, and a failed attempt to get into the James Madison Museum (closed), we wandered into downtown, where we stumbled on a gospel fair being held in Taylor Park. Here, too, everyone was eating barbecue, but with a lot more enthusiasm than the Friends of Montpelier had been the day before.

The James Madison Museum, an unassuming bricked-over storefront on Caroline Street, is said to contain the real artifacts of James Madison's life, but it's open only in the afternoon on weekends. The most valuable stop for us was the Orange County Visitor Center, where we picked up several brochures, one of which led us to a wonderful winery a few miles away.

The Barboursville Estate and Winery, just outside tiny Gordonsville, contains another Jefferson-inspired mansion, although his touch is a little hard to recognize among the brick ruins.

Designed by Jefferson in 1814 for a friend, Virginia Governor James Barbour, the Barboursville estate was considered the finest property in Orange County in its day, with a value twice that of Madison's Montpelier, but the house was destroyed by fire in 1884.

Legend has it that the Barbour ancestors were feasting on Christmas Eve dinner when the candles on the Christmas tree torched the tree and the flames spread to the rest of the house. With no nearby source of water, the family supposedly simply carried the dining table out-doors and continued feasting, watching their home burn.

Today, the ruins are a Virginia historic landmark, consisting of the bearing walls and pillars of the old house.

The winery produces some great wines. It was purchased in 1976 by the Zonin family, proprietors of Italy's largest wine company, who have brought European grapes, equipment, and vintners to Virginia.

As we headed for home, back through the rolling hills and graceful farmlands, I repeated the tale I had learned about how the Barboursville estate burned down.

The story caught Grace's imagination and she asked us to repeat it over and over again, each time elaborating on the details, until she finally fell asleep in the car. Even 4-year-olds, I thought, can get caught up in the magic of history.

—Jill Capuzzo

Directions from Philadelphia: Montpelier Station is four miles south-west of Orange, Va., on Route 20. Take Interstate 95 south to the Washington Beltway (I-495), go west to I-66 and west again to the Routes 29/15 exit at Gainesville. Follow Route 15 south to Orange and turn right on Route 20. The trip is about 260 miles.

For information on sights and accommodations, call the Orange County Visitor Center, 703-672-1653, or the Charlottesville Convention and Visitors Bureau, 804-293-6789.

∾

Beyond the Inner Harbor

BALTIMORE, MD.

SATURDAY IN BALTIMORE and the city is abuzz.

The headlines in the Sun say the Pope is coming in a few month to this, the oldest Roman Catholic diocese in the United States.

Another Page One story reports that Kurt Cobain, leader of Nirvana, is dead. Cobain's suicide is the main topic of discourse at Donna's Coffee Bar, an espresso stop off Mount Vernon Place, where a couple of bean-addicts are blaming the 27-year-old grunge rocker's death on terminally dank Seattle.

Down the road at the Charles Theater, the city's foremost art movie house, the marquee reads "Mike Leigh's Naked . . . Kurt Cobain, RIP."

Other rockers, still alive and kicking, are holed up at the Latham Hotel: NKOTB, formerly New Kids on the Block, are in town for a show, and while these onetime teen-throbs no longer attract the hordes of squealing baby-boppers they once did, there's an air of excitement among the hotel's guests and staff anyway—not to mention a clutch of die-hard fans in the lobby, their eyes wide with anticipation and trained on the elevator doors.

It's a crackling, crisp April morning, and we find ourselves in Baltimore—city of Barry Levinson movies, city of that pointy glass, packed-to-the-gills aquarium—with a challenge: Is it possible to "do" this city of 736,014 (founded in 1661, elevation: 32 feet) without going near the aquarium and the fabled, conventioneer-trodden Inner Harbor that surrounds it, or stepping into the neo-retro baseball stadium, that great, grassy Oriole Park at Camden Yards?

As it turns out, the answer is a resounding yes. Baltimore, on this particular spring weekend, is hopping with activity—culture, kitsch, concerts, black-tie soirées at the tony Engineering Center and fall-down-drunk pub-crawlers navigating the Belgian block byways of Fell's Point.

The latter, a neighborhood that juts into the water about a mile north of the Inner Harbor area, is Baltimore's answer to Philadelphia's South Street: bars, clubs, eateries, inns, punk shops, bookstore-cafés, a marketplace, crafts galleries, and, at Flashback, 728 S. Broadway, a shrine to John Waters, Baltimore's offbeat cinema auteur.

Our base of operations for this no-Inner-Harbor weekend is the aforementioned Latham, sister hostelry to Philadelphia's Latham (there's a third sibling in D.C.). Previously known as the Peabody Court Hotel, the Latham (612 Cathedral St.; 410-727-7101) is a restored 1924 apartment building facing Mount Vernon Place—one of the city's classier grids of garden, fountains, statuary, grand brownstone townhouses, churches, and the renowned Peabody Institute and Library. If you get a room overlooking the park (Baltimore's answer to Rittenhouse Square or New York's Gramercy Park), you'll find yourself eyeballing a sculpture of George Washington, towering atop a Doric shaft smack in the middle of Mount Vernon Place. This is the city's Washington Monument, erected in 1815—making it the first such memorial in the country to honor Our Founding Prez.

Even if you decide to break down and visit the Inner Harbor, the 13-story Latham is a good place to stay. It's less than a mile from the National Aquarium, but removed enough to offer you some respite from the megaconcentration of tourists. The rooms are big and nicely appointed; we could take advantage of a special weekend family rate; there's Michels, the new rooftop restaurant franchise from trendy Angeleno chef Michel Richard, and there's the clubbier, classical-music-themed Peabody Grill (where breakfast is served).

And by staying at the Latham, you're practically within spitting distance of one of the city's foremost institutions of art, the Walters Art Gallery. (However, we suggest that you don't spit: Baltimore, which in many ways physically and psychically resembles Philadelphia, has to be one of the cleanest cities in the nation. Even in the poorer neighborhoods, the sidewalks are clean, the signage good, and the roads devoid of killer potholes.)

The Walters (600 N. Charles St.; 410-547-9000) comprises two main buildings, one old and one new, and houses an impressive, centuries-and-cultures-spanning collection amassed by philanthropist William T. and his son, Henry. There's something for everyone here, from Egyptian and Mesopotamian artifacts, old masters' oils, Gothic altar pieces, illuminated manuscripts, Etruscan sculpture, and French Renaissance painted enamels. We spotted a Turner, some Ingres, a Delacroix, a small, beautiful John Everett Millais, a roomful of Impressionists (Pissarro, Alfred Sisley, Mary Cassatt, Degas, Manet) and some stunning early Renaissance Italian frescoes.

Just up the steep incline of Charles Street and facing Mount Vernon Place on the southeast corner is the legendary Peabody Institute and

Library (17 E. Mount Vernon Place; 410-659-8179). The institute is one of the oldest conservatories of music in the nation, and it is possible, on a fine spring day, to sit on a bench in the park beneath the Florentine-style edifice and listen to the sounds of a violin or a flute or a piano float out the open windows into the breeze.

You should also check out the Peabody's library, which can be done for free by just signing in at a guard's desk. A six-tiered sky-lit atrium rimmed with ornate cast-iron railings and crammed with some 250,000 volumes, the stack room is an amazing architectural space—and its display cases feature such bibliophilic items as a first edition of Harriet Beecher Stowe's *Uncle Tom's Cabin* and early editions of works by the Brontes and George Eliot.

Heading out on Charles Street in the opposite direction of the Inner Harbor, you'll find yourself passing Pennsylvania Station, Baltimore's restored Amtrak stop. And, a couple of miles down the road, the Baltimore Museum of Art (North Charles at 31st Street; 410-396-7101). If you're car-less, hop a cab or a bus (Baltimore boasts highly efficient public transportation), because there's a stretch of Charles here that's on the bleak and boring side.

This museum, housed in a main building designed by John Russell Pope (of National Gallery fame), occupies land contiguous to John Hopkins University's main campus, and the surrounding neighborhood is a handsome mix of pre-war apartment buildings and rehabbed rowhouses.

The museum itself is the perfect size—not overwhelming. With a strong collection of post-Impressionist art, an impressive African art exhibit, a beautiful sculpture garden, and work by Matisse, Picasso, Cezanne, Renoir, Gauguin, and van Gogh, BMA is well worth a half-day of your attention. The museum also boasts some key work by Andy Warhol and other purveyors of 20th-century pop art.

We could go on (and we did). A walk over to the Lexington Market (Lexington and Eutaw Streets; 410-685-6169) is worthwhile, although folks who frequent Philadelphia's Reading Terminal Market will find this bustling collection of food stalls disappointing by comparison. (While the Lexington Market is the city's oldest, the building it's housed in is not; it feels like a bus terminal, the floor has a peculiarly steep rake, and the surrounding neighborhood is in the throes of transition.)

Downtown Baltimore is full of neat architectural surprises, and if you walk past the city's municipal buildings—its City Hall, its courthouses —toward the Shot Tower, you'll find examples of everything from turn-of-the-century cast-iron facades to modernist slabs of concrete and glass. Shot Tower (East Fayette and Front streets; 410-837-5424), is an 1829 smokestack built of one million bricks where lead shot for guns was manufactured.

The city, renowned for its Harborplace shopping complexes, its National Aquarium with those giant tanks of exotic sea creatures, and all that other stuff we didn't bother with on this visit, is full of little surprises, including some delightful places to eat and snack. You get the feeling Baltimore is hiding many similarly great finds on streets all over town.

—Steven Rea

Directions from Philadelphia: Take I-95 south to Baltimore. Call your destination for local directions.

Good sources for additional information are the Baltimore Area Convention and Visitors Association, 800-282-6632 or 410-659-7300, or the Visitor Information Center, 300 W. Pratt St., 410-837-4636. Along with the usual big-name travel guides, an invaluable book for the pedestrian-inclined is A Walking Tour of Historic & Renaissance Baltimore by Donald T. Fritz. It is on display at most Baltimore-area bookshops.

The hub of "the war"

RICHMOND, VA.

THE CIVIL WAR HAUNTS THIS beautiful city.

The people here haven't forgotten the war, and many wouldn't want to, if they could. The defeat still rankles.

This was the heart of the Confederacy, the capital of both the Southern nation and the Confederacy's most important state. Richmond became the chief manufacturing center of the wartime South, the major rail junction in the Upper South, and the principal target of the North's principal army.

The city was in turmoil during the war. Its population quadrupled. In 1862, Gen. George McClellan came within sight of the capital before Gen. Robert E. Lee drove him away. Gen. U.S. Grant besieged Richmond in 1864 and 1865 and bled it white. "On to Richmond!" was the Union rallying cry for four years. Yet, until it had to be abandoned in April 1865, Richmond stood defiant and proud.

If you share my fascination with the Civil War, you have to come here. Richmond has more historic attractions than any other city in the South—more than you can crowd into one weekend, even if your feet don't give out. Be warned, however. There are unwritten rules for Yankees visiting Richmond, and you'll have a better time here if you follow them:

It was not the Civil War here—it was the War for Southern Independence. (You don't have to call it that; just say "the war," and southerners will know what war you're talking about.)

If any of your ancestors fought for the Union, keep it to yourself. At the Museum of the Confederacy, the news that my great-great-grandfather was a prisoner at Andersonville was greeted by an awkward, embarrassing silence.

Don't advertise that you're a Yankee. Talk slower. Schmooze a little before you ask questions. "How you? Chilly, isn't it? Would you mind telling me how to get to Monument Avenue?" You get the idea. You won't fool anyone, but your efforts will be appreciated.

Whatever you do, don't gloat. Southerners know who whipped whom, and they might just demonstrate why it took so long to do it.

On an earlier visit, we had toured the Richmond National Battle-field, a must for any serious Civil War buff. It starts at the site of Chimborazo Hospital, the largest military hospital ever built, and includes a self-guided, 97-mile tour of the major battlefields around the city—Seven Pines, Gaines' Mill, Savage Station, White Oak Swamp, Frayser's Farm, and Malvern Hill, all associated with Lee's great 1862 counteroffensive.

On the tour, don't miss Cold Harbor, Grant's great mistake. Here on June 3, 1864, he rashly ordered frontal assaults against Lee's fortified lines, and about 7,200 Union soldiers were shot down in 20 minutes. The Yankees knew what they were up against. They went into battle with scraps of paper bearing their names and next of kin pinned to the backs of their jackets. Dog tags began at Cold Harbor.

Also on the tour are a number of forts involved in the 1864–65 siege. The nature of war changed during the Civil War, and the trenches here are the ancestors of the trenches of World War I.

On this visit, though, we concentrated on the city itself—more specifically, Jefferson Davis, the only president the Confederacy ever had. When Davis came here he was 53, a West Point graduate who had fought in the Mexican and Indian wars and was President Franklin Pierce's secretary of war.

A senator from Mississippi when the Civil War came, Davis assumed that he would be a general and was surprised when he was elected president. Cold and aloof, Davis was not popular. He interfered with his generals, quarreled with his cabinet and was savaged by the southern press.

Our first stop was the home of Davis and his family, the White House of the Confederacy, a mansion that became the political and social center of the time. Built in 1818, it was reopened in the late 1980s after a major restoration. A guided tour took us through the magnificent public rooms and the private quarters upstairs. Davis' office looks as if he had just stepped away from his cluttered desk.

Probably the first Yankee to tour here was President Lincoln. He visited Richmond as soon as order was restored and was shown through the house.

Varina Davis loved to entertain, but her husband merely tolerated the social side of the presidency. "I can be a host, or I can perform my duties as president," he reportedly told her. "I believe I was elected to perform the duties of president."

Two of the Davis children, Billie and Winnie, were born here; another, Sam, was killed in a fall from the back porch. One bedroom still contains some toys. And, yes, the Davises had indoor plumbing, although apparently designed by an early-day Rube Goldberg.

Next door is the Museum of the Confederacy, a handsome new building containing the nation's largest collection of Confederate military and political artifacts, rare documents and manuscripts, and Davis memorabilia. Among its treasures are the sword that Lee surrendered at Appomattox; the plumed hat of "Jeb" Stuart, the great cavalry leader; the field uniforms of Lee, Stuart, Gen. Joseph E. Johnston, and Gen. Stonewall Jackson, and the coat that Davis wore when he was captured in Georgia. I was enthralled, but the many reminders of the human cost of the war depressed my companion.

A short walk from the museum is Capitol Square. The capitol, designed by Thomas Jefferson, was the seat of the Confederate government, and in April 1861, Lee assumed command of Virginia's armed forces in the Old Hall of the House of Delegates. In February 1862, Davis delivered his inaugural address in the square at the base of the Washington statue, which became a symbol on the Confederate seal. While Richmond burned, a volunteer bucket brigade saved the Executive Mansion, which is also in the square. Part of the mansion is open for tours.

After lunch, we strolled along Monument Avenue, a majestic boulevard with large monuments at intersections, statues celebrating Davis, Lee, Stuart, Jackson, and Matthew Fontaine Maury, pioneer marine cartographer known as the "Pathfinder of the Seas."

The outer defense of Richmond once ran just east of the Davis monument. The avenue is lined with rows of maples and oaks and classic buildings. After a 1924 visit, British historian John Buchanan wrote of Monument Avenue: "Conceived with such dignity and simplicity, it is infinitely the most impressive thing I saw on the American continent."

We then went to Battle Abbey, built in 1913 as a Confederate memorial hall and now the headquarters of the Virginia Historical Society. On display are portraits, battle flags, and weapons; the most impressive sight is a huge mural by French artist Charles Hoffbauer depicting the four seasons of the Confederacy: its formation, its battles won and lost, its fall, and its surrender at Appomattox.

In the late afternoon, we drove to Hollywood Cemetery, a Southern shrine, to visit the graves of Davis and his family. From the gravesite, a life-size statue of Davis looks out on the beautiful grounds, also the last resting place of Stuart, Gen. George Pickett, and about 15,000 Confederate soldiers who perished in the war. Two Virginians who might have argued against secession are also buried here, Presidents James Monroe and John Tyler.

Sunday morning we attended services at St. Paul's Episcopal Church, known as the "Church of the Confederacy."

On April 2, 1865, Davis was seated in the presidential pew (No. 63) with an associate. During the service, a young soldier entered the church and whispered to the sexton that he had a message for the president from General Lee. The sexton waited until the prayer was over, walked down the aisle, and handed the message to Davis. It began, "I think it is absolutely necessary that we should abandon our position tonight."

Within the hour, the evacuation of Richmond had begun. Rather than let Confederate assets fall into Union hands, Richmond was put to the torch. As the city burned, according to one Civil War historian, a Confederate soldier remarked that Richmond "seemed to prefer annihilation to conquest."

Richmond was rebuilt, of course. It is a modern city now, but it has a long memory. And if you leave your Yankee preconceptions at home and come and share its past, the city will give you a weekend you won't soon forget.

—Chuck Lawliss

Directions from Philadelphia: Follow I-95 south to Richmond.

~

Maryland's first capital

ST. MARY'S CITY, MD.

WE TOOK A GIANT STEP three centuries backward the day we met Godiah Spray at his tobacco plantation here. The farmer was barefoot and dressed in pantaloons, a loose-fitting shirt, and a broad-brimmed hat to protect him from the hot summer sun.

"Good day," he greeted us. Then, laying down his hoe, he led us through a field of broad-leafed tobacco, past corn growing one stalk to a hill and surrounded by squash. We passed pigs half hidden in the weeds and a clutter of chickens before we reached his plantation house.

We felt like 20th-century intruders as Spray introduced us to his four "indentured servants" who had been working nearby. His wife, he said, was at the neighbors' where she would stay until her baby—their seventh child—was born. One tenant farmer also lived on the plantation.

"Tobacco, of course, is our main crop," he explained. "The other crops we grow for food. We cut the tobacco leaves when they're ripe, cure them, then bundle them into barrels called hogsheads that we roll to the riverbank where they are put on a sailing ship to take them to the market in England."

Maryland tobacco, he said, is the slowest-burning tobacco in the world and serves as the economic mainstay of this colony. It is also believed to counteract such diseases as malaria, typhus, and influenza, which so many of his fellow colonists have died from. "It's a good laxative," he added, "and it calms down bee stings. If you have an earache, breathing in tobacco smoke will cure it."

Discovering the high regard for tobacco's medicinal properties in the 17th century was just one of the surprises we encountered on our trip to the southernmost tip of Maryland's western shore. At historic St. Mary's City, the restored first capital of Maryland, Spray offered us just one of many fascinating glimpses we had during the long weekend we toured the Maryland peninsula that lies between the Chesapeake Bay and the Potomac River.

Here, in a three-county region—St. Mary's, Calvert, and Charles counties—is where Maryland was born. Here, too, you will discover an open-armed hospitality among the region's people, a nautical flavor that derives from the area's proximity to the Chesapeake and a delightfully concomitant variety of restaurants where fresh seafood leads the menu. St. Mary's City offered the first surprise on our jaunt through history. Settled in 1634 by Leonard Calvert, the younger brother of Lord Baltimore, St. Mary's became the fourth permanent English settlement in North America, the Jamestown of Maryland. Like Jamestown, St. Mary's thrived for a time, then quietly faded into a ghost town when the colony moved its capital north to Annapolis. It slept undisturbed for more than two centuries until the state of Maryland undertook its restoration and in 1984 opened it to the public.

Today, thanks to years of painstaking archaeology and historical research, you can walk the streets of the restored area of the city and get the feel of what this wilderness capital was like when Calvert brought two shiploads of settlers here and guided the town's growth.

Magically, a few of the "original colonists" like Spray (portrayed by Aaron Meisinger) appear to guide you. With several others, we joined Mistress Farthing to stroll down the dusty streets. She pointed out the outline of the foundation of Governor Calvert's home, one of the first to be built. The house served not only as a residence but also as a meeting place for the first legislature and a gathering place for the populace.

As the capital of the colony, St. Mary's soon became a town of taverns and lawyers' offices. We looked through a protective glass window to admire the 17th-century brick kitchen floor of a partially reconstructed inn, where we were told members of the Governor's Council enjoyed some of the best cider in the colony. Travelers in those times were charged 50 pounds of tobacco to stay at the inn. The first printer in the Southern colonies ran a printshop near the inn, where he printed tobacco notes (used as cash) and government bills.

Down the street, we found William Farthing's Ordinary. An ordinary, Mistress Farthing explained, ranked a notch below an inn. The ordinary served but one meal a day and crowded four customers to a bed. Like all inns and ordinaries, Farthing's dispensed gossip and news along with food, drink, and lodging. We were glad to see that one of those is still available today. (In an outbuilding that blends with the period architecture, you can get a 20th-century lunchtime snack of a hamburger and soft drink, but the place is light on gossip.)

At the end of the lane stands the most imposing reconstruction of the restored town, a re-creation of the first state house, built originally in 1676. Rebuilt to mark the 300th anniversary of Maryland, this Jacobean-style brick structure was reconstructed using detailed plans that had survived from the original building. The legislature that met in the state house, Mistress Farthing said, was unique because both Roman Catholic and Protestant male landowners were able to vote. Maryland, founded by Catholics who came to this country to avoid persecution, did not discriminate as did other colonies. While the Catholic Calverts were in power, Maryland was one of the most religiously tolerant of the colonies.

Down a slope to the St. Mary's River, we came across the full-size replica of the *Dove*, named for one of the two ships that transported the first settlers and their supplies across the Atlantic. We climbed aboard and a sailor showed us around the compact square-rigger.

The sea and inland waters were important to the early settlers. What food the colonists couldn't harvest from the land they gathered from the surrounding bay and its tributaries.

We learned the ways of contemporary watermen when we spent a day at Solomons, a town that nestles at the tip of land where the Patuxent River meets the bay. The town's deepwater harbor attracts yachts from around the world and is home port for a few remaining oyster and crab fishermen. A good way to sample its nautical heritage is to drop in at the Calvert Marine Museum located at the Calvert County end of the nearby Thomas Johnson Bridge that arches high over the Patuxent.

We found plenty to do the day we strolled the grounds of this well-designed museum. We climbed a ladder to take a guided tour through the tight quarters within the Drum Point Lighthouse, one of three remaining "screwpile" lighthouses, which during its working years was located at the bay entrance to the Patuxent. We walked among a collection of small boats in a shed, boats that ranged from a log canoe to a crabbing skiff; watched as a woodcarver fashioned a duck decoy, and followed a boardwalk that angled through a salt marsh to learn how such marshes act as the nursery for much of the aquatic life of the Chesapeake.

In the aquarium within the main exhibition building, we came nose to nose with some of the prolific marine life that swim in these waters, from four-foot sturgeon to the famous Chesapeake blue crab. There is plenty to appeal to children, too. In a separate Discovery Room, youngsters dig in a big sandbox to find 15-million-year-old shark's teeth or build a playhouse out of whale bones. They are kept interested throughout the museum by volunteers, such as the woman who gave us a hands-on demonstration with a live horseshoe crab and the old salt who teaches landlubbers like us how to tie some useful knots.

A short walk down the street, and across the small bridge that makes Solomons an island, is another part of this innovative museum. The former J.C. Lore Oyster House, no longer in commercial operation, has been adapted to tell the story of the backbreaking tasks performed by fishermen, crabbers, clammers, and oystermen—and of the oyster pirates and oyster wars that occasionally disrupted the workaday routines of the Chesapeake watermen.

Today, Maryland has the only sail-powered oyster fleet in North America, the well-known skipjacks. If you want to get the feel of a skipjack, you can sign up a few miles away at Piney Point on the Potomac with Captain Jack Russell, who takes groups for a sail and "drudges" some oysters and shows you how to shuck them. At the museum, you can take a cruise around Solomons on a bugeye, a sail-and-power workboat that was once used to make the rounds of the oystermen and buy their catch.

Artifacts even more ancient are on display at the museum. It came as a surprise to learn that the steep cliffs of Chesapeake Bay near here have yielded fossils tens of millions of years old, dating from the time when shallow seas covered most of southern Maryland. If you walk the beach at Calvert Cliffs State Park, you can find fossils of your own.

In fact, so many fossils have been exposed that they fill not just one museum but two. Before the Calvert Cliffs nuclear power plant was built on the shore of the bay in 1968, scientists first carefully combed the site where the plant was to be built. What they found is on display at the attractive visitors center the Baltimore Gas and Electric Company built in an old tobacco barn near its operating power plant at Lusby. From the sands of time, the paleontologists have plucked a mastodon molar 14 to 16 million years old, a saltwater crocodile's jawbone, the molar of an Ice Age horse, and the huge jaw of a great white shark.

After seeing this evidence of the distant past, we stepped into the future. Interactive video presentations give visitors a chance to "tour" the power-producing nuclear plant itself, to see and hear the turbines roar and watch the blinking lights of the control room. Through a computer, you get to raise and lower control rods in a cutaway model of a reactor.

We uncovered a darker page of history at Point Lookout, a state park at the tip of the peninsula where the Potomac River flows into

Chesapeake Bay. Today, this 460-acre park provides a swimming beach, boat ramp, picnic areas, and campgrounds with recreational-vehicle hookups. But during the Civil War, Point Lookout was home to one of the largest Union prison camps.

Deplorable conditions faced the thousands of Confederate soldiers held here. Food was scarce, tents provided the only shelter, and diseases such as malaria, dysentery, and smallpox, combined with exposure, caused approximately 4,000 deaths.

To conclude our trail through southern Maryland's history, we swung inland and followed Route 301 north through Charles County. Several other historic points of interest proved irresistible.

Port Tobacco, where a reconstructed Federal-style brick courthouse and several restored 18th-century houses recall the days when Port Tobacco was the second-largest river port in Maryland, shipping a fortune in tobacco to Europe each year. But the once-busy harbor gradually silted in, the county seat moved inland, and Port Tobacco was a port no longer.

Thomas Stone National Historic Site is the partially restored country estate of one of Maryland's signers of the Declaration of Independence. Located five miles west of La Plata, the site's National Park Service rangers are on duty to tell you about plantation life in the 19th century and show you how the restoration is coming along.

Dr. Samuel A. Mudd House, five miles east of Waldorf, is furnished with authentic period furnishings of the 1800s. At the house, we met a granddaughter of Dr. Mudd who told us the well-known story of the highly regarded country doctor who set the broken leg of John Wilkes Booth shortly after Booth had assassinated President Abraham Lincoln. Accused of complicity, Mudd served nearly four years in prison until he was pardoned by President Andrew Johnson.

If you are thinking about making a trip to Williamsburg in Virginia to expose your family to early Colonial history—or if you've already been there—you might consider a weekend in southern Maryland. It may not have the extensive reproductions or the elegant hotels of Williamsburg, but you will discover reminders of a settlement a century older.

Moreover, a trip to St. Mary's and Solomons will be several hours shorter and put a correspondingly smaller dent in your wallet.

—Arthur Miller and Marjorie Miller

Directions from Philadelphia: Take I-95 south to Route 301, near Wilmington. Follow Routes 301 and 50 south and west to Route 2. Follow Routes 2 and 4 south to Route 235. Take 235 south to St. Mary's City.

❧

Where presidents relax

THURMONT, MD.

FDR ISSUED WAR UPDATES from this secret place he called Shangri-La. Jimmy Carter held a historic Mideast peace summit here. And Ronald Reagan broadcast his Saturday morning radio chats from the lodge's veranda.

While Camp David, just over an hour outside of Washington, may be the most famous weekend getaway place in the country, most people don't have any idea where it is. And those who do visit the Catoctin Mountains in western Maryland, where the presidential retreat is located, usually come for the natural beauty, not to spot presidents.

My husband and I got our first hint of the true character of this region when we set out to find one of the area's three covered bridges the first morning of our weekend visit. At Roddy Road Bridge, we stumbled upon the modern-day version of a barn-raising—30 local residents were draped across the sides, front, and roof, repainting the tiny red wooden bridge.

This was the final stage of a 16-month refurbishing of the bridge, after a trucker missed the "8½ foot clearance" sign and barreled right through, taking much of the support system with him.

Built in 1856, the one-lane, 40-foot-long bridge is Maryland's smallest, and one of its oldest. Thurmont was disheartened by the accident, particularly since the area's other most scenic bridge, at Loy's Station, had been closed since 1991, the result of arson. Determined to get the

Roddy Road Bridge up and operating, the group of volunteers had repaired it before our visit and were adding the finishing touches.

At noon, Jeff Yocum rang the dinner bell. He invited us to join the painting crew under the white tent in his front yard, where a full spread of burgers, dogs, homemade deer sausage, beans, slaws, and cakes awaited.

Yocum said he'd moved his family from suburban Washington to the 1820s brick house at the foot of the bridge so "the kids would have a sense of community."

The main reasons folks come to the Catoctin Mountains—whether to visit or to live—are to fish and swim, to soak up the country air, to get away from the hustle-bustle of the capital and experience a kinder, gentler lifestyle.

But if you are like us, the mystique of Camp David will also be a reason to come.

You won't get many clues about the camp at the Catoctin Mountain Park in which it's located. Your best bet is to go into Thurmont to the Cozy Restaurant & Inn. This 64-year-old establishment is a veritable shrine to Camp David and the last 10 presidents.

The Cozy offers a groaning-board buffet, but we were more interested in the half-dozen glass showcases containing aerial shots of Camp David, photos of a relaxed Ronald Reagan strolling across the lawn, teapots and containers of caviar sent by the Soviet delegation after their stay at the Cozy Inn, and signed photographs from Barbara Walters and Sam Donaldson, thanking the inn for accommodating them during the 1978 Middle East peace conference, arguably the most famous event to have taken place at Camp David.

While no president has ever actually eaten or stayed at the Cozy (FDR sat in his car outside while Winston Churchill ate here), the restaurant takes great pride in the sports figures, heads of state, and other celebrities who have, while on official business at Camp David.

By reading the yellowed articles at the Cozy, we learned that the camp site was "discovered" by FDR in 1942 when he was looking for a weekend getaway spot. Since it was wartime, he asked his scouts to look for a secure spot not too far from Washington so he could get back quickly if needed. They found "Group Camp #3," a secluded mountaintop cabin camp in the middle of the Catoctin Mountain Park, about 70 miles from the capital. FDR called it Shangri-La and held high-level war meetings there. The location was kept top-secret.

It was President Dwight D. Eisenhower who named it Camp David, after his grandson, and every president since has used it as a place to fish or hunt or simply to take a relaxing weekend break.

Strictly off-limits to the public, the retreat has 20 buildings, 16 of them residential. Two main lodges accommodate the president's family during weekend visits and the post commander's family year-round; the remaining buildings are mostly two-bedroom wooden cottages for guests.

President Clinton has spent very little time at the camp, according to the locals, who say they can tell when a president is in town because the traffic light goes on blinker mode and their windows rattle when the helicopter passes over.

Since we knew we weren't too likely to get an invitation to Camp David ourselves, we thought we'd try to duplicate a bit of its atmosphere elsewhere and checked into the Ole Mink Farm Cabins, about four miles from Camp David. The "cabin farm" is in the middle of Cunningham Falls State Park, at about the same altitude as Camp David (1,800 feet).

Finding it increasingly difficult to obtain a campsite in the park, Pat and Gordon Irons bought the abandoned 35-acre mink farm in 1963. They decided to create a new option for the growing number of campers, first for those with tents, and then those in trailers, which still occupy some sections of the property. Over the years, the Ironses cleared the thickly wooded land, built five cabins for overnight guests, and dug a huge swimming pool.

Our two-bedroom oak cabin, Hidden Spring, was the oldest and most secluded of the cabins, surrounded by trees and near a running brook. We guessed it might be similar to the cabins Menachem Begin and Anwar Sadat stayed in during their Camp David summit meeting.

Not exactly, according to Pat Irons, one of the few "average citizens" ever to have been invited to Camp David. She was lucky enough to get a glimpse of the presidential camp years ago when one of the members of her supper exchange group at church happened to be the post commander of Camp David. When it came his turn to have the other couples to his home for dinner, they were issued a formal invitation to Camp David (along with a lengthy security-clearance questionnaire and detailed instructions on how to approach the camp).

The rustic retreat nevertheless has perfectly manicured lawns and quietly tasteful cabin interiors, according to Irons.

For the most part, the public's exposure to Camp David is limited to the high-security entrance gate, exactly 1 1/2 miles along the Park Central Road in Catoctin Mountain Park, just off Route 77.

You can stop by the park's visitors center, where a guide will give you a map of the park and a big wink when asked where the presidential retreat is located. Although they are under strict orders to not even acknowledge its existence, signs reading "Camp #3," "Do Not Enter," "For Official Business Only," and "Restricted Area" make it hard to miss.

But there's much more to the park than Camp David.

Created in 1935 by the Civilian Conservation Corps, the park was intended to replenish hardwood trees depleted by loggers, charcoal-makers, and bark-tanners. You can still find remnants of the mountain farms as you explore the 5,000-acre park, and there are several hiking trails through the woods. The park also offers public demonstrations, including one on how the settlers made whiskey, an essential product for surviving this remote wilderness in the early days of our nation.

Across Route 77 is the Cunningham Falls State Park, which was split off as a state recreational site after the federal government decided to retain the portion of the park containing Camp David.

The 78-foot-high Cunningham Falls (the highest waterfall in Maryland) is considered the big attraction here, but we were a little disappointed to find there was no way to climb alongside the falls unless you were equipped to scale slippery cliffs. We hiked back from the falls on the moderately rated "lower trail," a scenic one-mile trek along Big Hunting Creek.

We spent a good part of an afternoon on the shores of Big Hunting Lake, the 44-acre manmade lake, fed by the creek, that is the main activity center of the state park. With three sandy beaches, grassy banks, wooded picnic sites, stocked fishing holes, and a full complement of rental canoes and paddle boats, this is a great place to pack a picnic and plan on spending the day.

It's best to fill up your daytime agenda, because other than the Cozy Restaurant, there's not much nightlife in Thurmont—a few pizza parlors, a couple of pool halls where you can get a burger, and a two-block "main drag" where, like everywhere else, teens cruise on a Saturday night.

Despite a population boom, there was little threat that Thurmont would become the next Aspen.

But we were happy with the escape this low-key mountain weekend offered. After our day at the beach, we returned to our cabin in the woods and sat on the Adirondack chairs on the screened porch, reading books. It might not have been Camp David, but then we're not Bill and Hillary.

—Jill P. Capuzzo

Directions from Philadelphia: Take Interstate 95 south to Baltimore and follow the signs for I-70 west to Frederick, Md. At Frederick, take U.S. 15 north about 20 miles to Thurmont. Thurmont is about 160 miles from Philadelphia.

For more information on Catoctin Mountain Park, call the visitors center, 301-663-9388. For information on accommodations, historic sites and attractions throughout Frederick County, Md., call the Frederick County Tourism Council, 800-999-3613 or 301-663-8687.

Back to the Revolution

YORKTOWN, VA.

WHEN WE ARRIVED, all we knew about Yorktown was that an important battle of the Revolution was fought here. That's true, but a visit here and to neighboring Jamestown will give you a new appreciation of Colonial America and its struggle for freedom.

In the early fall of 1781, Gen. George Washington had the British army bottled up along the shore of the York River. All the land routes were blocked, and the French navy prevented the British from escaping by sea. The siege of Yorktown was on. After a night attack captured two key British defensive positions, called redoubts, Gen. Charles Cornwallis surrendered and the last major battle of the Revolution was over.

We learned more about Yorktown's beginnings on a walking tour guided by Helen Myers, who came back to her hometown after a career on the stage. The town's history actually goes back to 1630, when free land was offered to those adventurous enough "to seate and inhabit" the 50-foot-high bluffs on the south side of the York River.

Yorktown, however, dates itself from 1691, when the Virginia House of Burgesses authorized a port here. The town grew rapidly and became a busy shipping center. Yorktown's great days were around 1750, when its population was about 1,800. It then declined, along with Tidewater Virginia's tobacco trade. Today's population is less than 300.

On the tour, Myers took us through the Nelson House, a Georgian mansion built in the early 1700s by "Scotch Tom" Nelson, the town's leading citizen. It later was the home of his grandson, Thomas Nelson Jr., a signer of the Declaration of Independence and the commander of the Virginia troops at the battle here. He went broke financing his troops and, after the war, never recovered his money or his health. His headstone, in the Grace Episcopal Church graveyard across the street, states that he "gave all for liberty."

Two British cannonballs that slammed into the side of the Nelson House during the battle are still there. Across the street, the Digges House, built around 1760, has battle scars on its inner timbers. All around town are grim reminders that the Revolution was not a quaint pageant but a war.

Grace Church was a highlight of our tour. Built in 1697, it survived damage in the Revolution, a devastating fire in 1814, and the Civil War, when it was used as a field hospital. The bell in the steeple, cast in 1725, was carried off during the Civil War. Its fragments later were recovered in Philadelphia, and they were used to recast the bell, which was restored to duty in 1889.

All the kneelers in the church are covered with needlepoint, lovingly made by the women of the parish: gold Christian symbols on a green background to match the hanging behind the altar. Each is different and signed with the initials of the woman who made it.

The last stop on the tour was the Yorktown Victory Monument, dedicated in 1881, which memorializes the victory here and the American-French alliance in the Revolution. Atop a 95-foot, elaborately ornamented granite column, a larger-than-life statue of Miss Liberty looks serenely down on the town.

After our short course in local history, we headed for the battlefield, which surrounds and includes part of the town. A 12-minute film at the visitor center dramatizes the battle, the events leading up to it, and its significance. The center displays the tent Washington used during the siege and a collection of firearms—the British Brown Bess and the more accurate Charleville flintlock used by the Americans and French. On the battlefield are the remains of the British fortifications (which, during the Civil War, were modified, strengthened, and used by Confederate troops), Redoubts 9 and 10, the American and French batteries, and the sites of the headquarters of Washington, Marquis de Lafayette, Frederick von Steuben, and Comte de Rochambeau, the French commander. The battlefield is surprisingly small and can be leisurely explored.

On an observation deck overlooking the Surrender Field, push a button and the gruff voice of actor William Conrad, over the music of fifes and drums, sets the scene as it was on October 19, 1781. That day, Cornwallis played sick and sent his second-in-command, Gen. Charles O'Hara, to surrender for him. O'Hara twice tried to hand his sword to the French commander rather than to Washington, whom the British considered a rustic commoner. After Washington received the sword, the 8,300 British troops marched out and laid down their arms.

We toured the Moore House at the edge of the battlefield, where the Articles of Capitulation were drafted. Then we stopped by the Yorktown Victory Center, built by the state for the 1976 Bicentennial, to see the collection of art and artifacts pertaining to the Revolution. The center also has excellent sight-and-sound exhibits and reproductions of a military camp and a small farm where living-history programs re-create domestic life in 18th-century Virginia.

The Watermen's Museum, on the riverfront, is housed in a 1930s reproduction of a Colonial tavern. It tells the story of the men who reaped the bounty of the Chesapeake Bay, its rivers, and their tributaries and displays models of the three traditional Chesapeake workboats—bugeye, skipjack, and dead-rise. Crusty retired watermen are on hand to explain their skills and share their lore. We learned how to tell male crabs from "she-crabs," for example.

As the sun was getting ready to set, we watched the Fife and Drum Corps of Yorktown strut its stuff. The young musicians assembled at the Fife and Drum Museum, which displays a collection of vintage martial musical instruments, and marched up Main Street to the Victory Monument for a short but stirring concert.

We made our weekend headquarters at the Cedars, a charming guesthouse in Williamsburg—which may sound strange, but Williamsburg is conveniently located between Yorktown and Jamestown. There is only one motel in Yorktown and no accommodations in Jamestown. More important, Yorktown and Jamestown represent steps in the early development of Tidewater Virginia. They also put Williamsburg into perspective. The next morning, fortified with an ample breakfast, we drove the six miles to Jamestown.

On May 13, 1607, thirteen years before the Pilgrims landed at Plymouth Rock, three ships—the *Susan Constant*, the *Godspeed*, and the *Discovery* —landed 104 people in a strange, hostile wilderness. Countless hardships lay ahead for the first permanent English settlement in the New World, but it was blessed with an able, hard-driving leader, Capt. John Smith. During the winter of 1609–10, called the "starving time," the colony, which had grown to 500 people, was reduced to about 60 emaciated, defeated survivors. They were ready to pack it in when Lord De La Warr, the first English Colonial governor of Virginia, arrived with reinforcements and supplies in June 1610.

The first settlers hoped to find gold. The only gold they found was tobacco, a crop that took skill, patience, and hard work to produce. But the "royal weed" was a cash crop and by 1612 the settlers were exporting it to England. In 1614, John Rolfe married Pocahontas, daughter of Chief Powhatan, and relations with the Indians improved. In 1619, the colony formed the House of Burgesses, the country's first legislative body. That same year, a Dutch warship brought the first indentured Africans to Jamestown.

When Jamestown became a royal colony in 1624, resentment of the highhanded government began to grow. In 1676, Nathaniel Bacon led a revolt and burned Jamestown, calling it a "stronghold of oppression." Though the town was rebuilt, it never prospered again, and in 1699, the government was moved to Williamsburg. By the time of the Revolution, Jamestown was a ghost town.

At the Colonial National Historical Park, nothing of the original Jamestown settlement remains above ground except the Old Church Tower. Since 1934, archaeological excavations have unearthed the outline of the town. Old streets, foundations, and property ditches have been restored, and the visitor can get a good sense of how the colony must have looked. In "New Towne," where Jamestown expanded around 1620, we saw the Governor's House and other historical buildings.

An introductory film and exhibits at the visitor center gave us a picture of early Colonial life. Near the center are statues and monuments to John Smith and Pocahontas, erected during the 1907 anniversary. We wound up at the Jamestown Settlement, a splendid living-history museum. Full-size reproductions of the three original ships are tied up at a pier. The original fortlike settlement and a Powhatan Indian village have been re-created, and young pseudo-settlers and Indians lured us back into the past. Inside the James Fort, a gentleman-soldier showed me how, with a cloth ball suspended from a limb of a tree, to sharpen my skills with a sword. My companion, meanwhile, was picking up tips on frying fish over a bonfire.

Driving home, we pondered some of the things we had learned and the questions they raised. Why did England give Spain a 100-year headstart in the New World? Why did mighty Britain call it quits after the defeat at Yorktown? And what was John Rolfe thinking of when he proposed to Pocahontas? Are we talking love here, or political expediency?

—Chuck Lawliss

Directions from Philadelphia: Take I-95 south to Richmond. Take 64 east and south to 238, and follow 238 north and east to Yorktown.